Brief Therapy

Brief Therapy

Short-Term Psychodynamic Intervention

Gregory P. Bauer, Ph.D.
Joseph C. Kobos, Ph.D.

JASON ARONSON INC.
Northvale, New Jersey
London

To Kathy and Carl
and
To Carolyn and Philip, Paul, and Adam

Library of Congress Cataloging-in-Publication Data

Bauer, Gregory P.
   Brief therapy.

   Includes bibliographies and index.
   1. Psychotherapy, Brief.   I. Kobos, Joseph C.
II. Title. [DNLM: 1. Psychoanalytic Therapy—methods.
2. Psychotherapy,Brief—methods. 3. Transference
(Psychology) WM 420 B344b]
RC480.55.B39   1987   616.89'14   87-1487
ISBN 0-87668-940-3

ISBN 0-87668-940-3

Manufactured in the United States of America.

Contents

Acknowledgments

We would like to acknowledge our gratitude to Mark Furshpan, Ph.D., and Gerald Thorner, M.S.W., for their encouragement, support, and invaluable suggestions regarding our work. We wish to thank Hilda Gutierrez, Janice Smith, and especially Terri Toci for their outstanding secretarial assistance. A most special thanks is expressed to Diane Bartella, a secretary whose patience, dedication, and excellent typing skills were of immeasurable value on the project. An additional thanks is expressed to Joan Langs of Jason Aronson Inc. for her excellent editorial assistance.

CHAPTER ONE
Introduction and Overview

Psychotherapists and the general public have come to accept and look for brief interventions in personal crisis and emotional turmoil. There is a growing professional commitment to provide services that are relevant and practical to more members of society. The community mental health movement, initiated in the 1960s, embodied this philosophy and has stimulated the growth of short-term approaches. Although federal funding for community mental health centers has declined in the past decade, psychological services have established formats different from the traditional long-term dynamic approach to treatment.

As psychotherapists have sought to meet the increased demand for psychotherapy, they have reconsidered the philosophy of treatment. There is an openness to consider that limited therapeutic goals may be the more correct response to patient needs, that brief intervention is often treatment of choice, and that long-term treatment may risk negatively gratifying a patient's dependency needs and perhaps complicate the individual's life rather than promote growth. A bias developed in the 1930s and 1940s that longer psychotherapy was better psychotherapy and that therapeutic change required a major reworking of the patient's internal psychic economy. Of late, mental health professionals are reevaluating the therapeutic process and have come to believe that, for many patients, shorter therapies may be more efficient, economical and effective.

This reevaluation of therapeutic strategy has come none too soon. In the last decade, the relationship between economics and provision of psychological services has changed. Governmental agencies and insurance providers are emphasizing cost containment and have dictated the emergence of short-term delivery programs (e.g., employee assistance programs, health maintenance organizations, crisis intervention services). By reducing coverage of outpatient psychotherapy, insurance companies are causing practitioners to consider briefer formats. At the same time, consumers regularly question whether they are receiving quality service for time and money invested. These considerations place a premium on the psychotherapist's ability to employ brief treatment formats.

PRESENT APPROACH

There exists no standardized procedure for implementing brief, dynamically based psychotherapy. In the past twenty years, numerous approaches have been presented. Malan (1963, 1976), Sifneos (1972, 1979), and Davanloo (1978, 1980) have made significant contributions to the development of brief intervention strategies. Careful study of the approaches of various short-term psychodynamic psychotherapy therapists—including Ferenczi, Rank, Alexander, and in particular Malan, Sifneos, and Davanloo—as well as our own clinical experience, has yielded a distinctive model of brief treatment.

This book presents a treatment technique that, when used with properly selected patients, elicits change in less time than is traditionally assumed necessary. Principles underlying this model are presented and explicated. The seminal works of Malan, Sifneos, and Davanloo in the development of modern short-term psychodynamic psychotherapy technique are emphasized. Our model of short-term treatment integrates and further develops their ideas. We offer a concrete and pragmatic model of therapeutic intervention that also allows the therapist flexibility and creativity.

The first section (Chapters Two and Three) presents the historical foundations of short-term psychodynamic psychotherapy. Short-term psychodynamic psychotherapy is based on principles elucidated in the development of psychoanalytic technique. It is a distillation based upon the understanding of personality dynamics and patterns of disturbed functioning delineated in more traditional, long-term treatment. Without the long-term psychotherapies, brief, dynamic psychotherapies would not exist. To more fully grasp concepts underlying short-term psychodynamic psychotherapy technique, its evolution from its psychoanalytic forebears is reviewed, starting with Freud. The contributions by Ferenczi, Rank, and Alexander are then highlighted. Chapter Three details the approaches to brief, dynamic psychotherapy implemented by Malan, Sifneos, and Davanloo. The essential components of their models — including selection criteria, treatment strategies, and results — are discussed.

Chapter Four outlines the assessment process. Proper patient selection is of paramount importance. The task of the assessing therapist is to identify those patients who have the capacity to readily enter into a therapeutic alliance, withstand the stress of a highly interactional treatment, and separate from the therapist once treatment is over (Bauer and Kobos 1984). An intact ego and ability to productively cope with painful affect are prerequisites for the emotionally intense interactions involved in treatment.

Short-term psychodynamic psychotherapy is most effective with patients who have achieved some maturation in personality development and whose emotional difficulties predominantly stem from unresolved oedipal conflict. These patients tend to function at a neurotic — as opposed to borderline — level of adjustment. Early developmental tasks (e.g., attachment, separation-individuation) have been sufficiently mastered to bring to the therapeutic endeavor the capacity to trust, to accept the therapist as a separate person, and to objectively view the therapeutic interaction. One aspect of assessment is to determine if the patient can work with perceptions of other people, including the therapist. The therapist works with the patient's habitual style of relating to people and attempts to elucidate the defensive and maladaptive aspects of this style. The therapist must assess whether the patient has the capacity to interact and also is able to observe the interaction without feeling self-conscious or defensive. An additional assessment determines whether the patient and therapist will become enmeshed and have difficulty terminating. Highly dependent transference relationships (i.e., the transference neurosis) are not encouraged.

The final section (Chapters Five, Six, and Seven) explicates intervention principles. In adherence to analytic principles, short-term psychodynamic psychotherapy helps the patient uncover, experience, and work through repressed emotional conflict by means of analysis of defense, resistance, and transference. Through this experience the patient is helped to learn new ways of functioning. This treatment may be characterized by the following principles:

1. *Reversal of the traditional analytic stance of passivity.* The therapist is an active participant in the interaction and avoids the role of impersonal conveyor of interpretation. The highly interactive, confrontive, and interpretive style leads to a great degree of emotional involvement by *both* therapist and patient.

2. *A focus of treatment is agreed upon and actively maintained.* Both patient and therapist must accept a limited treatment goal. A clear and circumscribed treatment plan provides direction and focus for therapeutic interventions and is an antidote for what Malan (1963) called therapeutic perfectionism. Successful therapeutic work on a specific conflictual theme enhances self-esteem and has a positive impact on other aspects of the patient's functioning.

3. *An early establishment of a strong therapeutic alliance.* The

establishment of a collaborative, investigative atmosphere is essential. The therapist rapidly works to achieve patient rapport with and confidence in the therapeutic method. Working with a psychodynamic understanding of the patient's ambivalent strivings towards growth, the therapist attempts to engage the patient's positive identifications with helpers, the wish for health, and strivings for competence and creativity.

4. *A persistent analysis of resistance.* Resistance is viewed as an enduring complex of defenses organized to maintain comfort and security and to avoid awareness of personal responsibility. A major activity is the persistent confrontation and analysis of resistance, especially as defenses are organized around the focal theme. The therapist actively identifies and examines patient resistance and encourages the patient to practice more adaptive and collaborative behaviors. Examination of resistance and defenses acquaints patients with defensive maneuvers and allows a reexperiencing of repressed feelings. Strong emphasis is placed on the emotional experience in therapy. This intense emotional involvement is intended to decrease the length of the working through process of therapy and the length of treatment. Though the short-term psychodynamic psychotherapy patient is assessed as possessing sufficient ego strength to cope with the anxiety elicited by this confrontational, interpretive style, patient reaction to therapist interventions is closely monitored.

5. *An early and vigorous use of transference feelings.* This increases the patient's self-understanding and provides an opportunity to examine and modify conflicted patterns of reaction and interaction. The therapist is alert for signs (e.g., silence, blocking, anxiety) that the patient is having difficulty in the therapeutic relationship. Negative transference is immediately explored and worked through as a means of gaining access to other repressed feelings and to foster the therapeutic alliance. There is an active interpretation of the patient's experience in the therapeutic relationship and its connection to

other current and past relationships. Therapist interest shifts from a focus on repressed instinctual material (id analysis) to an investigation of the defensive and adaptive functions of the patient's character style (ego analysis). Emphasis is placed on identifying and attempting resolution of problematic coping strategies within the here-and-now patient–therapist relationship. The therapist helps the patient examine how enduring, conflictual patterns of interaction are repeated in the therapeutic relationship, and to begin to practice changes in these patterns. Prolonging factors in treatment, such as the development of a highly dependent transference attachment or a regressive transference neurosis, are avoided. Issues of a preoedipal nature (e.g., dependency, passivity, acting out) are dealt with through immediate confrontation and interpretation. The establishment of a primarily oedipal focus and the avoidance of complex dependent transference relationships facilitate the patient's ability to engage in a successful and productive termination.

6. *An emphasis on learning how to solve emotional problems.* The therapist serves as a role model in demonstrating that intra- and interpersonal conflict is understandable and need not be frightening. Identifying with the therapist, the patient learns a method of recognizing feelings, working through emotional conflict, and gaining an understanding of one's conflicted interpersonal strategies.

7. *Careful attention to the time limit and the process of termination.* Depending on individual psychodynamics, termination may be experienced in a variety of ways. To some it represents the realistic end of a productive, meaningful collaboration. In such cases, termination occurs without difficulty and with minimal psychic pain. For most patients the termination process provides an opportunity to meaningfully examine, work through, and resolve conflicted feelings regarding attachment, separation, autonomy, and loss. Differential approaches to termination are outlined and discussed.

Short-term psychodynamic psychotherapy is challenging and gratifying work. It is not a panacea. Carefully selected patients respond well to the treatment format. This approach works most effectively for those patients who can work with issues of transference and metaphorical communication. The skill, training, and supervision of the therapist are important variables.

CHAPTER TWO
Historical Foundations

SIGMUND FREUD

Almost as soon as Freud made his revolutionary discoveries, it was recognized that psychotherapy should be efficient, effective, and inexpensive. Brief psychotherapy was born when Freud renounced hypnosis as an effective treatment technique. The patients he treated during, and immediately after, his early collaboration with Joseph Breuer were treated with brief psychotherapies. It was during this time that Freud learned that the therapeutic effect of treatment was due to the personal relationship between patient and therapist, an insight at the foundation of brief psychotherapy technique (Eisenstein 1980). In 1895, Breuer and Freud published *Studies on Hysteria,* outlining their ideas on the dynamics and treatment of patients whom they had treated, particularly those with hysterical symptoms. This text is recommended to the therapist studying short-term technique in that it attempts to identify and solve frequently encountered problems in such treatment. In *Studies of Hysteria,* Breuer and Freud highlighted many aspects of treatment now seen as crucial to modern brief technique. These include: (1) an emphasis on careful patient assessment and selection criteria such as motivation, intelligence, and psychological mindedness, (2) development of a strong therapeutic alliance, (3) persistent attention to patient resistance, and (4) maintenance of a consistent treatment focus (Flegenheimer 1985).

Freud initially believed that insight into the genesis of a neurosis would lead to its prompt resolution. The early emphasis of his psychotherapeutic work was on rapid diagnosis of patient dynamics and undoing through interpretation, which provided insight into unconscious intrapsychic conflict. Many of Freud's initial analytic treatments were brief. For example, in 1906 Freud successfully treated the famous conductor Bruno Walter in six sessions. In this treatment Freud combined insight through interpretation with a prescription of a vacation and a return to his normal activities (Sterba 1951). In 1908 Freud was able to relieve the impotency problem of the composer Gustav Mahler in four sessions (Jones 1955). In discussing Mahler's treatment, Freud stated that he was able to help Mahler because Mahler was rapidly able to understand the principles of psychoanalysis.

As Freud's theory of personality and psychopathology became more complex, his theory of analytic change became correspondingly more involved and ambitious. Freud (1937) noted that over the years a change had taken place in the nature and mode of his analytic work. In earlier days he dealt with patients who sought a cure to their neurotic suffering as quickly as possible. In later years he engaged mainly in training analyses and in the treatment of a smaller number of patients suffering from what he termed acute neuroses. Freud felt that in these cases treatment length was not a major consideration. The objective, according to Freud, was to learn as much as possible regarding psychodynamic functioning and to "completely exhaust the possibilities of illness and bring about a radical change in the personality" (Freud 1937, p. 380). As goals of analysis became more ambitious and its theory more complex, the length of analytic treatment began to increase (Marmor 1979). The increase in treatment length correlated with increased attention to the interpretation and working through of transference phenomenon, and a decreased focus on relief of specific symptoms (Malan 1963). In addition, the concept of resistance emerged in an effort to understand impasses in therapy. Resistance to insight and change required additional analysis and working through.

After tremendous initial enthusiasm, considerable pessimism developed about the growing length and decreasing effectiveness of psychoanalysis (Malan 1963). This pessimism is reflected in Freud's paper, *Analysis Terminable and Interminable* (1937). In this paper Freud discussed the efficacy and limitations of analytic technique. He stated that although psychic change occurs in analysis, it is often only partial. Parts of the patient's intrapsychic conflict, Freud observed, will always remain untouched by treatment. Even conflicts mastered during treatment are subject to reeruption in later life. Freud wrote that even the analyst who has undergone intensive personal analysis is subject to the reawakening conflictual instinctual demands. To counter this, he recommended that every analyst obtain personal treatment every four or five years. Freud's ideas were of seminal importance in stimulating other analysts' work on shortening treatment. In the end, however, he concluded that "psychoanalytic therapy—the liberation of a human being from his neurotic symptoms, inhibitions, and abnormalities of character—is a lengthy business" (Freud 1937, p. 373).

Freud's conclusions regarding analytic treatment must be understood from the perspective that psychoanalysis began not only as a method of psychotherapy but also as a method of research. The main emphasis in Freud's writings was on exploration of the human mind, on the development of psychoanalysis as a science of the psyche more than as a curative procedure (Jones 1957). Although analysis had potent therapeutic application, Freud foresaw that someday it would be superseded by more efficient methods (Lewin 1970).

SANDOR FERENCZI

The goal of creating a short and effective form of treatment, without abandoning basic analytic insights, was pursued by other early analysts. Notable attempts were made by two members of Freud's inner circle of followers, Sandor Ferenczi and Otto Rank. Ferenczi, an intimate friend of Freud for more than twenty-five years, was perhaps the most original thinker among early analysts. In the development of psychoanalytic theory, Ferenczi gave strong impetus to the practical application of Freud's discoveries. Ferenczi had an incessant urge toward therapeutic experimentation that sprang from his dissatisfaction with accepted analytic method. Although this experimental attitude eventually caused a rift with Freud, many of Ferenczi's therapeutic innovations have been proven valid over the course of years (Alexander and Selesnick 1966).

Active Therapy

Ferenczi credited the lengthening of analytic treatment, in part, to the passivity of the analyst. Counteracting this passivity seemed a logical step in shortening treatment. This was attempted with a technique called active therapy. Shortly after his analysis with Freud, Ferenczi began his technical experiments, which initially were strongly supported by Freud. In a paper before the fifth international psychoanalytic congress in Budapest in 1918, Freud reviewed the current status of analytic technique, commenting on Ferenczi's active technique as the possible avenue along which analysis would develop (Balint 1969).

Ferenczi (1919, 1921) opposed analyst passivity by such "activity" as:

1. Encouragement of activities avoided by the patient because of unconscious significance (e.g., exposing phobic patients to experiences that activated their phobias, in order to mobilize anxiety — which was normally avoided). Such anxiety could then be analyzed.
2. Prohibition of specific stereotyped behavior patterns (e.g., omitting rituals in obsessional patients, forbidding masturba-

tion, insisting that patients control certain body movements). Ferenczi noticed that some patients discharged repressed emotions by automatic and habitual behavior patterns. To force inadvertently discharged tensions to become conscious, Ferenczi forbade patients to carry out stereotyped patterns that occurred under emotional stress (e.g., crossing and uncrossing their legs). This was often successful in forcing unconscious tensions, formerly discharged, into consciousness.

3. Use of forced fantasies to speed up exposure to hidden conflict (e.g., Ferenczi encouraged patients to fantasize about topics that spontaneously appeared in their associations).
4. Assumption of a definite role vis-a-vis the patient, intended to bring out more intensely neurotic reactions in the transference.
5. Setting of a time limit for treatment.

Ferenczi's experimentations were based on an intuitive conviction that personality change is not caused solely by interpretation. With his active technique, Ferenczi attempted to intensify the patient's emotional experience. Active encouragement and prohibition of patient activities were utilized in hopes of increasing psychic tension, thereby mobilizing unconscious material. Ferenczi did not view active therapy as an active interference by the therapist on the patient's life. Instead, he saw his technique as an imposition on the patient of additional, within-session tasks besides the keeping of the fundamental rule of free association. Ferenczi used such technique to more rapidly remove patient resistance and thereby shorten analysis.

The tactics of active therapy were to be used only with certain patients (Ferenczi 1921) and with great caution (Ferenczi 1926). Active measures were advocated only after the failure of more orthodox techniques. Ferenczi felt that the basic tenets laid down by Freud were suitable for most patients. Certain patients, however, were seen as requiring special activity on the part of analyst and patient. Such steps were justified by a stagnation in the analysis, and once this was overcome, the analyst was to resume a more traditional attitude. Ferenczi found it difficult to provide specific indications for when active techniques should be used and suggested that the analyst proceed along individual lines. He taught that the use of active techniques required considerable therapeutic acumen, and he cautioned beginning analysts against overreliance on such tactics for therapeutic movement. In addition, Ferenczi noted that active strategies could cause a loss of the opportunity to gain an understanding of patient dynamics observable when the patient is under no external control and subjected solely to the fundamental role of free association. Since active techniques influence the development of transference, he felt they should be avoided in the beginning of treatment and used only when a stable, positive working relationship had been developed.

Ferenczi's active therapy was frowned on by many orthodox analysts who advocated a more neutral role. Fenichel (1941), for instance, saw Ferenczi's technique as creating the possibility of the analyst becoming, in the unconscious of the patient, "a punisher, a repeater of castration threats, or a magician waving away such threats" (p. 84). Ferenczi's techniques were criticized as destroying the analytic atmosphere of tolerance, making it difficult to obtain derivatives of unconscious conflict. Ferenczi defended his deviations from classical technique by stating that he merely elaborated on and experimented with principles Freud had already introduced into analytic treatment. In particular, Ferenczi (1921) pointed out that Freud had used such methods as setting a deadline for the end of treatment and asking phobic patients at some point in treatment to expose themselves to the phobic situation.

Ferenczi additionally argued that active strategies by analysts aren't new and are practiced in nearly every treatment. As an example, Ferenczi pointed out that making interpretation is an active interference with the patient's psychic activity; it turns thoughts in a given direction and facilitates the appearance of ideas that otherwise would have been prevented by resistance from becoming conscious. Ferenczi felt it important that analysts become more aware of how their interventions actively influence patient behavior. Only by doing so could analysts critically appraise and experiment with their procedures, thus improving technique.

Ferenczi helped dissolve the myth of analyst passivity. As analysts increasingly realized that they were, in fact, actively intervening with their patients (e.g., silence itself is an intervention), increased efforts were made at refining these interventions. Ferenczi's work was a forerunner of other active approaches to analytic therapy including those of Wilhelm Reich, Franz Alexander, and H. S. Sullivan. Ferenczi's emphasis on replacing therapist passivity with various forms of activity is an essential aspect of all modern forms of brief treatment. Active engagement with the patient characterizes the short-term therapy assessment process in which a rapid and accurate understanding of conflicts, defensive style, and ego resources are sought. This active interchange continues throughout treatment.

Therapy as an Emotional Experience

In his later work Ferenczi became increasingly interested in intensifying the emotional experience of treatment. His experiments were motivated by a conviction that therapy was an emotional experience, not an intellectual endeavor. The quality of this experience was the essential factor that induced the patient to change (Alexander and Selesnick 1966). To this end, Ferenczi experimented with adjusting the analytic atmosphere to meet the patient's specific needs. These particular experiments resulted from Ferenczi's attempt to treat "dried up" cases — patients who had been involved in numerous unsuccessful treatments. Such patients flocked to Ferenczi from all over the world, counting on him as their last hope (Alexander et al. 1966).

In 1929 Ferenczi introduced the technique of relaxation or neocatharsis, which was aimed specifically at increasing the emotional meaningfulness of treatment. This technique, in a sense, was very different than his active technique. Instead of increasing tension, Ferenczi tried to create a relaxed, secure environment in which patients were encouraged to express themselves as fully as possible. With this technique Ferenczi actively engaged his patients, encouraging expression of both aggressive and loving feelings, including the long-tabooed physical contact (Fine 1979).

Ferenczi believed that indirect contact through interpretation was insufficient with certain disturbed patients. He opted for a more direct approach to the childish infantile part of the patient. He felt that such patients needed to be "adopted" and to experience, for the first time in their lives, the advantages of a normal nursery (Ferenczi 1955, p. 124). Certain interventions involved the analyst directly expressing love based on the theory that the analyst as parent surrogate can make amends for rejections and traumata suffered by the patient with parental figures. Ferenczi's reparative efforts included hugging, kissing, and nonerotic fondling of his patients (Marmor 1979).

Ferenczi was preoccupied with the deprived and injured child in the adult patient. At times a literally maternal type of love was invoked to meet special therapeutic requirements. Such deep involvement led to the development of powerful conscious and unconscious reactions to the patient. Ferenczi's experiments led to the first intensive study of the analyst–patient relationship and the discovery of what is now called the technique of countertransference interpretations (Balint 1969). In his attempt to adapt treatment to specific patient needs, Ferenczi could be considered the forerunner of the "flexible approach" to therapy, which adjusts treatment to each patient's special problems and personality (Alexander and Selesnick 1966).

Freud took a dim view of Ferenczi's reparative efforts, predicting that they would eventually lead to greater excesses on the part of therapists. In a letter to Ferenczi, Freud wrote:

> A number of independent thinkers in matters of technique will say to themselves: Why stop at a kiss? . . . Bolder ones will come along who will go farther. . . . The younger of our colleagues will find it hard to stop at the point they originally intended, and God the Fa-

ther Ferenczi, gazing at the lively scene he has created will perhaps say to himself: Maybe after all I should have halted in my technique of motherly affection before the kiss [Marmor 1979, p. 150].

Freud additionally predicted it would prove impossible to satisfy unconditionally every need of a patient, and that such attempts would improve the patient's state only as long as the analyst was able and willing to be at the patient's beck and call (Balint 1969). Ferenczi subsequently abandoned these techniques, but he never gave up his efforts to develop a more active, emotionally meaningful approach to analytic therapy.

Ferenczi's attempt to effect patient change through direct, reparative interventions may be of dubious psychotherapeutic value. However, his emphasis on creating a therapy environment that is personally meaningful to the patient, and that elicits a high level of emotional involvement, is of particular importance to short-term psychodynamic psychotherapy. By means of careful selection, the therapist identifies those patients who are capable of a high degree of emotional involvement and able to use this involvement productively (i.e., a patient with a borderline personality disorder may become intensely involved with the therapist; however, this involvement involves such a slow development of an observing ego and therapeutic alliance that short-term psychotherapy is usually unproductive). Short-term psychodynamic psychotherapy places great emphasis on a high level of emotional involvement by both patient and therapist. This is created by means of active challenging of defensive operations, and persistent focus on anxiety-provoking conflicts while carefully monitoring the therapeutic alliance. The intense experience of this highly interactive treatment significantly decreases the amount of time needed to complete the working through process of therapy (Davanloo 1978).

Ferenczi's contributions to the development of short-term technique include: (1) an attempt to influence the therapeutic process by suggesting that therapists actively direct treatment focus and interact with the patient, (2) an emphasis on the emotional experience of therapy, and (3) a willingness to experiment with modifications of orthodox technique, despite the misgivings of his peers. Ferenczi served as a model for other therapists in their quest for increasing the efficacy of treatment. Many of his ideas, seminal in the development of brief therapy, were presented in his classic text, *The Development of Psychoanalysis* (1925), co-authored with Otto Rank.

OTTO RANK

Rank was one of Freud's most creative students. His 1907 treatise on artists (*Der Küenstler*) so impressed Freud that he was invited into the Viennese Psychoanalytic Society. Rank's contributions over the next two decades, particularly in the psychoanalytic understanding of art, literature, and myths, made him a highly respected, albeit controversial, member of the early psychoanalytic community. Rank's position as co-editor of the psychoanalytic journal *Internationale Zeitschrift fur Psychoanalyse* and founder of the Psychoanalytic Institute of Vienna made him an important figure in the early psychoanalytic movement.

As the years passed, Rank became progressively dissatisfied with psychoanalytic technique. He was highly critical of orthodox analysis, including its scientific tentativeness, the endless pursuit of infantile memories, the detailed interpretation of dreams, and the wearisome prolongation of treatment. Rank's attempt to improve on psychoanalytic method included: (1) setting an end to treatment as a key to the treatment process, (2) recognition that successful therapy involves the patient's motivation to change and a willingness to accept responsibility for one's behavior, and (3) emphasis on the analytic situation as a present experience rather than a reliving of the past.

Setting a Time Limit to Treatment: The Trauma of Birth

Rank believed that psychoanalysis was often used as an opportunity for furthering psychoanalytic investigation rather than an attempt to rid the patient of distress as rapidly as possible. To counter this, Rank experimented with setting a termination date with patients. The reaction of his patients to this tactic convinced Rank of its productiveness. In helping his patients work through the experience of enforced termination, Rank observed that patients responded to termination in a manner he described as "an affective reliving of the birth trauma." Rank felt that separation from analysis unconsciously symbolized the birth process and that the transference to the analyst was equivalent to the child's relation to mother on its deepest biological level.

In 1924, Rank's book, *The Trauma of Birth*, was published. In this book Rank attempted to build a psychological system on Freud's statement that the infant's physiological response at the time of birth (e.g., cardiac and respiratory acceleration) occurred because of overwhelming sensory stimulation, and that these responses are the prototype of all later anxiety (Alexander and Selesnick 1966). This was a new approach to the genesis of mental development. It was an approach that was based on the physical changes every infant experiences when born. Rank called this experience primal anxiety and felt it to be the most important element in personality development and the source of neurosis. Rank believed that the individual is forever seeking to return to the comfort and security of prenatal existence. This wish is later opposed by the wish to establish mastery and autonomy, the result being intrapsychic conflict.

Rank believed his theory carried through Freud's historical and biological explanation of the neuroses to their biological conclusions. Birth replaced castration as the ultimate and original trauma; the breast took precedence over the penis as the first libido object. It is of importance to note that Rank's theory minimized the importance of the Oedipus complex. Hatred, fear, and jealousy of father were of secondary importance to the anxiety relating to birth and separation.

Freud's initial reaction to Rank's concept of birth trauma was one of tolerance and curiosity. He initially stated that it was the most important progress since the discovery of psychoanalysis (Jones 1957). Freud, however, was startled by Rank's attempt to use this concept as the basis for a new psychoanalytic theory and technique. This, in addition to an unfavorable reaction to Rank's concept by other members of Freud's inner circle of followers, influenced Freud to admonish Rank for reducing psychoanalysis to a single theme that disregarded the impact of father upon the child (Alexander and Selesnick 1966). In *Analysis Terminable and Interminable* (1937), Freud stated that although Rank had made a determined effort to shorten analysis, his theory would not stand the test of critical examination. "Moreover, it was a premature attempt, conceived under the stress of the contrast between the post-War misery of Europe and the prosperity of America, and designed to accelerate the tempo of analytic therapy to suit the rush of American life" (Freud 1937, p. 373).

Although Rank's theory of birth trauma was rejected by the analytic community, his ideas stimulated a focus on the preoedipal period of development. The psychoanalytic exploration of the importance of mothering and the role of nurturance was pioneered by Rank. The primary emphasis in analytic thinking during Rank's time was on the oedipal period and corresponding anxieties of castration, competition, rivalry, and loss of love. Rank's concept of birth trauma, although biologically and psychodynamically dubious, laid the foundation for subsequent recognition of the importance in personality development of periods of early infancy and toddlerhood. The period of preoedipal development has subsequently undergone considerable productive investigation as evidenced by the works of such individuals as Melanie Klein (1948), Donald Winnicott (1965), and Margaret Mahler (1975). The concepts of good and bad mother, primal love, return to the womb fantasies, and fusion with mother, in part, owe their origins to Rank's innovative thinking (Alexander et al. 1966).

As Rank's ideas evolved, he began to downplay the importance of birth trauma and focus on issues of separation and individuation. Separation and individuation were considered critical to the process of adaptation and maturation. Rank used setting a time limit to treatment to promote a therapeutic examination of separation process. He advocated an early concentration on patient anxieties concerning separation from the therapist as a way of dealing in vivo with issues of attachment and autonomy. By setting a termination date, Rank attempted to use the issue of separation from the therapist to generate the broader problem of self-direction or dependence. The impending termination of therapy was believed to arouse the patient's emotional responses related to this central conflict. Skillful handling of the patient's reaction to the impending termination of treatment was seen as leading to a final resolution of the basic conflict of dependence versus independence.

Setting time limits on treatment has been adopted by many practitioners of brief therapy (e.g., Mann 1973) as an integral aspect of their technique. In an excellent review of short-term technique, Marmor (1979) stated that setting a time limit is a unique and essential element of the treatment process whose importance cannot be overemphasized. Even those therapists who do not rely on setting a specific termination date to force issues of separation, in their practice of short-term psychodynamic psychotherapy, *do* encourage examination of this dynamic by firmly insisting on the brevity of treatment.

The Concept of Responsibility

Rank thought the central problem in life to be the resolution of the dependence–independence conflict and the ultimate development of self-direction. Rank believed therapy would be ineffective if the therapist assumed responsibility for change. He continually sought to encourage the autonomy and responsibility of patients for their treatment.

Rank felt that the therapist's interpretations and explanations were not as therapeutic as the patient's own expression of thoughts and feelings. Self-expression was seen as facilitating autonomy and acceptance of responsibility, as well as deepening self-identity through self-discovery. Rank believed it was the therapist's task to encourage patients to talk further about their present emotional reactions as opposed to presenting them with a conclusion (interpretation) that might terminate such discussion. Rank rejected Freud's free association technique because it required patients to abandon responsibility for self-direction, thereby working in direct opposition to a major therapeutic goal (Ford and Urban 1963).

Rank's work foreshadowed the emphasis that modern therapists using short-term treatment place on: (1) helping patients gain awareness of how their own attitudes and predispositions are intimately involved in continuing their problems in living and (2) encouraging patients to take an active, responsible role in the therapeutic process, as opposed to assuming a passive-dependent role towards the therapist. In addition, Rank's emphasis on facilitating patient expression of thoughts and feelings, instead of interpreting them, foreshadowed the attention therapists of the short-term school give to the persistent use of questions and confrontations as a means to elicit a more active involvement in the treatment process.

Resistance

Rank's concept of resistance was closely related to his ideas about the importance of encouraging patient autonomy and self-direction. Rank criticized Freud's concept of resistance as representing therapist resentment with patients who were not doing what they were supposed to do. To the contrary, Rank suggested resistance was often an initial sign of progress in therapy. Resistance was viewed as representing the patient's first attempt at exercising a degree of independence (Ford and Urban 1963). Rank's accepting, affirmative view is basic to short-term therapy technique. For instance, Davanloo (1978) stated that resistive maneuvers in short-term psychodynamic psychotherapy should not be viewed pessimistically as a decline in the therapeutic alliance, but rather as an invitation for active interpretation and working through of defenses.

The Concept of Will

Rank believed it to be difficult for patients to consider themselves responsible for many of the unfortunate events of their lives, including distressing thoughts, feelings, and behaviors. He noted that patients have difficulty with therapy since it demands giving up the security and self-esteem maintained by neurotic defenses. Accordingly, Rank emphasized the importance of mobilizing a patient's will to counteract the tendency to avoid pain and conflict. Rank conceptualized will as that part of the personality that struggles to grow, to master conflict, to develop autonomy and self-direction. Rank believed that mobilizing the patient's will facilitated the course of therapy. In his concept of will therapy, Rank foreshadowed the overwhelming importance short-term therapy places on patient motivation for a positive therapy experience. Derivatives of the concept of will (i.e., willingness to actively participate in therapy, willingness to attempt self-understanding, and willingness to change) are employed by therapists in evaluating motivation for change when selecting patients for treatment. Willingness in this context is seen as the ability to mobilize one's will towards a particular task (Marmor 1979). Short-term psychodynamic psychotherapy is more effective with those patients interested in emotional growth and continued self-development than with patients primarily concerned with symptom relief. The former individuals are more willing (motivated) to cope with the emotional stress involved in the therapeutic encounter.

The Experience of Therapy in the Here and Now

Rank sought to improve analytic treatment with an emphasis on the use of the therapy situation as a present experience rather than a reliving of the past. Tracing the historical antecedents of an emotional problem was rejected unless it was used to highlight and more deeply understand a dynamic presently active within the therapeutic relationship. In a significant break from orthodox analytic thought, Rank stated that knowledge of the genetic origin of problematic behavior was not particularly useful in effecting change. The major requirement for the therapist is a knowledge of the disordered response sequences as they occur in the present relationship. Rank argued that a historic-causal explanation did not promote behavior changes, for it enabled patients to continue to deny responsibility for their present behavior (Ford and Urban 1963).

Rank rejected what he perceived to be Freud's great attention to content derived from free association. Rank saw no particular topic as in need of discussion, preferring instead to emphasize the process of the patient–therapist interaction. Attention to the here-and-now interaction between therapist and patient was viewed as creating more therapeutic anxiety than a discussion of memories of an infantile period of life.

Rank's attention to the impact of the therapeutic situation on patient behavior pointed the way towards a more in-depth understanding of the patient responses during therapy. The patient was seen as responding not only to personal projections of unconscious, repressed wishes and fears, but also to legitimate aspects of the therapy session (e.g., the therapist's own personality). In his attention to the process of the therapeutic interaction, Rank pointed to a means of developing increasing emotional impact in the session, thereby shortening the amount of time needed for treatment. Rank's attention to the interaction process foreshadowed the emphasis that current therapists of short-term psychotherapy (e.g., Sifneos 1972, Davanloo 1978) place on the within-session, here-and-now analysis of the patient's defensive and adaptive modes of interacting with the therapist.

Therapy as a Learning Experience

Rank placed great importance on the curative effects of the interpersonal relationship between patient and therapist. He felt that regardless of the conditions that resulted in the development of a conflictual mode of reaction, these reactions could be modified in the therapeutic relationship provided they occur within the session, are identified, and are examined. Rank believed patients react in the therapy situation with patterns of behavior learned to protect security and enhance self-esteem. Projections, rationalizations, denials, and distortions will occur in relationship to the therapist and may be examined and worked on if the interaction process is attended to. The key to change, according to Rank, was that therapy was a new situation and therefore could result in new learning. The identification, examination, and modification of neurotic patterns in relationship to the therapist was seen as the crucial occurrence.

Rank used the therapy relationship to help patients (1) examine their mode of interacting, (2) learn new and more effective patterns, and (3) learn a method of thinking about their problems that could be used after treatment was over. Rank's approach foreshadowed the attention modern practitioners of short-term therapy place on the therapy situation not only as a place to resolve conflict, but also as a place to provide the patient with a way of analyzing conflict that may be used after termination. By experiencing the examination and working through of behavior with the therapist, a method is learned that can be applied to future situations.

Rank's Break from Freud

With *The Trauma of Birth* (1924) Rank began his own movement toward autonomy and independence from the confines of orthodox analytic theory. By 1929, ideological differences created a chasm between Rank and Freud. At this time Rank formally separated himself from Freud, ceased to make apologies for his differences in thought, and no longer wrote in the Freudian idiom (Alexander and Selesnick 1966). Rank went on to develop a theory of behavior and treatment around the concept of will. This culminated in his book *Will Therapy: An Analysis of the Therapeutic Process in Terms of*

Relationship (1936). Rank's ideas, perhaps because they differed too greatly from accepted analytic thinking of the time, were destined to receive little attention from most analytically oriented psychotherapists. He was, however, an influential theoretical force at the Pennsylvania School of Social Work. In addition, Carl Rogers credited Rank with having a strong influence on the development of his client-centered approach to therapy. Therapists interested in the development of methods of dynamic technique designed to increase the efficiency of treatment can find much of value in Rank's writings.

Rank and Ferenczi

The dissatisfactions Rank and Ferenczi had for orthodox analytic technique led to a collaboration. For a number of years they worked together, developing various modifications to treatment with the overriding aim of increasing the efficacy of the analytic method. Their collaboration culminated with the writing of the monograph *The Development of Psychoanalysis* (Rank and Ferenczi, 1925). This volume was of great importance in the development of brief analytic technique. Although Rank and Ferenczi claimed to be in no way differing from Freud, their seminal work was an exposition and critical review of the analytic process. Rank and Ferenczi noted with pessimism the increasing length of analytic treatment. They attributed this to the "need to discover afresh, in every single case, the psychological and theoretical evidence on which psychoanalysis is based" (p. 52). Analysis was criticized as turning treatment into a proving ground for analytic theory, neglecting the actual therapeutic task for the sake of psychological interest. They pointed out that analytic treatment need not remain tied to investigative methods out of which the theory evolved (Marmor 1979). They insisted that experimenting in the interest of analytic theory is fundamentally antagonistic to treatment, which must concern the welfare of the patient only.

Rank and Ferenczi felt that analysis had become too theoretical. Patients dutifully recalled their childhood experiences but did not improve. Rank and Ferenczi concluded that a vital emotional relationship with the analyst was essential to cure. Analysts, they believed, had gone too far in eliminating their personalities from the treatment. In an attempt to carry out the concept of the analyst as a mirror reflecting back to patients pictures of themselves, Rank and Ferenczi viewed the orthodox analyst as creating a situation in which no true emotion could be experienced (Thompson 1952).

Rank and Ferenczi saw the goal of analysis as substituting affective factors of experience for intellectual processes. Anticipating Alexander's concept of corrective emotional experience, they placed central importance on the patient's emotional experiences in an attempt to correct the prevailing excessive emphasis upon cognitive insight through genetic reconstruction. Considerable therapist activity was advocated with a focus on current life problems and an avoidance of detailed probing of the past. Recollection of forgotten memories was not an absolute requirement for modification of neurotic patterns. Reliving maladaptive patterns in relation to the therapist and recognizing their inappropriateness were viewed as critical. Recognizing their inappropriateness was seen as therapeutic even without remembering the past events in which these reactions originally developed. Here-and-now transference interpretations were emphasized.

Ferenczi and Rank were first to underscore the concept of acting out in analytic treatment. They expressed the view that analysis and working through of neurotic behavior expressed in the patient–therapist interaction should take precedence over theoretical reconstruction of the patient's past life and developmental history. An emphasis was placed on the emotional experiences of the patient in the therapeutic relationship rather than the recovery of memories and intellectual reconstructions that characterized long-term psychoanalytic approaches (Marmor 1980). In addition to attempting to shorten analysis through emphasizing emotional experience over intellectual reconstruction, Rank and Ferenczi recommended that treatment would be shortened if in the last stage of the analysis a termination date was established and enforced in order to counteract the patient's fixation on the therapist.

Reactions to Rank and Ferenczi

The views of Rank and Ferenczi met strong opposition in the analytic circle. Although their ideas were of interest to some, Freud and his coterie were not responsive (Alexander and Selesnick 1966). In a letter to Ferenczi, Freud stated that their suggestions would lead to an abuse of psychoanalytic technique (Jones 1957). Alexander (1925), in a review of their monograph, stated that they overemphasized the abreactive experience in therapy and gave the process of working through insufficient attention. Alexander contended abreaction offered but passing relief from tension, whereas the working through process effected lasting alteration in the ego. Alexander also criticized the technique of enforced termination, stating that Rank and Ferenczi did not explain how this was connected to the patient's ability to give up the transference. Setting a time limit, Alexander argued, was only a formal activity and not a substitute for the patient's own renunciation of treatment. Until the inner willingness to give up the transference situation has been attained, Alexander believed that it was of no use to set a termination date, and if this willingness was already present, it was superfluous to do so. Alexander suggested that treatment was completed more quickly by progressively bringing the transferential aspects of the relationship into greater light. This would make it more difficult for the patient, as an adult, to act out the infantile part that s/he has to play in the transference. Alexander felt that resolution of the inner conflict between the adult and the infantile (i.e., neurotic) part of the patient determined when treatment would end. He argued that, in most cases, it would be a technical error to set a time limit in that the therapist ran the risk of converting this internal conflict into an external one — between the therapist and the neurotic tendencies of the patient.

The analytic community was not ready to accept Rank and Ferenczi's recommendations on how to conduct a more efficient treatment. Rank's ideas were vigorously attacked by contemporaries because they were correctly perceived as threatening the fulcrum of Freud's theories. His emphasis on the developmental tasks of attachment and separation, and the importance of preoedipal nurturing, threatened Freud's formulations regarding the oedipal period as the primary genesis of psychic conflict. Ferenczi's experiments were widely opposed. His active technique was seen as compromising the free associative communication of the patient and the neutrality of the analyst. His experiments with the indulgence technique were seen as presenting the possibility of dangerous overinvolvement with the patient. The unpopularity of the ideas of Rank and Ferenczi, in combination with Freud's strong negative reaction to them, inhibited development of short-term therapy for some time.

The role of reformer of analytic treatment has never been popular. Rejection by outsiders forced the pioneer analysts to stress conformity within their own ranks. Perhaps more important than the cultural need to conform is the bewildering complexity of the dynamic processes of treatment. The insecurity that these intricate processes necessarily provoke creates a defensive dogmatism. Almost any statement about technique can at best be tentative. Tolerance of uncertainty is generally low in human beings, and a dogmatic reassertion of a traditionally accepted view is a common defense against the ensuing anxiety (Alexander and Selesnick 1966). Such a stance had unfortunate consequences for the innovations of Rank and Ferenczi. Many of their ideas were thus fated to undergo the painful labor of rediscovery by future therapists seeking a briefer means of alleviating patient suffering.

FRANZ ALEXANDER

A significant upsurge in demand for brief therapy during and after World War II initiated renewed and more lasting efforts towards further development of brief, dynamically oriented therapeutic techniques. Franz Alexander was among the innovators of short-term analytic therapy. He, perhaps more than any other modern analyst, was responsible for leading the way toward application of analytic principles to shorter and more active dynamic therapies (Marmor 1979). Although trained in psychoanalysis in Europe, Alexander differed in orientation from most European analysts. Early European analysts tended to follow Freud's example and were primarily interested in understanding the functioning and structure of the personality. They believed that analytic knowledge was not far enough advanced to provide effective treatment. Psychoanalysis was more accepted as a source of knowledge, which at some future time might serve as the basis for improved treatment technique. Alexander's view of psychoanalysis was more pragmatic. As a member of the Berlin Institute for Psychoanalysis in the early 1930s, Alexander analyzed and trained numerous analysts, including many visiting Americans. These American trainees acquainted him with American thinking, which emphasized treatment results over theory development. A skeptical but treatment-directed attitude guided Franz Alexander throughout his life and was visible in his attempts to crystallize the essentials of the therapeutic process (Alexander et al. 1966).

Alexander believed his work to be a continuation and realization of ideas first proposed by Rank and Ferenczi. He felt that valid aspects of Rank and Ferenczi's work were overlooked due to strong negative reactions to certain parts of their theory (e.g., the concept of enforced termination). Alexander was particularly impressed by Rank and Ferenczi's efforts to highlight the emotional experience of the therapy situation as the major therapeutic factor in treatment. Their emphasis on emotional experience stimulated Alexander to experiment with methods of increasing the emotional impact of the therapy session in hopes of decreasing the length of treatment needed to induce intrapsychic change.

In 1946 Alexander co-authored an important volume on analytic therapy (Alexander and French 1946). This volume (highly rec-

ommended to all students of dynamic psychotherapy) was the cul-
mination of seven years of research on shorter approaches to
therapy at the Chicago Institute for Psychoanalysis. In the course
of their research, Alexander and colleagues experimented with frequency of interviews, optional use of chair or couch, long or short
interruptions of therapy prior to formal termination, and the combination of psychotherapy with drugs or other therapy. Above all,
they sought to learn how to control and use the transference relationship so as to achieve specific goals and to fit the particular psychodynamics of each patient.

Therapist Flexibility

An important principle evolving from the work of Alexander was
the principle of flexibility. Alexander thought it unsatisfactory to
view analytic treatment as a single procedure in which the therapist
(often unwittingly) selected patients to fit a technique. He insisted
that the therapist adapt technique to patient needs. He thought that
the nature of individual needs determines which technique is best
suited to bring about the curative processes of emotional discharge,
insight, assimilation of repressed material, and the corrective emotional experience. Alexander stressed that different patients need
different things in different phases of the treatment. The therapist
must adapt technique flexibly to these needs and avoid attempts to
force the patient to rigidly conform to a predetermined procedure.
Alexander's encouragement of increased flexibility in treatment intervention was a bold addition to analytic procedure. Although
such flexibility may seem obvious today, it was revolutionary in an
era dominated by the conviction that standard psychoanalytic
method was the optimum method of therapy for most neurotic patients (Marmor 1979).

The principle of flexibility led to heated arguments concerning
the relationship of psychoanalysis and analytically oriented psychotherapy. A controversy arose as to where to draw the line be-

tween analysis proper and analytic psychotherapy. Alexander contended his approach to treatment was psychoanalytic and therefore could be considered psychoanalysis. This contention led to conflict between him and analysts practicing more orthodox techniques. Such conflict made it difficult for many of Alexander's contemporaries to accept and profit from his contributions to analytic technique.

Treatment Planning

Alexander felt that every treatment could be made more efficient and pertinent by intelligent direction and planning. "In any properly handled flexible psychotherapy, a comprehensive plan is a sine qua non whether the therapy be one with a limited goal or an intensive analysis" (Alexander and French 1946, p. 108). Alexander noted that therapists often developed the unfortunate practice of drifting into treatment and becoming deeply involved in therapeutic responsibilities without having first formed a treatment plan. Often the result was an interminable therapy.

Alexander emphasized that in order to know what new emotional experiences were necessary to achieve therapeutic results, the therapist had to develop an early understanding of the patient's dynamics and their genetic development. Therapist interventions were planned on the basis of this dynamic insight. In this respect Alexander differed from Ferenczi and Rank, who tended to minimize the importance of genetic understanding.

Alexander believed it is easier to get a clear picture of the patient's problem and life history during the first few hours of treatment than at any other time until the treatment is almost complete. It is during the period before the patient became emotionally involved with the therapist that it is easiest to gain an adequate perspective on the patient's problem as a whole. Alexander compared the therapist during the initial interview to a traveler standing on top of a hill overlooking the country through which s/he is about to journey. At this time it was possible to see the whole anticipated journey in perspective. Once the traveler descends into the valley, one may examine small parts of the landscape in much greater detail than is possible when viewing them from a distance, but the broad relations will no longer be so clear. The emphasis Alexander placed on deliberate and thoughtful treatment planning as a means of increasing the efficacy of treatment foreshadowed the importance that modern therapists using short-term strategies place in a careful assessment process. Proper patient selection and planning of treatment through development of a therapeutic focus are critical for a successful treatment.

Alexander felt that a comprehensive treatment plan included an attempt to visualize: (1) what was to be attempted with the patient, (2) what was hoped to be accomplished, (3) what complications may occur, and (4) potential solutions to complications. He stressed the importance of anticipating the difficulties likely to be encountered in treatment; if and when difficulties occurred, the therapist would be less likely to be discouraged than if complications took the therapist by surprise. Alexander's attempt to anticipate difficulties in treatment foreshadowed Malan's recommendation (1963) that in assessing a patient for short-term psychodynamic psychotherapy the therapist look into the future therapy and forecast possible difficulties that may preclude use of short-term technique (e.g., potential decompensation).

The Corrective Emotional Experience

Clear understanding of the genetic development of the patient's emotional difficulties was seen as vitally necessary so that the therapist may revive for patients the original conflict situations from which they have retreated. The more precisely the therapist understands the dynamics and is able to reactivate the early attitudes, the more adequately the therapist can provide the new experience necessary to produce therapeutic results. Alexander termed this the corrective emotional experience and felt it to be the cornerstone of change in therapy.

The basic principle involved in the corrective emotional experience was to reexpose the patient under the more favorable circumstances of the transference relationship to emotional situations that could not be handled in the past. Alexander believed the corrective emotional experience resulted from the difference between the original parent response and the response of the therapist during treatment. The patient, experiencing the inevitable transference reaction, anticipates from the therapist parental attitudes that shaped the patient's neurotic behavior patterns. When the therapist responds differently than parents, the patient is provided with an opportunity to correct outdated perceptions. The fact that the patient continues to act and feel according to outdated earlier patterns, whereas the therapist's reactions conform to the actual therapeutic situation, makes the transference behavior a kind of one-sided shadowboxing (Alexander and French 1946).

Alexander explained the remediative effects of the corrective emotional experience in terms of the integrating function of the ego. One of the most basic functions of the ego is to integrate new experience and adapt to everchanging situations. Once the patient is aware of the immature origin of personal reactions, and at the same time faces a new interpersonal situation to which the old pattern does not fit, the ego actively searches for and develops a new response (Alexander 1956). Although Alexander placed great emphasis on a corrective emotional experience, he felt it of secondary importance whether this experience took place in the treatment relationship, or parallel with treatment, in the daily life of the patient (Alexander and French 1946).

The Emotional Experience in Therapy

Alexander reiterated Ferenczi and Rank's belief in the central importance of emotional experience in therapy. Emotional intensity was seen as influencing the progress and subsequent length of treatment. Strong emotional participation brought issues more clearly to the foreground and made insight more vivid, thus facilitating treatment. Alexander observed that one of the most common impasses to treatment was characterized by intellectualization and lack of emotional participation by the patient. He taught that treatment should be conducted on as high an emotional level as the patient's ego could stand without diminishing its capacity for insight. This level varied from patient to patient. Patients with stronger ego (good integrative abilities) were seen as being able to endure more intense sessions with less development of defenses (e.g., acute regression).

The level of emotional intensity was seen as varying within, as well as across, treatments. Patients in later stages of work were seen as capable of withstanding greater emotional involvement. Alexander's concern with increasing patient affect during treatment as a means of increasing treatment effectiveness anticipated the strong emphasis modern short-term therapists place on providing an emotionally intense therapeutic experience. Davanloo (1978) contended that the intense experience of short-term therapy significantly decreased the amount of time needed to complete the working through process of therapy.

Alexander's views regarding the centrality of emotional experience were similar to those of Rank and Ferenczi. He differed, however, in that he reemphasized the need for intellectual reintegration of previously repressed material, a reintegration he felt Rank and Ferenczi neglected. With this reemphasis Alexander attempted to combine what he considered to be the two trends in psychoanalytic treatment. One trend emphasized the ego's use of insight to stimulate adaptation. By providing information regarding patient dynamics, the therapist facilitated the patient's ability to master intrapsychic conflict. The other trend, highlighted by Rank and Ferenczi, concerned the importance of therapy as a meaningful emotional experience, without which intellectual understanding would remain ineffectual (Alexander 1956).

The Interpersonal Climate of Therapy

Alexander asserted that, whatever the form of therapy, whether an open-ended analysis or a brief therapy, use of transference reactions determined the course and success of treatment. He sought to improve analytic procedure by giving increased attention to interpersonal climate in hopes of increasing the effectiveness of the corrective influence of transference. Control and manipulation of the transference relationship, as assessed and determined by patient needs, was a central goal.

Alexander was among the first to question the concept of analyst as a blank screen. Alexander believed that a total blank screen was nonexistent, nor was it desirable. He held that unless this was recognized by therapists, there would be a significant discrepancy between the theoretical model of the analytic process and what actually took place in treatment. Alexander encouraged the therapist to avoid attempting to be a blank screen upon which patients projected pictures out of their own imaginations. Instead, the therapists should endeavor to put the patients at ease by behaving in a way expected of a person offering help and counsel. "When we project the patient's behavior not against a blank screen but against a background of normal behavior, the very fact that our behavior does not encourage the patient's irrational tendencies makes them all the more conspicuous when they do occur" (Alexander and French 1946, p. 87).

Control of the Transference Relationship

Alexander disagreed with the widespread belief among analysts that a complete transference neurosis was unavoidable, as well as the sine qua non of analytic treatment. (The transference neurosis was viewed as the reliving of the patient's neurotic past in his/her relationship with the therapist.) Alexander felt that the attempt to develop a transference neurosis accounted for many long, seemingly interminable cases. He saw the transference neurosis as complicating treatment, impeding progress, and becoming a focus of resistance to treatment (Alexander and French 1946).

Alexander believed that the control of the transference relationship, not the development of the transference neurosis, was the axis around which treatment proceeded. The most frequent means of controlling the transference relationship was interpretation of patient actions, attitudes, dreams, and fantasies. Alexander believed skillful use of interpretations (in choice, timing, and manner of presentation) was the most powerful means of regulating the type and intensity of the transference relationship at the therapist's command. For example, if the therapist directed interpretations towards the infantile past, regression and a dependent transference relationship would be encouraged. Conversely, by avoiding mention of infantile conflict and by directing interpretations towards present, current-life problems, the potential for development of a transference neurosis would be decreased.

Alexander believed that therapists could control the intensity of transference reactions by changes in interview frequency and by assuming a deliberately planned attitude towards the patient which was opposite the original parental attitude. Changes in interview frequency counteracted patient dependency and attempts by the patient to avoid active work on life problems. Alexander felt that daily interviews often gratified dependency needs more than was desirable and encouraged a patient's regressive and procrastinating tendencies. Frequent interviews on an unlimited basis were believed to support the neurotic tendency to evade confronting problematic issues.

The most fundamental factor in a neurosis, according to Alexander, was the patient's withdrawal from life situations. A highly dependent transference relationship served the purpose of the original neuroses — withdrawal from real participation in life. Manipulating interview frequency offered the patient less opportunity to substitute safe, regressive therapy experiences for life experiences. Constant pressure was placed on the patient to actively struggle with life problems and to continuously apply what was learned in therapy to outside life experiences.

Alexander further attempted to influence the interpersonal climate of treatment by deliberately behaving towards the patient in a manner which he felt was opposite to the original parental attitude. By being different from the parent, whose attitudes were judged as pathogenic, Alexander tried to provide a corrective emotional experience for the patient. Alexander believed that therapy should highlight the discrepancy between the patient's transference expectations and the actual situation as it exists between patient and therapist. For example, if the original childhood situation repeated in the patient's transference relationship involved a frightened son relating to a strict, punitive father, the therapist should behave in a calculatedly permissive manner. If the pathogenic factor was the father's doting, all-forgiving attitude toward his son, the therapist should take more of an impersonal and reserved attitude.

Alexander's suggestion that the therapist deliberately assume an attitude opposite to the patient's expectations was questioned by many analysts. The conscious and purposeful adoption of attitudes was criticized as artificial and as being readily recognized as such by patients. Stone (1961) wrote that such a tactic calls upon the analyst to "adopt attitudes which aren't necessarily immanent in the analyst's identity. . . . [and] creates a hazard to the basic sense of thorough reliability which the patient should experience in this deeply important relationship" (p. 58). Stone criticized the strategy of using a current attitude to undo the effect of an earlier attitude, as if they were interchangeable; in fact, they are remote from each other in time, place, state of development, and personal meaning. Alexander countered by stating that the therapist's objective and emotionally detached attitude is itself artificial in that it does not exist between human beings in actual life (Alexander and Selesnick 1966).

Therapy as Learning

Alexander believed therapy to be a learning process. He felt this was in accord with Freud's statement that analytic treatment was a process of reeducation. Through normal development, behavioral patterns were progressively modified; early patterns were corrected in light of later learning. Problems occur when certain problems became too disturbing to face. Conflictual issues were repressed and avoided, thus making it difficult for the individual to learn how to resolve them. The natural learning process was interrupted. Subsequent attempts to master problems often became repetitions of previous unsuccessful attempts. Alexander defined neurosis as stereotyped reactions to problems the patient had never learned how to solve. The task of therapy was to help the patient resume and complete an interrupted learning process.

A Focus on the Current Life Situation

Alexander's therapy focused on current life problems. A guiding principle of his work was that therapeutic interest should be focused on the patient's problem adjusting to present life demands. The more closely the therapist kept the patient focused on actual life problems, the more intensive and effective the therapy. Alexander stressed that focus on disturbing events of the past had utility only when it threw light upon the motives for irrational reactions in the present. Therapist interest in past history, at the expense of the present, was seen as a residue of the historical period when research in personality dynamics was necessary for developing a treatment method.

Alexander believed that observation and systematic influencing of the patient experiences in life to be an integral part of every treatment. He encouraged the patient to assume management and responsibility for personal affairs and to face conflictual life situations as soon as possible. Alexander assumed that the normal, adaptive response to conflict was continued effort towards mastery or resolution, and that withdrawal or avoidance of conflict was neurotic. Patients were thus continually urged to confront and master their problems. The sooner the patients were helped to face those obstacles in life from which they retreated, and the sooner they could be induced to engage in new experimentation, the more quickly therapeutic results were achieved. Inevitably, patients had to solve problems in actual life: relationships to spouses, children, superiors, competitors, friends, and enemies. The experiences in therapy were only a preparation, a training for the real battle. The most powerful therapeutic factor was the performance of activities formerly neurotically impaired or inhibited. No insight, no emotional discharge, no recollection was as reassuring as accomplishment in the actual life situations in which the individual had previously failed. With such success, patients regained confidence, the fundamental prerequisite of mental health (Alexander and French 1946).

Regression in Therapy

Alexander felt regression in therapy was manifested in what patients chose to discuss and in the nature of the relationship they formed with the therapist. Alexander (1956) distinguished two types of regression. In one type of regression, patients, when confronted with an overwhelming conflict, sought security by reverting to modes of functioning more typical of earlier stages of development; security and protection were sought according to an old pattern. In the second type of regression, patients relived a conflictual event or phase of development in order to accomplish a subsequent mastery of unresolved issues; a solution was sought for something which had not been solved in the past. Alexander felt it important to determine whether the regression induced by treatment was an attempt to return to a more secure phase of development or an attempt at mastering an unresolved conflict. The former regression was seen as unhelpful, an evasion of current adaptive tasks. Alexander (1954) wrote that the so-called deep regression toward material of a pregenital nature was not always a sign of penetrating the depths of the patient's psychopathology; the emergence of early material is often the manifestation of the regressive attempt by the ego to avoid dealing with a later pathogenic conflict.

Alexander's ideas regarding regression are helpful to the therapist practicing brief treatment. In selecting patients for short-term therapy, the therapist must identify patients who have suffered early and severe emotional deprivation. During treatment such patients tend to regress to a more immature emotional relationship with the therapist (e.g., a highly ambivalent and dependent transference seeking literal gratification rather than understanding). Identification, working through, and mastery of such transference phenomena is more appropriate for long-term treatment. Early identification of patients with the propensity to experience deeply regressive transference reactions is essential in an assessment task.

In addition, Alexander warned of patients who, while able to profit from short-term therapy, also had a tendency to readily regress. Such patients developed passive-dependent relationships with the therapist to avoid conflicts of a more advanced phase of development (e.g., the feeling of rivalry and competition with the therapist). With such patients, the therapist must persistently counteract the patient's tendency to sink into a safe, comfortable transference neurosis. Without continuous, alert pressure from the therapist, even relatively mild neurotic disturbances may lead to a disproportionately prolonged treatment. Alexander contended that gratification obtained in the transference relationship in therapy sooner or later outweighed the patient's desire for change. In support of this contention, Alexander cited Freud's observation that treatment often reaches a point where the patient's wish to be treated outweighs the will to be cured.

Free Association

Free association was seen as a double-edged sword. While an integral part of analytic technique, it also provided the patient an opportunity to avoid anxiety-arousing material. Alexander believed that strict adherence to the technique of free association supported the patient's avoidant defenses. A more limited, therapist-directed approach to free association was favored. In his observation that patients, left to their own devices, avoid therapeutically relevant issues, Alexander foreshadowed two essential aspects of modern short-term therapy technique: (1) maintenance of a treatment focus and (2) active confrontative and interpretive work around patient avoidance of anxiety-provoking issues.

Termination

Alexander used temporary interruptions from therapy to ascertain a patient's readiness for termination. Interruption of regular therapy appointments allowed the patient to cope independently for a time and gave evidence whether the patient was able to lead a satisfactory life without regular therapy contact. This method was a modification of Ferenczi and Rank's concept of enforced termination. Temporary interruptions depended on trust in the natural recuperative powers of ego, which Alexander felt were underestimated by analysts. Alexander believed many patients used therapy as a comfortable retreat from real-life problems — the patient presented interesting material to allay therapist impatience and to give the impression of steady progress and deepening analytic insight; while seemingly working through issues, in reality the patient often was procrastinating and avoiding.

During a temporary interruption, patients often discovered they could live without treatment. In addition, unresolved difficulties came more clearly to the forefront. Through treatment interruptions, patients became more aware of dependency strivings, rendering them more available for analysis. Alexander advised against too short an interruption from treatment; patients needed the opportunity to struggle with their problems without the therapist and were not encouraged to return at the first hint of relapse. Patients, however, were assured of being able to return to treatment if needed. Such assurance was seen to counteract the panic reactions observed in the patients of Rank and Ferenczi when their termination technique was used (Alexander and French 1946).

Alexander made no predictions as to the precise number of therapy sessions. This was seen as varying with the case. The task of the therapist was to help the patient develop self-reliance and a sense of mastery. This was accomplished by blocking the patient's neurotic retreat into fantasy and the past and by encouraging an active confrontation of current life difficulties. The number of sessions needed to produce mastery or modification of patient difficulties varied according to patient motivation and ego strength.

Reaction to Alexander

The initial reaction of the psychoanalytic community to the work of Alexander was harsh. An example of this reaction can be found in Ernest Jones' review of Alexander and French (1946) in the *International Journal of Psycho-Analysis* soon after the book's publication (Jones 1946). Alexander's ideas were controversial; to some they symbolized progress, to others analytic impurity. Hostility of contemporary analysts stemmed, in part, from Alexander presenting his work as a modification of orthodox analysis rather than a method of brief therapy based on analytic principles (Malan 1976). Today, however, the principles he elucidated have become part of the daily repertoire of almost every therapist. By developing a more flexible and efficient approach to analytic treatment, Alexander provided a fertile soil for the germination of new ideas regarding therapeutic strategies leading to successful short-term treatment. Grotjahn (1966) observed that if Freud disturbed the sleep of the world, Franz Alexander disturbed the sleep of the psychoanalysts.

The attempts of Ferenczi, Rank, and Alexander to develop a brief psychodynamic treatment met with mixed enthusiasm from their contemporaries. More recently, however, we have witnessed a dramatic acceptance and demand for short-term yet effective treatment. This upswing in the demand for brief treatment is motivated by many factors including: (1) a growing professional commitment to provide immediate treatment, relevant and practical, to all segments of the community, (2) an increasing emphasis on preventive and emergency therapeutic measures, and (3) increasing consumer demand for economically feasible services. The works of Ferenczi, Rank, and Alexander have provided a foundation for other developing systems of brief treatment. While challenging classic analytic concepts, they remain loyal to dynamic design. Among the best-known contemporary contributors to the development of brief, dynamic treatment models are David Malan (1963, 1976), Peter Sifneos (1972, 1979), and Habib Davanloo (1978, 1980).

CHAPTER THREE
Key Contributors

David Malan, Peter Sifneos, and Habib Davanloo have played core roles in the development and implementation of short-term psychodynamic psychotherapy. Their seminal contributions require a summary of their individual approaches.

DAVID MALAN

David Malan is a pioneer in the systematic study of the nature of therapy. His studies were carried out in Britain with aid from a number of analysts, most notably Michael Balint. Their approach was initially called focal therapy, later, intensive brief psychotherapy, major concepts of which are derived from analytic theory and practice. All techniques of analysis are used — with the exception of passivity in the analyst's role, which Malan opposed as a prominent lengthening factor in treatment. Using concepts and procedures of analysis, Malan molded a therapeutic technique that initiated psychological change in less time than required by classical analytic

An earlier version of this chapter appeared in *Psychotherapy: Theory, Research and Practice* 21:153–170 (1984).

methods. His study of treatment outcome provides evidence that therapy is effective when specific techniques are employed.

An evaluation of brief therapy must concern itself with three related factors: selection criteria, technique, and outcome. To study these variables, Balint brought together a team of therapists, one of whom was Malan. Malan (1963) published a report on this endeavor and continued with further research. What follows is a discussion of Malan's research and his therapy technique.

Selection: Importance of Evaluation Criteria

Malan asserts that successful brief therapy is as much dependent on selection criteria as on technique. Certain patients are eliminated before the interview process by means of referral information. These include alcoholics, drug addicts, and those with a history of serious suicide attempts, long-term hospitalization, more than one course of electroconvulsive therapy, grossly destructive or self-destructive acting out, and incapacitating chronic obsessional or phobic symptoms. The next step in patient selection is a thorough psychodynamic evaluation, which aims to develop an understanding of the patient's illness, forecast specific dangers if the patient is accepted for therapy, assign the patient to an appropriate form of therapy, and formulate a therapeutic plan for the form of therapy chosen. As with Alexander and French, the idea of therapeutic planning is central to Malan's therapy.

The elements of a psychodynamic evaluation are psychiatric history — a full-scale dynamic history that attempts to understand events of the patient's life in emotional terms — and an assessment of patient–therapist interaction. The patient–therapist interaction is assessed on the patient's capacity to speak honestly about himself, to see the problem in emotional terms, and to allow the interviewer some degree of emotional closeness. Trial interpretations are used in the assessment. Patient response to interpretation is an essential element in evaluation. At the end of the evaluation it should be possible to make a full diagnosis. Evaluation frequently takes more than one session and often includes projective testing.

Evaluation data is assessed on the basis of a set of criteria. First, the therapist is asked to visualize future therapeutic interactions with the patient and to predict the possible dangers of an interpretive therapy. Injudicious use of interpretation with potentially depressive or latently psychotic patients may precipitate a depressive or psychotic breakdown. Such patients are generally not accepted for intensive brief psychotherapy, but when they are, care is used to avoid such breakdowns. Rigid defenses, poor motivation, and inability to make emotional contact typically lead to rejection. Such aspects of personality functioning prevent the patient from rapidly entering an effective therapist–patient interaction. Potentially extreme and complex transference situations are forecast and avoided since these lead to difficulty in termination. The second and third evaluation criteria deal with focus of treatment. The therapist must feel that there is a conceivable focus that can be separated from the overall pathology the patient brings to treatment. The therapist must delineate a circumscribed problem that would be useful to the patient to work through. Patient and therapist must agree on an acceptable treatment focus. Interpretations based on the emerging focus are given during the evaluation. It is important that the patient respond positively to interpretations based on this focus. The fourth criterion is patient motivation. Motivation for insight and therapeutic interchange is considered an essential ingredient in successful therapy (Malan 1976).

The process of evaluation, though complex, may be formulated briefly: a focus is delineated, patient responds positively to isolating the focus, motivation is sufficient, and specific dangers do not seem inevitable. Of all factors in prognosis, motivation for insight and ability to focus on significant material are of primary importance. Severity and chronicity of pathology are of less importance in patient selection.

Patients are impressed that treatment is to be brief in duration. Malan favors setting a definite time limit to treatment. Malan uses a 20-session limit and an upper limit of 40 sessions as a definition of intensive brief psychotherapy. Malan stresses setting a time limit in terms of a definite date rather than number of sessions. This eliminates the necessity to keep count and avoids complications of missed sessions. Malan offers aperiodic sessions to the patient after therapy is over.

Technique: Active Therapist Involvement with Limited Focal Aim

Malan proposes an intensive brief therapy of an interpretive mode aimed at resolving the patient's central problem, or at least important aspects of it. To Malan, the most important lengthening factor in analysis is passivity in the analyst. In intensive brief psychotherapy Malan replaces therapist passivity with activity in various forms. This begins with selective planning of a limited aim. Selection of a limited aim, in part, is a reaction to an attitude of therapeutic perfectionism Malan views as common in analysis. Malan believes that therapeutic perfectionism is a deterrent to brief therapy. The limited aim is formulated in terms of a desired therapeutic effect. Because therapeutic effects are difficult to predict, Malan formulates the aim in terms of a particular area that needs work, hence a particular theme for interpretation.

The focus of treatment is usually developed within the first two interviews. This is communicated to the patient as part of the description and structure of therapy. Balint was responsible for introducing the concept of focus (Balint et al. 1972). Others have used this concept in a somewhat different manner. French (1958), for example, used the phrase focal conflict to refer to conflict in the patient's current life that is nearest the surface in any given session and is contrasted with the nuclear conflict originating in childhood.

Malan views the strategic aim of intensive brief psychotherapy as uncovering, reexperiencing, and working through repressed emotional conflict. Use of interpretation is deemed essential. Initially, Malan was concerned with the depth of interpretations. The term depth here means: far from consciousness, disturbing, and belonging to an early stage. Since one of the lengthening factors of therapy is therapist preoccupation with developmentally deeper and deeper feelings, one way of shortening therapy may be to keep interpretations superficial. Should interpretations be made only in terms of current life problems, or should they include the developmental roots of the patient's neurosis as well? Depth interpretation was feared to increase treatment duration through fostering regression and deepening patient dependency. Malan feels that these fears are groundless. Sensitive depth interpretations are seen as a necessary element of intensive brief psychotherapy. It is essential, however, that depth interpretation focus on the circumscribed area of conflict.

Transference interpretations play a major role in intensive brief psychotherapy. This is especially true when interpretation links feelings about the therapist to past feelings about parents. Interpretation of the transference–parent link is essential in successful therapy. It is important to interpret and work through negative transference. The patient must experience and understand negative feelings toward the therapist in order to learn to tolerate such feelings toward others.

Provided the formulation is correct, the course of therapy can be predicted. The initial stage of therapy is concerned with clarifying the impulse–anxiety–defense triad, working toward deeper, more disturbing material; the middle part is concerned with making the transference–parent link; and the later part of therapy will be concerned with bringing out feelings about termination, expressing these in terms of the nuclear conflict, and making the transference–parent link in this area as well.

Outcome: Support for the Radical Views of Brief Therapy

Malan saw two outstanding features in previous therapy research: (1) lack of impact of research on clinical practice and (2) despair about research expressed by leading workers in the field. Malan attributed this to failure to devise outcome criteria that do justice to the complexity of the human personality. He found that the majority of research on therapy was based on clinical impression and attempted to reduce confusion on brief therapy to a polarity of conservative and radical views. According to the conservative view, brief therapy was suitable only for mild illness of recent onset. Techniques should be simple and transference interpretation avoided. Results could only be palliative. According to the radical view, far-reaching changes could be brought about in relatively severe and chronic illnesses by a technique of active interpretation containing all essential elements of full-scale analysis. A complete spectrum of these views may be found in the literature (Malan 1976).

Malan (1963, 1976) published two series of studies on brief therapy. The 1963 study was based on the case histories of patients seen in brief therapy by Malan and his co-workers. Findings were based on a clinical and statistical analysis of highly condensed therapy summaries. Successful treatment was found to be correlated with early emergence of transference, thorough interpretation of negative transference, interpretation of the transference–parent link, ability of patient to work through grief and anger about termination, and therapist enthusiasm.

Malan (1976) published a replication of this study using a more rigorous methodology to obtain more objectively quantitative data. The 1976 report provided no confirmation for the negative transference finding and little for the early transference, termination, and therapist enthusiasm findings. Successful treatment was found to be highly related to the ability to formulate a focus and patient motivation to work with this focus. Strong support was found for the importance of making the transference–parent link. Since the central therapeutic mechanism in analytic therapy emphasized by many writers is working through the transference relationship, the fact that the transference–parent link has been shown to have an important relevance to outcome in both studies was seen by

Malan as constituting validation in a clinical setting of a fundamental analytic principle (Malan 1976).

A number of generalizations can be made from Malan's work: (1) certain neurotic patients have a far greater capacity for genuine recovery than previously thought, (2) there exists a type of patient who can benefit radically, within the limits of brief therapy, from partially working through nuclear conflict in the transference, (3) such patients can be recognized in advance through a process of dynamic interaction, and (4) there exist certain more disturbed or complex patients with whom a carefully chosen partial focus can be therapeutically effective. Some of these generalizations are new, some are not, but even those that are not new have never been generally accepted. The work of Malan has supplied empirical evidence for these convictions and has expanded the boundaries of brief therapy to include more than the traditional criterion of acute and recent onset. Malan's studies provided support for the radical view of brief therapy. With careful selection, relatively disturbed patients can be helped toward permanent change by an active technique containing the essential elements of analytic treatment.

Malan attempted to systematically study the process of therapy. Case histories were qualitatively and quantitatively analyzed. Though much was done to broaden and sharpen the application of brief therapy, there are problems with his research. Ratings of outcome and type of interpretation were made by the same people; thus ratings were not independent. Much of the evidence was taken from highly condensed summaries, not verbatim transcripts, suggesting a possible bias. Also, findings were largely based on correlations that do not yield causal relations.

PETER SIFNEOS

While Malan's work on brief therapy was being carried on at the Tavistock Clinic in Britain, Peter Sifneos was involved in comparable work at Massachussetts General Hospital in Boston. Though unaware of each other's work until 1964, many of their publications reached similar conclusions. At this time brief therapy in the United States emphasized crisis intervention and restoration of previous functioning. Sifneos saw crisis intervention as the treatment of choice for certain severely disturbed individuals. He also recognized a less severely disturbed group of individuals with relatively stable ego functioning. He offered this group a different form of brief therapy. He referred to this therapy as short-term anxiety-provoking psychotherapy.

Based on analytic principles, short-term anxiety-provoking psychotherapy aims to resolve psychic conflict and help patients learn new ways of functioning. This is done by actively focusing the patient on oedipal problems. Given proper selection of subjects by specific criteria, the effectiveness of short-term anxiety-provoking psychotherapy has been documented in clinical studies (Sifneos 1979).

Selection: Development of an Oedipal Focus

Sifneos considered the selection of appropriate patients for short-term anxiety-provoking psychotherapy to be essential and used the following criteria: (1) circumscribed chief complaint, (2) previous meaningful relationship, (3) capacity to relate flexibly during interview and access to feelings, (4) above-average psychological sophistication and intelligence, and (5) motivation for change.

Based on information from the patient, the therapist arrives at a dynamic formulation and a therapeutic focus that crystallizes the specific conflicts to be resolved during treatment. The focus is communicated to the patient and efforts are made to obtain cooperation and agreement. The focus becomes the central point of the treatment. Mutual agreement about the focus constitutes the therapeutic contract, which establishes limits to therapeutic work and lays the foundation for the therapeutic alliance. In addition, the contract serves the purpose of making the patient take an active responsibility in treatment.

The underlying conflicts involved in the therapeutic foci of patients in short-term therapy have to do with oedipal/genital or triangular/interpersonal interactions. Sifneos differentiates three categories of oedipal problems: (1) The situation in which patients linger too long in their attachment to the opposite-sex parent and fail to pursue a suitable surrogate among peers. These patients are seen as prime candidates for short-term therapy. (2) A more complex situation in which the patient is subtly encouraged by the parents to remain attached to them. An example of such a situation would be a father who clearly prefers his daughter over the other children and behaves seductively. (3) The most complicated category, in which a major external event has occurred during the oedipal period creating difficulties that cannot be changed, thus clearly interfering with oedipal resolution (e.g., death of parent). Sifneos believes that the majority of short-term therapy failures are due to faulty evaluation and acceptance of patients with pregenital character traits. Such traits include passivity, excessive dependency, poor impulse control, and manipulative tendencies.

The final task for the therapist, though not central to evaluation, is valuable to outcome assessment. This is the specification of criteria for successful results. The therapist states what would constitute a resolution of the patient's idiosyncratic difficulties, both dynamically and phenomenologically. It is specified, for example, what symptoms will be eliminated, in what way interpersonal difficulties will change, and how self-esteem and self-understanding will be effected. These specifications are tested by independent evaluation at the end of treatment. Sifneos credited Malan (1976) with the concept of specifying outcome criteria for brief therapy.

On the basis of this extensive evaluation, Sifneos feels that patients fulfilling these criteria are capable of withstanding a great deal of anxiety. For this reason the treatment is called anxiety provoking. Anxiety is not decreased in treatment. No medication is given. The therapy does not support the patient or tell the patient what to do. It is maintained that the patient is able to explore resistances and underlying dynamic conflicts.

Technique: Interpretation of the Therapist–Parent Link

Short-term anxiety-provoking psychotherapy is a dynamic therapy based on analytic principles. The face-to-face interview is used to discourage rambling, ruminative behavior, which may occur in an attempt to avoid unpleasant material following an anxiety-provoking confrontation. Interviews are weekly. Although it is made clear that the treatment is expected to last several months, no rigid number of sessions is specified. In practice, treatment averages four months with a range of two months to a year. The therapist attempts to establish good rapport with the patient as soon as possible in order to create a therapeutic alliance conducive to the problem-solving task at hand. A rapidly developed therapeutic alliance is considered of extreme importance. The patient's initial transference feelings, which are usually positive, are used to strengthen the alliance and help create a joint venture where understanding and learning can take place. The strong positive feelings of the patient in the beginning of treatment are seen as resulting from the intensive patient–therapist interaction during the evaluation, which has prepared the patient for treatment.

The therapist utilizes the patient's transference feelings in a vigorous and explicit manner. This is a golden opportunity to bring old family conflicts into the atmosphere of the developing patient–therapist relationship. The therapist confronts the patient with transference feelings and uses them as the main therapeutic tool. Rather than waiting for the transference to develop into a resistance (transference neurosis), it is interpreted as soon as it appears.

The transference neurosis is also avoided by an active avoidance of characterological complications. Material pertaining to pregenital characterological issues is systematically avoided. In addition to prolonging treatment, discussion of such issues as passivity, dependency, and acting-out tendencies is frequently used defensively to avoid discussing focal oedipal issues that create anxiety. When the patient presents such material, the therapist's task is to interpret and reestablish the oedipal focus.

Two features characterize short-term anxiety-provoking psychotherapy: (1) the therapist regularly focuses on unresolved oedipal conflicts underlying the patient's emotional problems, and (2) the therapist avoids the difficulties involving primitive character traits. The best technical tools used for remaining on therapeutic focus are questions, clarification, and confrontations timed appropriately, aimed at creating enough anxiety to maintain the patient's motivation for problem solving on a high level (Sifneos 1972).

Confrontation and anxiety-provoking questions are used to increase the emotional intensity of the session and to explore areas of difficulty that the patient tends to avoid. Short-term anxiety-provoking psychotherapy emphasizes that a certain degree of anxiety is necessary during the interview. Anxiety is seen to motivate the reluctant patient to understand the nature of emotional conflicts, to recognize defensive reactions utilized to deal with them, and to enable the patient to have a corrective emotional experience (Sifneos 1967). Interventions frequently involve the patient's illogical conclusions, ineffectual responses, irrational wishes, and maladaptive behavior patterns. The anxiety-provoking quality of these tactics highlights the importance of a detailed assessment of ego strength in candidates for short-term therapy.

Interventions most likely to produce anxiety are invariably associated with oedipal material and/or transference feelings. Such interventions are used repeatedly by the therapist to make the all-important therapist–parent link. This link brings into the therapeutic relationship the old oedipal problems and the feelings associated with them. It enables the patient and therapist to examine these feelings "alive" in the interview. The opportunity to create an atmosphere for a corrective emotional experience takes place. The displacements onto the therapist of feelings, attitudes, and behavior patterns the patient experienced toward parental figures can be examined and analyzed. The possibility of new learning is made available to the patient.

Sifneos places great importance on therapy as a learning experience. The patient learns not only about himself but also new ways of solving emotional problems. Learning problem-solving techniques is strongly emphasized in anxiety-provoking psychotherapy. Sifneos believes that the problem-solving, cognitive component of therapy is just as important as the affective element, which up to that time had been viewed as playing the dominant role in successful outcome.

Problem solving and new learning cannot take place without the therapist's repeated interpretations. The interpretation must be effectively timed and based on evidence provided by the patient. Such interventions constitute novel explanations and potential solutions the patient had not previously considered. The patient begins to identify with the therapist and imitates this technique of analyzing information. The patient quickly realizes that old ways of handling problems are outmoded and that new patterns of behavior offer better opportunities for success. When this occurs, a crucial aspect of therapy has been accomplished.

Evidence of problem solving, changes in attitude, and altered behavioral patterns suggest a change in the patient and signal to the therapist that treatment is approaching termination. The therapist must watch for hints about termination from the patient. If not forthcoming, the therapist initiates the discussion, emphasizing trust that the patient can carry on this work alone.

One of the best ways to evaluate change is to scrutinize the therapy relationship. Demonstration of progressive independence, self-assurance, improved self-esteem, and less reliance upon the therapist are important measures of progress. Satisfied with the progress, but realizing all difficulties are not overcome, the therapist must avoid the temptation of prolonging treatment.

When dealing with the issue of termination, one is frequently confronted with the patient's ambivalence about loss of the therapist. The Sifneos approach, however, by focusing on oedipal issues, generally experiences little termination difficulty. Although loss does play a role in the oedipal period, it is not the devastating loss that occurs in patients fixated at earlier pregenital states. Termination is viewed by most patients as the logical conclusion of hard, problem-solving work.

Outcome: Learning a Method of
Examining and Solving Emotional Problems

Sifneos (1961, 1964) presented results of follow-up interviews with twenty-one patients treated with short-term therapy. Patients reported moderate symptom relief, increased self-understanding, striking improvement in self-esteem, successful resolution of the crisis that was instrumental in bringing them to therapy, and more realistic expectations of therapeutic outcome. Encouraged by the findings, it was decided to more systematically investigate therapeutic outcome by a controlled study of patients chosen according to short-term anxiety-provoking psychotherapy selection criteria and treated according to the technical requirements discussed earlier.

The patients were seen by two independent evaluators before and after treatments. Patients were designated "experimental" or "control" and matched to age and sex. The control patients waited for the approximate time that the experimental group was in treatment and were seen again to assess any changes that had taken place while they were waiting. Following this, they were also offered treatment. The groups were then compared and followed as long as possible. There were numerous difficulties with the study, the most prominent being loss of patients in the experimental and control groups, leading to a small number of subjects per group.

Results of this work were similar to earlier findings. Improvement was seen in problem-solving ability, self-esteem, and self-understanding. Although the control group showed only minimal improvement at the end of their waiting period, after treatment they compared favorably with the experimental group. Moderate symptom improvement and conflict resolution was seen in the majority of both groups (Sifneos 1979).

The results of short-term therapy were classified under three main categories of change: intrapsychic, interpersonal, and psychodynamic. Intrapsychic changes, as reported by the patients, included moderate symptom relief, increase in self-esteem, more realistic expectation of therapy, new learning and problem solving, increased self-understanding, and absence of desire for more therapy. The findings demonstrated that while only partial symptom relief was achieved, the patients' attitudes regarding their symptoms changed. The symptoms no longer seemed overwhelming nor did they interfere with normal functioning. Sifneos observed that many patients did not want to abandon their symptoms completely because they were viewed as a solution. It was nice, so to speak, to keep them "in reserve."

Interpersonal relationships were scrutinized, and specific changes were noted. It was found that patients had predominantly positive feelings toward their therapist. Overall improvement in relationships with key people in their environment were noted, as were development of new meaningful relationships. Psychodynamic changes, as observed by the evaluator, were also noted. To Sifneos, psychodynamic change involved substituting more adaptive and useful defense mechanisms for maladaptive ones, as a result of moderate or complete resolution of the underlying dynamic conflict. This was noted in a number of patients. However, although Sifneos presented evidence of limited dynamic change, he found that no basic characterological changes occurred.

Long-term follow-up of up to four years reflected the overall trend of the above findings. The most significant follow-up finding was that short-term anxiety-provoking psychotherapy, with its emphasis on learning and problem solving, continued to facilitate the solving of emotional problems long after treatment.

HABIB DAVANLOO

Davanloo has been involved with short-term dynamic psychotherapy at Montreal General Hospital in Canada since the early 1960s. Davanloo's research began when he noted the inefficiency of long-term therapy in the hospital's outpatient psychiatric unit.

Davanloo began a twenty-year project of experiments, publishing the majority of his results since 1975. In 1973, Davanloo became aware of the research efforts of Sifneos and Malan and began a collaboration. Largely through Davanloo's efforts, international symposia were organized in 1975, 1976, and 1977, bringing together professionals interested in brief, dynamic therapy. The proceedings of these symposia, in particular the 1977 symposium, provided much of the impetus for a book on brief treatment edited by Davanloo (Davanloo 1980).

Davanloo's technique, grounded in analytic theory, also reverses the trend toward therapist inactivity originally initiated by Freud. When a particular topic makes a patient resistant and uncomfortable, rather than the therapist becoming passive and waiting for further developments, Davanloo thought it correct to challenge defenses forcefully. This inevitably would arouse anger in the patient as well as the patient's typical defenses against these feelings. In this model patient anger is brought into the open as it occurs, as is any other manifestation of transference. While using a very focused interview, Davanloo adheres strictly to three fundamental analytic principles: (1) release of repressed feelings by actively working on and interpreting resistance, (2) strict attention to transference, and (3) linking transference phenomena to both past and current relationships (Davanloo 1978).

Initial reaction to Davanloo's work from professional peers was somewhat hostile. In his therapeutic demonstrations patients seemed hounded and persecuted. Patient reports of success and lasting behavioral change, however, forced clinicians to consider his theory and not only react to his aggressive style.

Selection: Trial Therapy Model of Evaluation

Short-term dynamic psychotherapy refers to a spectrum of brief, dynamic therapies based on analytic technique. Therapists accept for treatment patients suffering from a wide range of neurotic disorders. Good candidates for short-term therapy can be categorized into four major groups: (1) patients with a predominantly oedipal focus, (2) patients in whom the focus is primarily a loss, (3) patients suffering from phobias and/or obsessional neuroses with one or more foci, and (4) patients suffering from long-standing, neurotic characterological problems.

Evaluation focuses on assessment of ego functions of primary importance to dynamic therapy. The process of evaluation should enable the therapist to make a psychiatric, dynamic, and genetic diagnosis, and on this basis, a therapeutic recommendation.

To establish a patient as suitable for short-term dynamic psychotherapy, a set of criteria must be fulfilled. These criteria are related to: (1) the ability to establish therapeutic focus, (2) the quality of object relationships, (3) the capacity to experience and tolerate anxiety, guilt and depression, (4) psychological-mindedness, and (5) the motivation and response to interpretation (Davanloo 1980).

Davanloo felt that the most crucial selection criterion is response to interpretation. The evaluation is more than an assessment of the patient's history and current situation. To properly determine how a patient will respond to short-term therapy, Davanloo initiates certain aspects of the therapeutic process in the opening interview. This trial therapy is an essential part of the evaluation process and determines whether a patient can withstand the impact of uncovering unconscious material and can be responsive to interpretive treatment.

Technique: Persistent Challenge and
Analysis of Resistance and Defense

Short-term dynamic psychotherapy includes a spectrum of therapies used in accordance with the particular needs of the patient. The technique and principles of short-term therapy are based on analytic technique with the exception of the increased activity of the therapist. Short-term technique consists of analysis of defense, resistance, and transference. The technique used in the initial interview is essentially the technique used in the therapy. The patient is continuously confronted with feelings regarding the transference, current life, and past situations; when possible, links are made between these three areas. Short-term therapy is characterized by the following:

1. Active maintenance of a focus with liberal use of confrontation and interpretation. The early use of confrontation and interpretation frequently leads to a seeming lack of differentiation between treatment and evaluation. Such intervention is deemed necessary to both test hypotheses concerning dynamics and to test patient receptivity to uncovering work.

2. Rapid establishment of therapeutic alliance. This allows therapist and patient to collaborate and direct attention to the therapeutic focus.

3. Early utilization of transference with intensive use of interpretation and clarification. Positive transference feelings are utilized both to strengthen the therapeutic alliance and, through interpretation, to increase the patient's self-understanding. Early interpretation of negative transference is considered essential for the maintenance of the therapeutic alliance.

4. Active working through of resistance. Manifestations of resistance are not interpreted as a decline in the therapeutic alliance, but rather as an invitation for active interpretation and working through of defenses.

5. Meticulous attention to patient feedback. In initial stages feedback frequently consists of increased resistance, but, as soon as the core problem is touched, the patient almost invariably experiences relief and hope, which is reflected in an increased willingness to collaborate, i.e., an increase in motivation and therapeutic alliance. This assures the therapist of the correctness of the approach. Attention is given to signs of extreme regression, fluidity of thought processes, and other

symptoms of adverse patient reaction, which suggest more supportive techniques.

6. Active avoidance of symbiotic transference, particularly in passive-dependent and severe obsessional characters. This is initially done through patient selection and, during treatment, by means of frequent confrontation. Actively bringing out passivity and dependency with confronting techniques does not allow development of symbiotic transference. The transference neurosis is actively avoided.

7. Active interpretive work to help the patient develop an emotional understanding of the relationship between their defensive patterns, the impulse/feeling being defended against, and the anxiety experienced at the threatened breakthrough of the impulse resulting in the defensive pattern. The relationship between defense, anxiety, and impulse is called the triangle of conflict.

8. Active interpretive work involving the transference-current-past triangle. In this crucial aspect of short-term therapy, links are developed between current behavior patterns (C), past behavior with parents or parent substitutes (P), and behavior in the transference (T). The complete transference-current-past interpretation is preceded by pointing out parallels between the patient's reaction to the transference and current people (the transference-current link) and between the transference and the past (the transference-past link). Early and frequent use of meaningful transference-current-past interpretation has been found to positively correlate with treatment success.

9. Emphasis on emotional experiences of the patient in the transference. A definite rise in the transference during the first session and a continual high level of transference in the first few sessions has been correlated with successful outcome.

Conflicts that emerge during short-term therapy are the same as those encountered in analysis. These consist of buried feelings the patient has from childhood experiences. Compared to analysis, these conflicts emerge in a more overt and unmistakable form, rather than through gradual inference and reconstruction.

Repeated confrontation of the patient with painful feelings frequently leads to the development of angry feelings toward the therapist as well as defense against those feelings. Focusing on this anger is essential. Demonstrating to the patient the defense against anger in the three areas of transference, current, and past is a powerful therapeutic tool and frequently leads to the expression of other repressed feelings involving love, hate, loss, and forbidden childhood wishes. With the uncovering and reexperiencing of these conflicts, therapeutic effects begin to occur. This usually happens by the sixth or eighth session. Active confrontation in the form of pointing out defenses forces the patient to experience repressed feelings. This results in the core neurosis being unrepressed and more fully experienced. Rather than being complicated and overdetermined, it frequently has to do with simple things concerning feelings left over from childhood — love and hate, loss and grief. Davanloo shows that the intense experience of this highly interactional treatment significantly decreases the amount of time needed to complete the working through process of therapy. Short-term therapy averages from 10 to 15 sessions with an upper limit of 25. Davanloo considers therapy successful when the patient no longer has symptoms, has given up maladaptive behavior, and has cognitive and emotional insight into the core neurosis that caused the difficulties (Davanloo 1978).

Termination usually occurs without difficulty. This is especially true where the focus is primarily oedipal. Where the focus is loss, the process of working through termination becomes an essential part of therapy, taking up to five sessions. Dependence on the therapist is rarely an issue (Davanloo 1980).

Outcome: Resolution of Core Neurosis

Davanloo began his research in response to long waiting lists, high dropout rates, and low staff morale at the outpatient psychiatric clinic of Montreal General Hospital. An appraisal of the clinic highlighted additional difficulties, including lack of clear-cut therapeutic goals, fragmented therapy contact, and inadequate assessment. In 1963, Davanloo began research in short-term dynamic therapy. Patients were selected by means of criteria revised in response to therapy results. Patients not qualifying for short-term therapy received supportive therapy.

In developing short-term dynamic psychotherapy, Davanloo recorded all therapy contacts using a tape recorder or videotape. Playing and replaying tapes, Davanloo determined which ingredients in his technique seemed to lead to progress, and which to failure. When he thought he had identified an important factor, he systematically employed it in his next half-dozen cases. As effective ingredients in short-term therapy were identified, Davanloo began to shorten therapy. Initially therapy lasted from ten to thirty sessions with an upper limit of forty; at present therapy lasts from ten to fifteen sessions with an upper limit of twenty-five.

The outcome of short-term dynamic psychotherapy was evaluated by a sophisticated technique involving interviews by both the therapist and an independent evaluator immediately after termination and a second set of interviews up to five years later. In addition, the patient also evaluated the therapeutic process and outcome. Six months after treatment the patient observed five randomly selected recorded therapy sessions and determined the changes as well as important variables in treatment outcome. Successful outcome in Davanloo's research applied to those patients fulfilling outcome criteria for dynamic change: disappearance of symptoms, definite change in patterns of defense mechanisms and mode of ego function, insight into emotional conflicts, and understanding of symptoms in dynamic terms. Such changes begin to occur between the fifth and eighth sessions, permeating the patient's entire life by termination. At termination successful outcome means definite evidence of the total resolution of the patient's core neurosis.

Davanloo has treated more than 170 patients in three studies.

The majority of the work, consisting of initial interviews, therapeutic sessions, and outcome evaluation, has been recorded audiovisually and is in the process of systematic analysis and publication. In his largest research project, lasting from 1963 to 1975, Davanloo evaluated 575 prospective patients, 130 of whom fulfilled the criteria for short-term dynamic psychotherapy. Of the 130 patients, 115 were treated successfully within an average of 20 sessions. Treatment success was still noted in these patients with follow-ups up to seven years (Davanloo 1980).

Improvement in the patient was found to begin after certain types of events in therapy, particularly the open acknowledgement of hostility in the transference, followed by an interpretation linking patterns in the transference relationship with similar patterns in current and past relationships. Davanloo feels that persistent challenging of defense makes short-term therapy effective even with very resistant patients suffering from chronic symptomatic and characterological problems. Davanloo estimates that short-term therapy is applicable in 30 to 35 percent of the patients presenting themselves at the Community Mental Health Center of the Montreal General Hospital.

Table 1 summarizes the major characteristics of the therapy models developed by Malan, Sifneos, and Davanloo.

Table 1. Comparison of Malan's, Sifneos's and Davanloo's Approaches to Short-Term Dynamic Psychotherapy.

	Malan	Sifneos	Davanloo
SELECTION			
Interview	Formulate dynamics, treatment plan, and success criteria. Attention given to patient–therapist interaction. Trial interpretations.	Formulate dynamics, treatment plan, and success criteria. Thorough history-taking for signs of early pathology and to clarify oedipal issues.	Highly interactive formulation of dynamics, treatment plan, and success criteria. Trial therapy model used; neurotic defenses challenged with attention given to response to interpretive intervention. Therapist flexibility emphasized.
Patient characteristics facilitating treatment	Motivation, ability to develop treatment focus.	Ability to develop focus, introspect, and interact flexibly. Previous meaningful relationship. Motivation essential.	Ability to develop focus and become involved in flexible emotional interaction. Ability to tolerate painful affect, introspect, and develop high motivation. Patient works with early interpretations.
Problems treated	Limits not fully explored. Nature of pathology and symptom duration of minor importance. Potential depressives, latent psychotics, and addicts rejected.	Interpersonal difficulties and circumscribed symptoms resulting from oedipal conflict. Pregenital character traits avoided.	Oedipal conflicts, long standing neurotic characters, recent losses. Rejections include paranoid conditions, previous psychotic decompensation, severe self-destructive tendencies, and poor impulse control.

Therapy contract	Treatment focus agreed upon. Brevity of treatment stressed. Time limit set. Therapy lasts 10 to 40 sessions with optimal limit of 20.	Agreement on focus constitutes contract. Emphasize brief therapy but no limit set. Therapy lasts 8 to 52 sessions with average of 16.	Focus agreed upon. Therapy averages 10 to 15 sessions with upper limit of 25.
TECHNIQUE Initial maneuvers	Crystallize focus. Establish alliance.	Develop rapport. Rapid establishment of alliance. Education about role activities of therapy stressed.	Rapid establishment of alliance. Therapy technique essentially that of trial therapy model used in initial interview.
Patient–therapist interaction	Therapist passivity replaced with activity.	Highly interactive. Therapist confronts, clarifies, and questions unresolved oedipal conflicts. Emotional intensity is high. Anxiety is deemed necessary.	Emotional engagement emphasized. Therapist not merely impersonal conveyor of intepretation but an active participant in interaction.
Focus	Maintained by selective attention and neglect. Importance of staying on focus increases with severity of pathology.	Maintained through confrontation, questioning, and interpretation.	Maintained through confrontation and interpretation.
Significant therapeutic maneuvers	Limited therapeutic aim is selected to combat an attitude of therapeutic perfectionism.	Problem-solving, cognitive component of therapy seen as important as affective element.	Interpretation of relationship between current, past, and transferential feelings.

(Continued)

73

Table 1. *Continued*

	Malan	Sifneos	Davanloo
Transference management	Transference manifestations interpreted, especially transference–parent link. Negative feelings towards therapist pointed out and worked through.	Transference feelings immediately confronted. Transference neurosis avoided through early interpretation and avoidance of pregenital issues.	Transference feelings discussed immediately, especially negative transference. Symbiotic transference actively avoided through confrontation of dependency strivings.
Role of interpretation and insight	Interpretation an essential intervention. Directed towards focal issues of conflict. Understanding transference–parent link emphasized.	Intervention focus on triangular/oedipal relations. Transference–parent link essential. Interpretations focus on impulse as opposed to defense (resistance).	Active interpretive work involving triangle of conflict (impulse–anxiety–defense) and triangle of insight (past–current–transference).
Resistance	Dealt with through interpretation.	Dealt with through confrontation and anxiety-provoking questions.	Strong emphasis on analysis of character defenses (resistance) to force a reexperiencing of repressed feeling. Meticulous attention given to patient responses to deep interpretations.

Working through	Accomplished in regard to a specific, limited focus.	Emotional and cognitive education concerning oedipal conflict and its manifestations.	Intenseness of emotional experience decreases length of working through.
Corrective emotional experience	Not emphasized.	Intense reexperience of oedipal anxieties in relationship to therapist results in realization that old ways of handling problems are outmoded.	Strong emphasis on emotional experience in the transference.
Termination	Limit set in terms of date. Extra sessions after termination offered if necessary.	Changes in and out of therapy signal approaching termination. Therapist must initiate discussion if patient doesn't. Oedipal focus makes termination less painful.	Occurs without difficulty. Dependency on therapist rarely problem.
OUTCOME	Successful treatment related to: 1. ability to formulate treatment focus; 2. patient motivation; 3. active interpretation of transference–parent link.	Successful treatment related to: 1. active focus on oedipal conflict; 2. avoidance of transference neurosis; 3. concentration on problem solving.	Successful treatment related to: 1. response to trial therapy; 2. open acknowledgement of negative transference; 3. active interpretation of relationship between the transference, current, and past relationship.

(Continued)

Table 1. *Continued*

Malan	Sifneos	Davanloo
Patients found to benefit greatly from a partial working through focal conflict in the transference relationship.	Treatment results included improvement in self-esteem, self-understanding, and moderate symptom relief.	Persistent challenging and analysis of defenses felt to make therapy effective even with chronic characterlogical problems.
Such patients can be recognized by means of a highly interactive assessment.	Though only moderate symptom relief reported, attitudes regarding symptom changed. Symptoms no longer seemed overwhelming.	Successful treatment considered to be total resolution of core neurosis.
Certain more disturbed patients can benefit from concentration on a carefully chosen partial focus.	Most significant long-term effect is increased ability to "problem solve" emotional difficulties.	

CHAPTER FOUR
The Assessment and Selection of Patients

The assessment of a patient for psychotherapy is a complex and subtle procedure. The development of an accurate understanding of the patient is affected by: (1) the presentation of the patient, (2) the level of knowledge and experience of the interviewer, and (3) the interviewer's countertransference to the particular patient being assessed. The assessment process is not the taking of a psychiatric or social history, nor is it a psychotherapeutic session — it contains elements of all three. The complexity of the assessment interview arises because of the diversity of tasks the interviewer must accomplish. These tasks include: (1) understanding the patient's presenting problems, (2) assessing level of crisis, (3) understanding the genetic development of the patient's difficulties, and (4) gaining a sense for the patient's current life situation and past history. The interviewer constantly "thinks on one's feet," switching roles and modifying the therapeutic approach according to a continually developing view of the patient and the possible treatments that seem appropriate (Malan 1980). To illustrate:

A young woman (TA) presented for therapy with mild depressive symptoms and difficulties concentrating on her studies. TA was attractive and expensively dressed, although her clothing and make-up seemed more appropriate for a woman considerably older. As TA presented her concerns, the therapist noted her willingness to discuss rather intimate aspects of her life with what seemed a great degree of insight. Her response to questions concerning her depression were responded to with a wealth of memories about past experiences. Her apparent psychological mindedness and willingness to explore her feelings and past experience suggested that TA was appropriate for an uncovering as opposed to a supportive psychotherapy. This assessment was quickly modified as TA explained that her difficulty in concentration was due to people talking inside her head as she tried to study. As she discussed these voices, she became increasingly anxious and agitated. She wondered if she was going crazy again. She was afraid it would be like the last time when she ended up in the hospital. As this interchange proceeded, the interviewer developed a vastly different picture of TA, as well as the most appropriate treatment interventions. A more tenuous, emotional balance and potential for regression now suggested a more ego-supportive approach.

Proper assessment demands considerable knowledge of personality development, the various character disorders, and the ability to apply this understanding in vivo to the patient being interviewed. The ability to integrate theoretical understanding with practical application is developed with experience, supervision, and continued study. Patient assessment also requires that the interviewer understand the treatment process, the various options and alternatives available within it, and the demands various treatments will make on the patient's internal and external resources. Without such knowledge, the treatment recommendation may not dovetail with patient needs and capacities. For example, failure of an interviewer to accurately assess a patient's ego strength and ability to tolerate anxiety may result in a treatment plan that places too great a therapeutic task on the patient. Assuming a patient has the ability to rapidly develop a therapeutic alliance when, in fact, the patient is strongly conflicted around issues of trust and dependency may result in a therapeutic impasse and ineffectual treatment.

PATIENT SELECTION

Proper patient selection by means of careful assessment is an essential aspect of successful short-term psychodynamic psychotherapy. Malan (1963) stated that in brief treatment, selection of patients is as important as the technique used. Sifneos (1972) believed that the majority of his failures with brief therapy were due to inaccurate assessment. Davanloo (1980), by means of his trial therapy model of assessment, paid meticulous attention to the initial therapist-patient interaction. The time-limited nature of short-term therapy does not afford the opportunity of allowing patient assessment to gradually unfold as treatment progresses. Such a stance may be taken in long-term therapy. In the latter, treatment may be conceptualized as diagnostic investigation in which the inner situation of the patient gradually unfolds in an eversharpened form (Singer 1965).

In short-term psychodynamic psychotherapy the therapist cannot allow the diagnosis and assessment process to reach its climax with the end of therapy. The specific demands this therapy places on patient resources requires an early and accurate assessment of the patient's character structure and level of functioning. The feasibility of short-term therapy rests in large part on the interviewer's ability to develop a clear understanding of the patient during the assessment phase of treatment. In their classic presentation of brief therapy technique, Alexander and French (1946) emphasized the importance of the active development of an accurate and in-depth understanding of patient dynamics. It was their opinion that to work rapidly the therapist must know a great deal about the patient.

In this chapter we outline a diagnostic procedure to be used in assessing patient suitability for short-term psychodynamic psychotherapy. In addition to aiding therapists in identifying those patients best suited for this therapy, we hope this discussion will enable therapists to strengthen their understanding of the underlying treatment principles. Understanding the type of patient most effectively treated by a particular modality often facilitates a deeper grasp of that particular treatment. Our discussion draws from the ideas of David Malan, Peter Sifneos, and Habib Davanloo. Additionally, discussions on patient assessment by Dewald (1965) and Palino (1981) are integrated into our work.

Aims of Assessment

The psychotherapy assessment interview has the goal of developing sufficient understanding of the prospective patient to make an appropriate treatment recommendation. In assessment for short-term psychodynamic psychotherapy this goal is accomplished in the following manner:

1. Explore the patient's presenting difficulties and current state of functioning.
2. Obtain a history of the patient's emotional development.
3. Relate current difficulties to patient's underlying psychological structure.
4. Assess ego functions of importance to uncovering psychodynamic treatment.
5. Develop therapeutic focus and treatment contract.

The above tasks overlap and blend into each other. For instance, to understand the psychodynamic significance of the patient's presenting problem, knowledge of past development is needed. This in turn is provided by means of history taking. We find it helpful to differentiate these various tasks of the interviewer as a means of clarifying the responsibilities of the assessment process. It should be recognized, however, that in treatment such a division is not static, nor is it sharply circumscribed.

Presenting Difficulties and Current State of Functioning

To understand a patient's present state of functioning, the interviewer must attempt to define the current forces in the patient's life that are operative in producing the patient's emotional difficulties. The interviewer strives to understand the purpose and meaning of particular symptoms and behavior in terms of the individual's personality structure and environmental realities. To aid in exploration and understanding of the patient's current intrapsychic functioning, the interviewer may consider the following questions: (1) What is the exact nature of the presenting problem? (2) How much of the patient's problem is the result of conflict between internal forces (e.g., id drives versus superego prohibitions)? (3) How much is a reaction to external forces (environmental constraints)? (4) What are the primary and secondary gains of the problem? (5) What is the current level of crisis? (6) How well is the patient adapting to this crisis?

Obtaining a Patient History

It is of critical importance during the assessment interview(s) to obtain a history of the patient's emotional development. A meaningful therapeutic plan cannot be developed without knowing, for instance, that a patient has had numerous psychiatric hospitalizations as a result of suicide attempts or that a psychotic disorganization was experienced upon entering college resulting in withdrawal from school and return to home. The taking of a psychiatric history during assessment allows the interviewer to eliminate certain patients as potential candidates for short-term psychodynamic psychotherapy. Patients for whom this therapy is contraindicated include those with a history of serious suicide attempts, long-term hospitalization, grossly destructive or self-destructive acting out, and incapacitating chronic obsessional or phobic symptoms. Patients presenting chronic alcoholism or drug addiction and confirmed homosexuals asking to be made heterosexual also may be eliminated from consideration.

Sifneos (1979) outlined several principles to be adhered to in history taking:

1. Allow patient sufficient time to describe presenting complaint. Questions for the interviewer to consider include: Where and when was the problem first noticed? How long has it been a problem, and under what circumstances?
2. Pay particular attention to the events surrounding the first onset of the difficulty. Tracing a problem back to its first occurrence often provides the interviewer with the clearest picture of the psychodynamics involved. To illustrate:

   A young woman (NT) sought treatment for anxiety attacks stemming from being informed by her boyfriend that he was leaving her in favor of another woman. Careful inquiry determined the original onset of these panic attacks to be at age 5 when NT's stepmother threatened to send her to an orphanage unless she more willingly attended kindergarten. Knowledge of only the current onset of the symptom was suggestive of issues of competition, rivalry, and unexpressed anger, primarily an oedipal focus. However, the original onset of the problem highlighted preoedipal issues of attachment and separation. Such information has important treatment implications.

3. Consider how the patient's problem affects daily life activities. For whom is it a problem? (This is particularly important in assessment of motivation for therapy). How would things be different if the patient didn't have the problem? What are the specific circumstances leading to the present consultation? And finally, why does the patient present for treatment at this specific moment in life?
4. Ask patient to recall one's earliest memory. This recollection frequently illuminates the way in which the patient views life.

5. Obtain specific information about family structure and atmosphere that prevailed when growing up.

6. Scrutinize nature of relationship with each parent. A perspective should be gained as to what the parents were actually like and what they actually did for the patient. Emphasis is placed on specific interactions between the patient and each parent. This assessment throws light on conflicts of the oedipal period. These conflicts often become the focus of treatment.

7. Gather data concerning patient's move from home to school, relationships with peers, teachers, and academic performance.

8. Assess patient's experience at puberty. This helps illuminate successful or unsuccessful strivings to resolve oedipal transactions.

9. Assess adolescence with special emphasis on interpersonal relationships.

10. Obtain information about early adulthood and current life. Focus on work, intellectual achievements, interpersonal relations, and critical life events such as marriage, divorce, and family deaths.

Although the history taking contains certain organized sets of areas to question, the process doesn't follow a cut-and-dried pattern. The patient's history should be explored in a manner that is relevant to presenting concerns. Rather than abruptly introducing seemingly unrelated topics, it is helpful for the interviewer to follow the patient's cues and to flexibly flow with the presentation of material.

Clinical Diagnosis

Taking a full history allows the formulation of a clinical diagnosis, which is often essential in determining treatment choice. For instance, therapeutic success with a patient suffering from a major affective disorder may depend on appropriate application of psychoactive medication in addition to psychotherapy. It is essential that the interviewer be able to identify these patients.

The suitability of a patient for short-term psychodynamic psychotherapy, however, requires an assessment that encompasses more than developing a specific diagnosis. Marmor (1979), for example, stated that short-term therapy is effective with a wide variety of patients presenting neurotic symptoms, personality disorders, and reactive transitional crises. The critical issue, according to Marmor, is not diagnosis so much as the possession of certain personality attributes plus the existence of a focal conflict and a high degree of motivation.

One cannot always predict response to treatment in terms of the presented symptomatology and resultant diagnostic impression. Patients assigned a similar diagnosis may vary considerably in terms of individual psychodynamics, ego resources, and environmental support for emotional growth. For example, the diagnosis of compulsive personality disorder is but a shorthand method used in describing individuals who present similar spectrums of thoughts, feelings, and behaviors. It describes, in a very general manner, adaptive and defensive functions of the ego. An individual presenting a severe compulsive personality disorder with an extremely rigid defensive system and few successful adaptive skills has a much poorer prognosis in short-term therapy than does an individual with a compulsive personality structure functioning at a higher level in terms of flexibility of defensive operations and coping strategies.

Psychodynamic Significance of Current Difficulties

Short-term psychodynamic psychotherapy is guided by the interviewer's ability to accurately conceptualize how present difficulties relate to underlying character structure and psychological development. The interviewer has two tasks. One is to relate the presenting complaint to the current dynamics. For example, a college student, procrastinating on a paper, may be involved in current issues of autonomy and performance anxiety. The second task is to relate the complaint to historical background and developmental dynamics. For example, the student had a harsh father with high expectations who required his child to attend his alma mater.

Effective therapeutic interventions require the therapist to develop a clear picture of the patient's central dynamic structure. To accomplish this task, a general overview of the patient's life is needed. The interviewer attempts to understand the forces that have affected the patient's early life, as well as reactions to these forces. This exploration facilitates the reconstruction of the historical determinant of the patient's current conflicts. The interviewer strives to determine the emotional significance of past events and to see how they have contributed to the patient's present impasse. In addition, study of past life events gives evidence of the patient's ability to cope with previous difficulties and to master earlier anxieties. To illustrate:

FL was a 20-year-old college student who sought treatment for dysphoria, apathy, insomnia, and lack of energy. He reported study difficulties and weight loss. The onset of these feelings was the recent breakup of a brief romantic relationship. FL's severe reaction to this brief encounter was initially perplexing. This puzzlement was short-lived as FL related his past history. FL's mother had died when he was 6. An only child, FL reported being extremely close to his mother. After her death, FL's father withdrew into his career, leaving FL in the care of a series of live-in housekeepers. FL reported severe depression and several suicide attempts during his latency years. After his last attempt FL became involved in what he felt to be a very successful psychotherapy and integrated his life well enough to graduate with honors from high school and to obtain entrance into a prestigious college. During this time FL maintained an emotional distance from people, with occasional development of brief, intense relationships that left FL depressed and determined to avoid further involvement.

FL's history suggested acute sensitivity to loss and abandonment and shed light upon his present problems. His previous success in treatment and ability to reorganize his life after his mother's death indicated that FL was a strong candidate for uncovering psychotherapy. However, his sensitivity to loss and his distancing mechanisms would contraindicate short-term psychodynamic psychotherapy.

Psychotherapy assessment involves the formulation of working hypotheses based on the detailed information obtained from the patient during interview. As the patient's problems and life situation are discussed, certain ideas are formed regarding underlying emotional conflicts that may help to explain the patient's symptoms and interpersonal difficulties. For instance, FL's intense reaction to losing his girlfriend was puzzling and suggested to the interviewer that loss was an important issue in FL's life. This led to an investigation of past losses in FL's life. The interviewer looks to substantiate these tentative dynamic formulations. These hypotheses, explored at length in the interview, often become the foundation upon which the whole therapeutic structure is built. FL's treatment, for example, focused on working through feelings of loss and abandonment relating to his mother's death, as well as in modifying self-defeating interpersonal defenses (i.e., detachment, withdrawal) used to insulate himself from future losses.

Assessment includes a thorough history of the patient's relationships, with particular reference to any clear-cut patterns that emerge. Such patterns may include, for example, becoming romantically involved with significantly older figures, forming many relationships but no close friends, or compulsively needing to compete and "best" one's peers. Malan (1980) suggested that the interviewer keep the following formula in mind: (1) look for a precipitating event or experience, (2) make an effort to understand the emotional impact and complexity of the event, (3) look for a genetic antecedent in the person's life that has some emotional and interpersonal similarity to the current event. To illustrate:

PT was a 25-year-old dental student who sought treatment for difficulties in her relationship with a man she had been dating. He wanted greater emotional and physical intimacy with her. PT found herself very anxious and increasingly detached from him since he brought up this topic. This was distressing in that she deeply cared for him. Careful investigation of PT's history revealed an insecure and dependent father who dealt with an unsatisfactory marriage to a narcissistic partner by investing a great deal of energy in PT while simultaneously demanding an equal investment from her. While initially pleasurable, this became increasingly uncomfortable for PT and was responded to with rebellion and counterdependent behavior. PT had learned to protect her autonomy and psychological integrity by placing emotional and physical distance between herself and her father. The similarity between her current and past reactions to important males subsequently became an important focus of treatment.

SHORT-TERM PSYCHODYNAMIC PSYCHOTHERAPY SELECTION CRITERIA

The underlying goals of assessment are to identify those patients with the capacity to: (1) rapidly enter into a therapeutic alliance, (2) work effectively in an interactional, uncovering treatment, and (3) separate from the therapist once treatment is over with a minimum of distress. Through their study of brief therapy technique, Malan, Sifneos, and Davanloo have identified a number of criteria that facilitate the identification of such patients. Individual contributions of each theorist are briefly summarized, with a more detailed discussion of the criteria to follow.

Motivation

Motivation for insight and therapeutic interchange is an essential ingredient in short-term psychodynamic psychotherapy. Sifneos (1968), finding direct correlations between motivation to change and successful outcome, considered motivation for psychotherapy to be possibly the most crucial contributing factor to successful

Table 2.   *Selection Criteria of Malan, Sifneos and Davanloo.*

Malan	Sifneos	Davanloo
1. Strong motivation for change. 2. Area of conflict on which to focus treatment may be delineated. 3. Patient responds positively to interpretations based on the emerging focus. 4. Patient presents no clear evidence to contraindicate an uncovering treatment (e.g., serious suicide risk, potential psychotic decompensation).	1. Strong motivation for change. 2. Circumscribed chief complaint (focus). 3. Previous meaningful relationship. 4. Capacity to relate flexibly during interview and to have access to feelings. 5. Above average psychological sophistication and intelligence.	1. Strong motivation for change. 2. Ability to establish a therapeutic focus. 3. Quality of object relationships. 4. Psychological mindedness. 5. Capacity to experience and tolerate anxiety, guilt, and depression. 6. Response to interpretation.

treatment. He further noted that patients who appeared to be highly motivated, even if they were quite disturbed, tended to do much better than patients more superficially healthy but not particularly motivated. Davanloo (1978) also found a strong positive correlation between motivation and successful outcome and considered its evaluation to be a significant aspect of assessment.

A high level of motivation is of particular importance in short-term therapy due to the active, interpretative nature of the technique. Treatment requires that the patient engage in an emotionally immediate examination of personal resistances and underlying dynamic conflicts. This is accomplished, in part, by investigating the nature of the reciprocal interaction between therapist and patient. Such a task is often stressful and anxiety-provoking. Patients lacking a strong desire for emotional growth tend to be reluctant to engage in this process.

A healthy motivation for therapy arises out of a sincere wish for intrapsychic change, which includes insight, less psychic pain, and increased emotional growth. Not all motivation to seek treatment arises out of a wish for further psychological growth and maturation. The interviewer must distinguish between the desire to achieve constructive psychic change and the desire to receive treatment to make one's problems go away. Motivation for change should not be confused with motivation for symptom relief. The former implies activity on the part of the patient, whereas the latter is a passive trait involving expectations that someone else is going to relieve discomfort. An example of the latter is provided.

HK was an 18-year-old male college student presenting for therapy with complaints of lack of concentration, inability to study, and occasional depressive episodes. HK explained that he knew why he had problems (his parents got divorced; he was too close to his mother, who was neurotic), but he didn't know how to change. He wanted the therapist to tell him how to do so. HK stated that he wanted his problems to go away and that it was the therapist's job to make this occur. HK responded to the therapist's explanation of therapy with frustration and impatience. He was unwilling to reflect on present feelings, to talk about past experiences, or to consider suggestions the therapist made regarding relieving his present difficulties (e.g., study skills suggestions). HK remarked that all those things would take time and that he did not have time.

In discussing the difference between neurotic motivation (i.e., motivation to enter treatment based on conflicted childhood needs) and motivation based on genuine desire for change, Palino (1981) observed that motivation for treatment is often based on a wish to reinforce rather than alleviate the neurosis. For example, a person conflicted around assertion and self-worth issues, with subsequent needs for perfection, may enter therapy in order to eliminate inhibitions in order to reach the goal of exceptional professional success.

Interpretive psychodynamic therapy can be attractive for other unconstructive reasons. A patient may seem highly willing to tolerate the anxiety and stress of therapy, when, in part, the patient is acting out a masochistic wish for punishment. Such an individual's masochism may not allow therapeutic progress. Other unconstructive motivations for therapy include wishes to (1) obtain confession and absolution, (2) decrease anxiety through emotional abreaction, (3) gain the secret answer to life's mysteries thought to be withheld by one's parents, and (4) receive validation that someone else is responsible for one's emotional hardships (i.e., parents, spouse).

The failure to determine the patient's motives for seeking treatment results in an unproductive relationship between therapist and patient. Both individuals will have differing expectations of their relationship, often dooming it to failure. The patient may not consider the problem to be psychological at all. Patient difficulties may be seen as stemming from a physical illness or the unreasonable behavior of others. Failure to attend to such attitudes results in the therapist struggling to identify and resolve emotional problems the patient does not see. The patient and therapist may continue indefinitely to talk in terms that the other does not understand or appreciate. To avoid such complications, it is important for the therapist to determine what it is the patient wants. It is the patient who must furnish the incentive for whatever is to be accomplished in treatment. No amount of reforming zeal by the therapist will be of any avail unless some strong motive of the patient's can be put to therapeutic use (Alexander and French 1946).

> ZA was a 32-year-old female graduate student who sought consultation due to her internist's recommendation. She was an only child and presently living at home. Although ZA had been experiencing stomach problems for the past year, medical tests could not identify the cause. She stated that she agreed to psychological consultation out of respect for her internist and that she didn't have any emotional problems. Although ZA was reticent to offer information about herself, the interviewer gradually developed the impression of a rather immature young woman with an ambivalent attachment to her parents, towards whom she felt dependent yet highly resentful. At the end of the hour the interviewer presented a brief summary of his understanding of ZA's problem, including a pattern of stomach pain following arguments at home. He suggested a possible connection between ZA's stomach distress and her feelings for her parents and living situation. ZA said she needed some time to think and would return next week. Upon her return, she stated that her stomach problems had dramatically improved and that she no longer was in need of treatment. Attempts to explore these feelings were unproductive. Though the therapist felt ZA could benefit from treatment, she did not seem interested or motivated for therapy. Further confrontation would undoubtedly lead to increased resistance. As she left, ZA was offered the opportunity to return if she felt like continuing their discussion at a later point.

Primary and Secondary Gain

The wish to be free of emotional distress (psychic pain) is a powerful motivation for psychotherapy. We are warned, however, not to overvalue this wish (Kuiper 1968). Palino (1981), in support of this notion, cited Freud's observation (1916) that the patient who complains the most about his/her distress often presents the greatest resistance in treatment. Resistance to change is influenced by the gains that one's problematic symptoms/coping strategies incur for the individual. All symptoms have a primary gain, and in general, a secondary gain. Although it is often difficult to clearly differentiate between primary and secondary gain, it is important to attempt to evaluate these gains as they have a great effect on the motivation for, and the ultimate success of, therapy.

From Freud onward, primary gain has referred to the importance of the symptom for the patient's internal psychic economy (Krohn 1978). The primary gain of a symptom involves the original attempt to achieve a homostatic balance to psychic functioning. It is this attempt that led to the formation of the symptom. The symptom is a compromise developed between narcissistic wishes and ego defenses that strive to allow both partial expression of these wishes, as well as providing a protection from superego or environmental punishment. A brief vignette illustrates primary gain:

> NF, a young woman, presented for therapy with feelings of depression, inadequacy, and self-depreciation. NF related the onset of these feelings to her fiancé's decision to end their engagement. Through therapy it was found that a primary gain of NF's depression was to allow expression of her anger towards her ex-fiancé while simultaneously avoiding retribution for this expression (further rejection by her fiancé). In a manner quite out of her awareness, she directed anger toward herself through self-depreciative and berating behavior. This allowed her to ventilate her feelings while at the same time avoiding a hostile confrontation with her ex-fiancé which might have permanently sealed the fate of their relationship.

The secondary gain of an emotional difficulty involves an advantage accrued from the illness that may have nothing to do with the psychodynamic forces existing at the time of its original development. Emotional disturbances may attain a practical importance in the patient's life and become difficult to relinquish. For instance, bouts of depression, originally a compromise between anger and fear of retribution, may be used to manipulate significant others or one's current life situation. Neurotic problems may be used to gratify dependency and exhibitionistic needs or to obtain financial compensation.

Secondary gain is often more quickly recognized than primary gain. The therapist is encouraged to focus on it as soon as it is determined. Failure to do so may lead to complications that severely compromise treatment in that the patient's ongoing motivation for change is significantly affected by the particular gratifications that are given up as change occurs (Glover 1956). As Rank (1936) observed, emotional growth involves loss of the security afforded by past coping strategies.

Criteria to Assess Patient Motivation

Sifneos has offered the following criteria for the assessment of patient motivation (Sifneos 1972).

1. *An ability to recognize the psychological nature of symptoms.* Such awareness demonstrates a degree of psychological sophistication. This may be contrasted with an attitude of denial of emotional difficulties, often accompanied by the insistence that the only reason for seeing a psychotherapist is because of the recommendation of the referring physician. For example, a 35-year-old garage mechanic demonstrated a degree of psychological awareness with the following statement: "I thought that my headaches were due to some physical cause. I was angry when the Nerve Clinic made an appointment for me to see a psychiatrist. When the doctor explained to me that nervousness can aggravate headaches, I realized that when I was tense my headaches became worse. I know that I am nervous, but I did not put the two together" (Sifneos 1972).

2. *A tendency to be introspective and to give an honest and truthful account of emotional difficulties.* A 28-year-old graduate student described it this way:

   For a long time I had tried to understand why I break out in sweating and nausea when I have to make presentations in my classes. At first, I thought I had some kind of skin disorder and a weak nervous system. But this doesn't really make sense. I think it has something to do with how I feel about myself, and how I want other people to feel about me. I don't know what it's all about, but I know I've got to stop avoiding my problems and take an honest look at myself.

3. *Willingness to participate actively in the treatment situation.* The implication here is that the patient does not want to be a passive participant. Sifneos (1972) presented the following as an example of a desire to remain passive. A 22-year-old girl, in describing her reactions to a recent date, related the following:

> I lie in bed, tossing back and forth, and I keep thinking about my date, the way he looked, the way he danced, and the girls he talked with. I feel quite jealous. I finally get exhausted trying to figure everything out, and I fall asleep. My priest tells me what to do and so does my mother. But it isn't enough. I want everyone to guide me because I am so confused I cannot think straight. After all, I cannot be with my mother and my priest all the time. I expect you to work for me. Isn't it your job?

4. *Curiosity and willingness to understand oneself.* Active curiosity signifies self-inquisitiveness, introspection, and a willingness to understand oneself. Such curiosity may indicate a motivation train that can be utilized constructively in psychotherapy. Positive indicators are such questions as: "Do you think my reactions to my family still influence what I do?" "Is it possible that by trying to understand my past relationships that I can somehow behave differently now?"

5. *Willingness to change, explore, and experiment.* These attitudes reveal some flexibility and are indicative of the turning to psychotherapy as a new way to deal with his problem. For example, a 42-year-old man, presenting with fear of airplane travel, said, "I'm to a point where I need to get a handle on this problem. My job requires that I make occasional trips. It's difficult always trying to arrange my situation where I can get

around my fears. I am tired of it and am willing to put some effort in changing."

6. *Expectations of the results of psychotherapy.* A distinction should be made between unrealistic and realistic expectations. Unrealistic expectations are vague, nonspecific, exaggerated, and magical. They are the remnants of childhood wishes that are omnipotent in nature and give the indication of a poor assessment of reality. For example, a patient who had never written or published anything expected that, as a result of the treatment, he would be able to write a novel and become a best-selling author. Realistic expectations, on the other hand, are usually modest, specific, and circumscribed. A 20-year-old single student stated:

I have talked with you about my worries, about my poor grades, my problems with my father, and my feelings of guilt. I don't know why, but at the present time I am mad at my roommate. This makes my life very difficult. Of course, I could move out of our apartment. However, this would not explain what makes me angry at him. If psychotherapy can help me realize what lies behind these angry feelings, I would be quite satisfied.

7. *Willingness to make reasonable sacrifices.* Most patients are willing to make compromises, but occasionally a seemingly well-motivated patient may prove to be unwilling to make specific sacrifices, such as arranging transportation to the clinic or changing one's schedule to meet clinic appointments. In such cases, what was believed to be motivation is better understood as a wish for change to take place without too much effort by the patient.

It is often difficult to initially gauge motivation level. Malan (1980) noted that until a patient knows what is involved in therapy, motivation for treatment may be unrealistic. A patient may be very interested in therapy as long as it is believed that one can remain passive while the therapist does something. True motivation may only emerge after the patient — and his/her unconscious — have been given a taste of what to expect (i.e., after the therapeutic process has been experienced). To illustrate:

> SS, a 21-year-old young woman presenting with chronic loneliness and difficulties in relationships, initiated treatment by stating that she was a firm believer in psychoanalytic therapy and wanted as much therapy as possible to get at the roots of her problems. Assessment revealed a histrionic character style with strong needs to be nurtured and to remain dependent. As her therapy progressed, SS's initial burst of enthusiasm and interest began to wane. She came late to sessions and had little to say. After the sixth session, her therapist was called out of town for a week. Upon his return, SS failed to attend her next session. SS subsequently phoned and informed her therapist that she was through with therapy. The therapist invited her to come in and discuss her decision. During this discussion SS stated that therapy wasn't what she thought it would be and that the therapist wasn't helpful. SS felt he didn't like her and didn't want to work with her. She based these feelings on the therapist not offering reassurance and agreement with her analysis of her problems. She felt unable to trust what he said, yet was afraid to let him know. Interventions were focused on sorting out the transference and nontransference components of her reaction, most specifically helping her identify how needs for reassurance and fears of rejection impeded effective communication. This helped SS gain understanding of a significant interpersonal difficulty in her life and resulted in renewed and sustained interest in the therapeutic process.

Davanloo (1978) observed that motivation for treatment often greatly increased with the second or third interview, as the patient became more aware of the nature of therapy and how it may be used to identify and work on the patient's problems. A correlation was noted between patient motivation and the interviewer's ability to focus on core aspects of the patient's problem. Whereas the focus on the central core of the patient's problem increased the patient's motivation, an inability to develop and sustain such a focus often decreased patient motivation for therapy.

Psychological Mindedness

When assessing patient suitability for short-term psychodynamic psychotherapy, attention must be given to the patient's psychological mindedness and capacity for introspection. Psychological mindedness involves the ability to verbally communicate one's thoughts, feelings, fantasies, and inner psychic life. It involves an awareness of inner emotional reactions and the ability to see how these psychic processes are integrated and related to past experience. Short-term therapy requires the patient to become increasingly aware of emotional reactions, thoughts, feelings, and fantasies, and to reflect on how these experiences are integrated and related to past experiences. The more a patient is initially capable of introspection, and has awareness of one's inner emotional life and reactions to others, the more likely it is that the patient will be able to benefit from an uncovering therapy (Dewald 1965).

Psychological mindedness is characteristic of individuals who are intrigued and excited by the psychological side of human nature. Such people often wonder why people behave in a specific fashion and attempt to understand present reactions in terms of prior thoughts and feelings (Palino 1981). This is to be contrasted with more nonpsychological minded people, who express little interest in causation, and perhaps even doubt whether there is any meaning behind people's behavior. To illustrate briefly:

> EM was an 18-year-old female college student who sought therapy because she lacked motivation to study. When the therapist's comments did not directly offer suggestions about how to increase motivation, EM became frustrated and angry. Attempts to understand her motivation problems in terms of a larger life picture were either ignored or attacked as not offering any immediate help. EM stated she was not interested in understanding her feelings. She further inquired if there were any exercises or medicines that would make her feel differently.

When assessing psychological mindedness, the interviewer should keep in mind that extreme introspection may cause its own complication of the therapeutic process. Individuals exhibiting introspection to the point of excessive and continuous rumination, or rigid internal preoccupation to the point of exclusion of reality and external life situations, make difficult short-term patients. This therapy calls for the patient to make adjustments and changes in present interactions with the external environment on the basis of learning gained through the treatment process. Patients bound to strict introspective and ruminative patterns are often relatively incapable of effective external action and find it difficult to convert the understanding gleaned from therapy into behavioral change (Dewald 1965).

Other patients, by virtue of psychological organizations centering around defenses of projection, denial, and displacement, are relatively unaware of their intrapsychic world and tend to focus almost exclusively on external current realistic events. Such patients will generally have a difficult time in an uncovering therapy and are not promising candidates for short-term therapy. Though some patients are able to increase psychological mindedness by means of participation in the therapy process, such work requires time and is more congruent with the strategies of open-ended treatment.

Intelligence

The use of short-term psychodynamic psychotherapy makes the presupposition that the patient is capable (and motivated) towards conceptualizing and integrating complex ideas regarding intrapsychic and interpersonal functioning. The strategy of short-term therapy, and the nature of the processes of introspection, psychological perceptiveness and communication needed for successful treatment, require an average to above-average level of intellectual resources. The interviewer assesses intellectual resources available for adaptive tasks by examining current academic achievement and work performance, as well as accomplishments in other creative activities. In assessing intelligence, the issue is not intellectual power, but intellectual resources that are conflict-free and available for meaningful psychological work. The extent to which emotional conflict and resultant stress interfere with intellectual effectiveness must be assessed. For instance, an individual may perform at a superior level in high school and on college entrance exams only to flunk out of college due to an inability to cope with being away from home and on one's own. In addition, Davanloo (1978) cautioned the interviewer assessing intellectual functioning to keep in mind that patients with superior intelligence may use this ego function in service of resistance by means of an overreliance on intellectualizing and concept integration to the detriment of emotional reexperience. Such resistance must be confronted and worked through for treatment to be effective.

The emphasis that short-term therapy practitioners place on intellectual resources is related to the importance of the cognitive integrative component of this therapy. The patient's ability to grasp the principles underlying dynamic treatment and to learn to solve emotional problems (i.e., analyzing one's own conflicts) play an important role in successful outcome. The more intelligent patient is seen to possess greater potential to more rapidly and effectively use short-term therapy technique (Sifneos 1979). This is not meant to imply that use of brief therapy is limited exclusively to patients of above-average or superior intellectual functioning. Patients with less available intellectual resources may do very well. Success in such cases, however, is most often related to the possession of other qualities that facilitate treatment success (e.g., strong motivation, high level of psychological mindedness). In selecting patients for short-term therapy, all aspects of the individual must be evaluated. Strengths in one area of functioning often effectively counterbalance deficits in others.

Capacity to Verbalize

An ego function closely related to psychological mindedness and intelligence is the capacity to verbalize. Short-term psychodynamic psychotherapy requires the patient to communicate a variety of emotional experiences. The effectiveness of this process of communication is dependent on the patient's ability to make oneself understood. For the therapist to understand the unconscious or latent meanings of conscious thoughts and feelings, the patient's conscious or manifest meanings must first be comprehended. The patient's ability to articulate conscious thoughts and feelings thus becomes an important assessment variable (Palino 1981). The patient who hesitates, blocks, has difficulty in talking clearly or coherently, or who uses limited verbal stereotypes will have greater difficulty in effectively communicating the specific inner feelings, thoughts, and ideas that are necessary for a successful treatment (Dewald 1965). Palino (1981) noted that talkativeness is not always a sign of communicative ability. Speech may unconsciously/consciously become a means of concealing, as well as expressing, one's inner experience. Excessive talk characterized by evasiveness and vagueness can be a harbinger of untreatability by expressive psychotherapy.

General Ego Strength

Ego strength reflects the effectiveness with which the ego performs its various functions. A strong ego effectively mediates between internal pressures and external realities. In addition, it does so with enough flexibility that psychic energy remains for creativity and other needs (Hinsie and Campbell 1977).

The assessment of a patient's ego strength is important in the selection process for two reasons: (1) available ego resources must be used to advantage, and (2) an assessment must be made of the patient's ability to withstand uncovering work. Short-term therapy is characterized by an active investigation of emotional conflict and a persistent confrontation of patient resistance. This process subjects the patient to increments of psychic stress, within limits of the patient's tolerance. The patient must be able to withstand and work with this stress. Success is dependent on the capacity of the ego to constructively integrate such experience. Patients possessing low ego strength (i.e., low integrative capacities) tend to react to stress induced by this highly interactional treatment by increased defensiveness and regressive behavior. Regressive behaviors may include: (1) high levels of cognitive and emotional confusion that threaten the patient's psychological organization and maintenance of constructive coping strategies, or (2) an increased rigidity and constriction of thought and affect to protect remaining security. Such behaviors compromise the effectiveness of the patient–therapist collaboration.

RT, a 42-year-old college instructor, sought treatment for inability to get along with colleagues. Although relating in a controlled and reserved manner, RT discussed his concerns in an appropriate manner. He took initiative in explaining his problem and made efforts to answer therapist questions. As the interview progressed, and as new material and novel connections were made, RT became increasingly guarded and nonresponsive. When the interviewer pointed this out, RT became visibly anxious and agitated. He requested their session be continued outside to give him some breathing room. The therapist informed RT that he was free to leave and that the therapist would be available until the end of the hour. The therapist additionally pointed out the importance of understanding what was bothering RT, and the therapist encouraged its exploration. RT responded to these comments with silence but seemed less anxious. He soon began to explore his reactions to the session, including the feeling of being out of control when the therapist commented on an aspect of his behavior he had been previously unaware of.

RT's reaction to therapeutic investigation was initially resistant. Feeling insecure and vulnerable, he became closed, defensive, and wanted to escape his anxiety by leaving the office. After this initial wave of resistance and after reflecting on the interviewer's comments, which were meant to reinforce RT's autonomy and to encourage therapeutic investigation, RT responded by working with the therapist on discovering why his reaction to therapy was so intense. RT's response to the therapist's interventions suggested that RT would profit from an interactional, uncovering treatment such as short-term psychodynamic psychotherapy.

Alexander recommended that the integrative capacity of the ego (ego strength) be assessed by appraising the patient's past adaptations, as well as how the present crisis was being handled. The patient's typical reactions to life situations — early school experiences, puberty, work situations, marriage — are indicative of the efficiency of one's adaptability (Alexander and French 1946). The degree of success or failure in school, work, or play gives some idea of the patient's perseverance and ability to release psychic energy in a constructive fashion. It also sheds light on the patient's ability to make internal adjustments and psychic compromises in order to adapt to, as well as influence, the environment. The patient who has been successful in school, work, or play is usually someone who has adjusted to unpopular but necessary rules of life (Palino 1981).

Good previous adaptational functioning predicts a better prognosis with short-term psychodynamic psychotherapy. The patient who is capable of meeting and dealing with the ups and downs of life, who maintains various constructive activities and relationships in spite of emotional distress, presents good evidence of the capacity to tolerate and resolve the stresses of treatment. Additionally, the more a pattern of persistent goal-directed effort has been established, the greater the likelihood the patient will sustain effort during the course of the treatment, and ultimately achieve some measure of success. A less promising prognosis is held for the patient whose life pattern has been one of repeated failures, ineffectual adaptation, or of major disturbance in ego functions (i.e., judgment, reality testing, impulse control). Behavior patterns tend to be repeated in the therapeutic situation, and even though the patient may develop some awareness and insight, s/he may be incapable of using this insight effectively to modify previous patterns of disturbance by virtue of inadequate overall ego capacity (Dewald 1965).

Capacity to Tolerate Anxiety, Depression, and Guilt

Assessment of patient's capacity to tolerate and experience various affects is an essential task in the selection process. Short-term therapy requires patients to recognize and express a broad range of feelings. Successful treatment hinges on the patient's ability to experience and constructively manage feelings as they occur in the treatment process. The process of therapy is compromised when a patient is unable to tolerate the various painful feelings evoked during the therapy session without resorting to rigid avoidance maneuvers or regressive behavior. The ability of the patient to tolerate frustration, anxiety, depression, guilt, and other painful feelings during therapy provides an opportunity to progressively master these feelings. Such mastery often enables the patient to give up previous self-destructive methods of expressing or avoiding awareness of such feeling. Individuals unable/unwilling to cope with painful affect through psychic means (e.g., reflection, understanding, working through) may seek relief through drugs, alcohol, impulsive acts, or the development of psychosomatic symptoms.

The patient's capacity to deal with the painful feelings of anxiety and depression is assessed through a careful history taking and sensitive observation of the patient's manner of dealing with affect during the interview. The interviewer evaluates how the patient copes with feelings that easily enter into consciousness, as well as mobilizing latent affects.

Anxiety

In evaluating the capacity of the patient to experience and tolerate anxiety, the interviewer should differentiate between anxiety as a stimulating factor and anxiety as an inhibiting factor. A distinction is to be made between a primitive form of separation anxiety, which Freud (1933) termed primary anxiety, and anxiety arising as a signal of internal danger, called secondary anxiety. Primary anxiety has its roots in the earliest period of life. Often referred to as traumatic anxiety, it is a psychic and psychological experience in which a person feels helpless and unable to relieve overwhelming excitation or tension. Palino (1981) described it as a type of psychic panic situation in which the person feels abandoned by all beneficial objects and vulnerable to attack from bad objects. With the mobilization of primary anxiety the patient becomes helpless, much like an infant confronted with an overwhelming situation. The patient may report feeling blank and unable to use ego resources in a purposive way. Patients readily experiencing primary anxiety are seen as having a poor prognosis in short-term psychodynamic psychotherapy. An example follows of a patient prone to experiencing primary anxiety:

> NY was a 28-year-old college student majoring in English who presented for treatment with complaints of isolation, loneliness, and social anxiety. She was a slightly built woman with a wavering voice and timid demeanor. Upon entering the office, NY took a seat and looked at the floor. It seemed a struggle for her to be there. She responded to interviewer questions with brief comments or with silent agitation. When asked about her present feelings, NY was initially unable to respond, but with some encouragement she reported feeling uptight, nervous, and unable to think. The therapist's questions had thrown her into a panic, and she couldn't respond. In subsequent sessions the therapist worked to develop a stable and trusting relationship which NY used to help her strengthen her ego and improve her functioning. This work progressed at a very gradual pace with the therapist constantly aware of NY's tendency to freeze up and block when experiencing anxiety.

Secondary anxiety is associated with a higher level of ego organization than is primary anxiety. Often called signal anxiety, secondary anxiety is a defensive phenomenon in response to the ego's observation of an internal threat. In secondary anxiety, the individual experiences uncomfortable physical sensations but maintains usual mental alertness and the ability to use one's ego resources. Anxiety acts as an ally. It is the mind's way of warning the ego of the possible development of a situation that may threaten its security. In contrast to primary anxiety, which is maladaptive since it leads to further impairment, secondary anxiety is adaptive in that it stimulates the ego to use its resources for mastery of the anxiety-provoking situation. Through constructive response to signal anxiety, the patient is able to deal with the onset of threats to one's security and self-esteem, thus minimizing the occurrence of primary anxiety reactions. The development of secondary anxiety is necessary for normal psychic development. Without an adequate development of secondary anxiety there can be no defense system against dangerous intrapsychic situations. The development of secondary anxiety is thus a protection against psychic disaster (Palino 1981). Patients who tend to experience secondary rather than primary anxiety are more promising candidates for successful resolution of the intrapsychic conflict engendered by the uncovering strategies of short-term therapy.

When assessing how the patient experiences and manages anxiety, the interviewer is alert to those patients who report little or no anxiety in their life. The inability to experience anxiety may indicate an inflexible and rigid defensive structure that does not allow awareness of virtually any type of feeling. A schizoid-like stance such as this may be the most successful adaptation available to the individual in terms of available ego resources and environmental constraints and is difficult to remediate. Successful short-term psychodynamic psychotherapy requires the capacity to become aware of and investigate one's experiential world. Patients unable to do this are inappropriate candidates for this treatment.

Depression and Guilt

An important aspect of assessment is a consideration of the patient's capacity to experience and tolerate depression and guilt. Distinction should be made between depression resulting from loss in a relatively mature individual with well-internalized attachments and realistic ideals, and the overwhelming, empty, hopeless, and frustrated experience of depressive affect associated with individuals who have experienced severe trauma in early nurturing situations. The former is much more able to experience and tolerate painful affect in a therapeutically productive manner.

In assessing a patient's capacity to bear and tolerate depression, Palino (1981) considered the following questions to be of importance: (1) Is the patient able to experience depressive affect without significant maladaptive ego regression and/or severe narcissistic injuries such as feelings of rejection or abandonment? (2) Is the patient able to utilize adaptive coping strategies to mobilize available resources to minimize inevitable frustration and to maximize substitutive gratifications? (3) Can the patient develop new relationships despite persistent desires for unavailable ones?

The patient's ability to manage depression is assessed by a careful study of his/her developmental history and current relationships, giving particular attention to situations of loss and separation. The following two vignettes illustrate differential capacities to constructively cope with depressive affect and to work in an intensive, brief treatment. The first (LZ) is an inappropriate candidate for short-term therapy whereas the latter (BB) has a promising prognosis.

> LZ was a 32-year-old female who sought therapy for feelings of depression, hopelessness, inferiority, and loss of appetite. She sought therapy on the advice of the Crisis Service Counseling Line. LZ appeared disheveled, lethargic, and spoke in a slow monotone. She related feeling down since being fired from her position in a local bank. Her job had been the most important thing in her life in that she had few friends and didn't get along with her parents. Since being fired, LZ had done little except sleep and watch TV. While initially seeking out her friends for comfort, she now found herself withdrawing into herself. LZ related past episodes of depression, some of which she related to specific events (e.g., the loss of a boyfriend) whereas others seemed to occur "out of the blue." She related a history of depression in her family, particularly on her mother's side.
>
> BB was a 25-year-old male graduate student in engineering who sought treatment for social anxiety and discomfort with people. During the past semester BB's academic success resulted in being invited to join an engineering fraternity. Initially pleased, BB soon found himself dreading fraternity meetings and dreaded having to talk with so many people he didn't know. BB felt that other members were beginning to avoid him. He felt increasingly isolated and began to berate himself for his inadequacies with people. Over the next few weeks, BB became increasingly pessimistic and self-critical. At first

his studies were some solace, but soon his dysphoria affected these as well. A failing grade on an exam jolted BB into a serious soul-searching. He decided he didn't have to live this way and that he had worked too hard to throw everything away. He subsequently enrolled in a YMCA exercise course, took a university-sponsored workshop on coping with shyness, and made an appointment to see a psychotherapist.

In addition to assessing the capacity of the patient to tolerate anxiety and depression, the presence and importance of guilt feelings in the patient's psychic economy must be assessed. The development, structure, and functioning of the superego should be explored. There are individuals who have never internalized a set of usable moral values. There are also those in whom the superego function is externalized and projected onto others. Both types of individuals tend to be problematic candidates for short-term psychodynamic psychotherapy—the former because of difficulties in establishing trust and a therapeutic alliance, the latter because of the tendency to become involved in intense dependency strivings towards the therapist.

Organization of Ego Defenses

The defensive organization of the ego influences the patient's ability to benefit from short-term therapy. We elucidate the most common defensive patterns found to contraindicate brief therapy.

Rigid Use of a Few Defenses

Davanloo (1978) noted that patients presenting a greater variety and flexibility of defensive patterns are able to use brief treatment most effectively. Short-term therapy calls for the gradual reduction in the intensity of ego defenses, permitting the emergence of previously unconscious or preconscious conflict in such a way that the patient is not flooded with major anxiety or with the sudden intense eruption of primary process thinking. With patients who rely on the rigid and inflexible use of a small number of defenses, the possibility exists that by reducing the strength of these defenses, the capacity to organize and integrate experience may be seriously disrupted, producing overwhelming anxiety and further disorganization. The larger the number of psychological defense mechanisms available, the less dependent the patient will be on any one specific mechanism to maintain adaptation and, therefore, the more easily s/he will be able to reduce the intensity of any one particular defense (Dewald 1965). Said another way, the greater the flexibility of the ego's organization, the less the ego is dependent upon any specific defense mechanism to solve emotional conflict and maintain healthy adaptation. This increases the likelihood that the patient will be able to find more effective modes of integration as therapy progresses and self-understanding increases. Patients relying on primitive, stereotyped, defensive patterns that are indiscriminately applied to different situations tend to respond best in a long-term treatment that allows a gradual and repetitive examination of problematic defenses.

Patients Presenting a Current, Relative Failure of Ego Defenses

This includes patients in whom there is an active, ongoing regressive process and who are consciously aware of thoughts, fantasies, or drives that are ordinarily unconscious. In instances of acutely failing defenses, further uncovering and reduction of defenses will lead to more psychological disruption and general disturbance. Such patients may appear to be suitable for intensive uncovering treatment since they seem to have so much awareness of thoughts and feelings that are normally repressed. They tend, however, to lack the ego capacities to integrate and deal with such insight. Initially, these patients respond best to a supportive therapy that stabilizes and strengthens the patient's ego to prevent further disruption in psychic functioning.

Patients Presenting Strategies that Represent the Attempt to Gratify Intense Dependency Needs

Included here are patients whose problems are of such severity and whose ego resources are so limited that they need an ongoing dependent relationship for a great part of their lives to maintain a minimal adaptation to life. Such patients will utilize therapy for purposes of support and reassurance regardless of the goals and interventions of the therapist (Wolberg 1965).

Patients Who Rely Primarily on Primitive Defenses Such as Massive Denial, Withdrawal, Regression, and Avoidance

Such defenses indicate significant deficits in ego functioning and major maladaptive coping strategies.

Patients Who Rely Primarily on a Pattern of Projection and Externalization of Conflict, Particularly When Combined With Impulsive Acting Out

These patients have difficulty assuming responsibility for their behavior. They tend to act out to reduce psychic stress rather than use such stress as a catalyst for emotional growth and behavioral change. The following vignette presents a patient with such a defensive organization.

MG was a 19-year-old college student who sought treatment due to the request of his dormitory director. MG felt his difficulties related to being unjustly treated in a class co-taught by two instructors. MG felt he deserved higher grades on his essay exams and felt he was being discriminated against. Recently, upon getting an exam back, MG engaged his instructors (a male and female) in a shouting match and stormed out of the class. MG returned to his dormitory room and began drinking heavily. He subsequently punched a hole in the wall of his room and was referred for counseling. MG felt the female instructor was a militant feminist who resented intelligent men and that the male instructor was her pawn. Further discussion revealed a similar pattern of feelings during high school, this time in relation to a certain clique he felt snubbed him due to their jealousy of his skills. Attempts by the therapist to discuss similarities between these two situations and to further understand why people responded as they did to MG were met with bristling indignation and the charge that the therapist was working for the system and trying to protect the instructors. MG abruptly terminated the interview, stating he had better things to do with his time. Although MG later returned and had relatively successful treatment, the initial work of developing a stable therapeutic alliance involved much time and effort. The severity of his interpersonal conflicts and externalizing defenses were more appropriately addressed in a long-term treatment.

The defensive patterns outlined above are indicative of patients experiencing conflict that has its roots in an early stage of psychological development, a preoedipal as opposed to oedipal level. Sifneos (1972) felt that the majority of failures in his method of brief therapy were due to faulty evaluation and acceptance of patients with preoedipal character traits. Such traits include poor impulse control, self-destructive tendencies, and severe obsessive-compulsive and masochistic trends. Patients presenting these traits often lack the ability to rapidly enter into a therapeutic collaboration and to productively work with the therapist's confrontations and interpretations. Other preoedipally oriented traits include intense passivity, deep and excessive dependency, and symptoms representing deep-seated issues regarding early loss (e.g., chronic depression, severe separation anxiety). Patients with these traits tend to be unsuccessful in a brief therapy due to inability to give up the therapeutic relationship once treatment is over.

Wolberg (1977) noted that, in general, the problems that do not yield to short-term measures are those that have persisted a long time and date back to early childhood. "These obdurate attitudinal and behavioral patterns usually cannot be resolved except by a prolonged therapeutic experience. Time is an essential part of treatment in instances where emotional growth has been thwarted by unfortunate traumas in early life, and where the therapeutic goal is a maturation of the personality structure" (p. 839).

Object Relations

Successful therapeutic technique involves the establishment of an emotional relationship between therapist and patient which, while varying in form and intensity, exists throughout treatment. This relationship, often called the therapeutic alliance, is, in part, based on the patient's conscious rapport and willingness to trust and work with the therapist in striving towards the therapeutic goal. The therapeutic alliance provides the patient motivation to work in therapy and to withstand the psychic stress that treatment imposes. Short-term psychodynamic psychotherapy requires the patient to have the capacity to quickly form a therapeutic alliance and to maintain this collaboration while experiencing the stress involved in a highly interactive treatment.

Information regarding the potential quality of the therapeutic alliance is gleaned from an assessment of the patient's object relations. The capacity to establish and maintain emotionally significant ties with other people (object relations) significantly influences his/her ability to participate in the establishment and maintenance of a therapeutic alliance. Both theory and clinical experience suggest that the patient will bring to the treatment relationship the same general patterns of response, interaction, and defense that have been manifested in earlier life with other people. Where past experiences and relationships have been relatively satisfying, the same will be anticipated in the treatment situation. The patient who has developed close emotional ties with others is more likely to emotionally invest in the therapist and therapeutic situation.

Sifneos (1972) emphasized as a selection criterion that the patient be able to demonstrate at least one meaningful relationship with another person, particularly during early life. This relationship should contain trust, give-and-take, a sense of altruism, and usually involve a parent or parent surrogate. Sifneos viewed such a relationship as constituting the prototype of which all future interactions with people are patterned. For a relationship to be judged meaningful, it must involve willingness by the patient to make a tangible sacrifice for the other person. The patient must additionally be able to view this person as a unique and separate individual having his/her own feelings and needs, and not just a potential satisfier or frustrator of patient needs.

Viewing others as sources of individual gratification or frustration has strong implications on how the patient will view the therapy relationship; for such individuals, therapy is often seen as a source of supportive nurturance or punitive withholding. This perception severely compromises the patient's ability to rapidly develop a therapeutic alliance and to collaborate with the therapist on understanding the patient's problems in living. Such patients often exhibit intense dependency needs, an egocentric orientation, and, for an extended period in therapy, are resistant to the therapist's attempts to educate the patient on the cost of such coping strategies.

Sifneos (1972) recommended that the way to assess a patient's interpersonal relationship is not to accept at face value the patient's statement about having had good relations but to closely examine the nature of these relationships. Information about participation in groups, such as work, family, and clubs, may give an overall picture. Such questions as "What did you do for this person? Did you sacrifice anything for this person's sake? Is your relationship continuing at the present time? How often do you see each other?" may give the interviewer considerable and specific information about interpersonal relations.

The assessment of a meaningful relationship in the patient's past history does not necessarily have to involve a member of the immediate family. There are individuals who appear to have been devoid of human contacts in the past, yet appear to be fairly well adjusted in the present. Persistent scrutiny and review of interpersonal relations will almost invariably reveal a meaningful contact which, at first glance, had been obscured and was not obvious. When interviewing such patients, one frequently finds a grandmother or favorite uncle who provided support, guidance, and an object for identification when little was available elsewhere.

It is helpful to note any discrepancies between a patient's discussion of past relationships and the ability to interact with the interviewer. Presenting a history of painful, unsatisfying relationships while relating to the interviewer an open, honest, and engaging fashion suggests that a meaningful emotional attachment existed some time in the patient's life. Such a patient is a more appropriate candidate for short-term therapy than a patient who discusses past relationships in glowing terms but relates to the interviewer in a manipulative, distant, or uninvolved fashion. The latter patient is often employing rigid defenses (e.g., massive repression, denial) to avoid awareness of past emotional trauma. To illustrate briefly:

> AF was a 28-year-old college student who sought therapy for feelings of confusion, panic, and inability to concentrate. AF had been unable to study for the past few weeks, had fallen behind in classes, and wanted help in getting his act together. While AF spoke in glowing terms of his mother, his father, and a perfect childhood, he presented evidence of significant intrapsychic and interpersonal disturbance. During the months of therapy that followed, AF engaged in a difficult yet productive examination of his life. Of great importance to his therapy was his ability to take a new look at his relationships with his mother and father. These relationships were eventually found to be much more painful than AF originally acknowledged to the therapist or to himself.

Discrepancies between reports of past relationships and present functioning require close scrutiny to optimally plan a course of treatment. For example, a history of satisfactory nurturing relationships in conjunction with highly disturbed functioning and symptom formation may suggest an emotional problem with a largely biological — and not psychological — basis (e.g., some types of schizophrenia, or a major affective disorder). Patients having such problems are best treated with a combination of psychoactive medication, as well as psychotherapy, and must be quickly identified to offer the most appropriate treatment.

There are some individuals presenting for treatment who, while unable to share much in the way of gratifying emotional ties, are able to discuss a relatively stable but highly conflicted and ambivalent emotional involvement with a significant other. While not prime candidates for short-term therapy, such individuals respond to long-term treatment more successfully than do those who have never experienced, and sustained, significant emotional involvement. The former display the ability to invest in people, even though it is in a very conflict-laden fashion. Such capacity may be productively used in the eventual establishment of a therapeutic alliance.

Patient–Therapist Interaction

Further information regarding the patient's ability to interact meaningfully will be gleaned by examining the patient–therapist interaction. The patient's characteristic style of relating to others, including both adaptive and maladaptive aspects, is often discernible in the first interview. The patient–therapist interaction is assessed by the patient's capacity to speak honestly, to see the problem in emotional terms, and to allow the interviewer some degree of emotional closeness. The capacity to interact with the interviewer may be viewed as a test of the patient's development of previous meaningful relationships. Is the patient collaborative, flexible, and responsive to verbal and nonverbal interaction? Does the patient communicate satisfaction with the emotional contact that is achieved in the interview?

The ability of a patient to enter into an emotional interaction with the interviewer, in the process confiding personal thoughts and feelings, was found to be positively correlated with successful outcome (Davanloo 1978). Inability to make meaningful emotional contact suggests that the patient is not a prospective candidate for short-term therapy in that such difficulty prevents the rapid development of a therapeutic alliance and a productive patient–therapist collaboration.

The appropriate expression of feelings within the interview is not necessarily limited to warm, friendly feelings. The patient who is able to acknowledge and express anger and disagreement during the interview is often a more appropriate candidate for short-term therapy than the patient who represses such feelings or who, while aware of being angry, attempts to avoid its expression. The former patient shows greater awareness, ego strength, and comfortableness with affect, as well as a greater willingness to take a risk within an interpersonal interaction.

Sifneos (1972) noted that good candidates for short-term psychodynamic psychotherapy have the ability not only to recognize and express emotions, but also to verbalize them. Some patients, when asked to talk about how they feel, repetitively and endlessly discuss somatic sensations, without being able to relate them to any accompanying thoughts, fantasies, or conflicts. Other patients, while aware of the importance of their affective experience, are unable to specify what it feels like to be angry or sad. Still others fail to differentiate between pleasant and unpleasant emotions. Such patients usually respond to questioning by describing the actions they take under those circumstances and, when pressed for further details, show irritability and annoyance. Limited emotional vocabularies make it difficult for a fast-paced treatment, which relies heavily on shared understanding and communication of thoughts and affects.

The ability to acknowledge and express a range of feelings within the interview provides evidence for flexibility in interpersonal relating and is indicative of a good short-term therapy candidate. Another evidence of flexibility involves the patient's willingness to attempt to view personal conflicts from more than one perspective. Statements such as "My difficulties with my professor may not be totally caused by his 'power trip' " or "My need for definite answers may place others in an uncomfortable spot" denote an attempt to gain some perspective on problems and to view a situation from more than one perspective.

When evaluating the therapist–patient interaction, the interviewer should assess the degree of narcissistic preoccupation of the patient. Granted, the patient entering treatment is likely to be personally preoccupied. However, significant narcissistic pathology will adversely affect the patient's ability to use short-term psychodynamic psychotherapy. Levin (1960) noted that patients who live by the self-centered code of "I have the right to have what I want when I want it" very often lack the capacity for a collaborative patient–therapist relationship. Such individuals tend to view therapy as a place to get something from the therapist (e.g., reassurance, mirroring, love) rather than a place whereby the therapist and patient work together for the patient's benefit (Palino 1981). Significant narcissistic pathology is indicated by such traits as an unusual degree of self-reference, a great need to be loved and admired, a sense of entitlement, a curious contradiction between an inflated self-concept and an inordinate need for tribute from others, lack of a sense of humor, an inability to form and maintain meaningful relationships, lack of empathy for other people's feelings and needs (including the interviewer), and an inordinate sensitivity to empathic failures by the interviewer (Kernberg 1975, Kohut 1971).

The patient–therapist interaction presents important information regarding the patient's basic trust in relationships. The ability of the patient to experience a level of trust within the therapeutic relationship significantly affects the type of relationship the patient is capable of developing with the therapist. Some degree of basic trust is essential for a successful uncovering therapy. It is through basic trust that the patient is able to establish and maintain the distinction between transference phenomena and reality. The ability of a patient to collaborate with the therapist to make sense of conflictual aspects of their relationship is dependent on the patient's confidence in the ultimate benevolence and helpfulness of the therapist.

Palino (1981) suggested that an individual's capacity for basic trust may be assessed by observing the person's willingness to: (1) relax censoring of thoughts and feelings, (2) abandon the usual expectations of regular, verbal, and perceptual feedback, (3) accept certain rules of therapy that may at first appear to be illogical, (4) accept the limitations of reality, (5) separate wishes from needs, (6) accept the fact that the therapeutic relationship is in some ways not reciprocal, and (7) accept the fact that the therapy is often painful and embarrassing and will not provide immediate gratification.

Lack of basic trust results in an inability of the patient to internalize the nurturing aspects of the therapeutic relationship (Palino 1981). A patient, for example, who has rarely experienced unconditional acceptance from others may find it difficult to trust and accept the therapist's intentions. Inability to accept what can be realistically given (i.e., acceptance, empathy, increased perspective) often results in increased demands for more literal gratification and increased anger and frustration as therapist interventions fail to satisfy emotional needs. These dilemmas are most effectively dealt with in a long-term treatment.

Assessment of the patient–therapist interaction includes an assessment of how transference is manifested within the session. Transference reactions begin with the first thought or suggestion of psychological help. Childhood-based fears and wishes are stimulated even as the prospective patient telephones for an initial consultation. The individual's conscious and unconscious attitudes toward the therapist usually manifest themselves from the very beginning of the interview. Sifneos (1979) felt that interviewers often fail to carefully scrutinize the patient–therapist interaction for manifestations of transference. This scrutiny is often avoided in an effort to discourage early development of transference feelings, particularly negative transference. Although such technique may be sound for severely disturbed patients, it does not apply to short-term therapy candidates. Transference feelings (i.e., feelings the patient has about the therapist, their interaction, or the interview setting) are discussed as soon as possible. Early focus and work with transference is an important component of this therapy.

Although all behavior has a transference component, not all individuals profit from its examination. The ability to work with transference manifestations may be assessed by providing mild interpretations regarding patient behavior while carefully monitoring patient reaction. It is most helpful to attend to nonverbal behavior. Nonverbal behavior (e.g., gestures, facial expressions) often conveys the patient's emotional reactions to the interview, including transference reactions to the interviewer. Responding to nonverbal behavior and determining whether the patient can participate in such an interchange can often supply the first sign of whether the patient can deal with immediate feelings and reactions in the here-and-now therapist–patient interaction.

Trial Interpretation: Assessing Patient's Ability to Use Uncovering Therapy

Although uncovering therapies such as short-term psychodynamic psychotherapy are extremely beneficial to many patients, they are not indicated for everyone. The interviewer has the task of assessing the capacity of the prospective patient to use short-term therapy for optimal benefit. Malan (1980) stated that the best way of assessing the patient's capacity to use uncovering therapy is to try it. He recommended, therefore, the use of trial interpretations during assessment. The intent of these interpretations is to: (1) deepen rapport, (2) decrease resistance, (3) test out hypotheses about the patient's conflicts, which will be used in planning therapy, and, most importantly, (4) assess the patient's capacity to work in an uncovering therapy.

Use of interpretations during the assessment interview has developed into a critical aspect of the assessment process. Davanloo (1980), for example, contended that patient response to interpretations is the most crucial of all short-term therapy selection criteria. The importance modern theorists such as Malan and Davanloo place on the use of trial interpretations in the assessment interview is congruent with the thoughts of an earlier innovator of dynamic technique, Franz Alexander. Alexander (1944) recommended trial interpretations be used in the assessment interview and that patient response be assessed as an indicator of the capacity to transform insight into adaptive behavior.

A trial interpretation often consists of identifying a behavior or an emotional reaction and providing the patient with some understanding of what may underlie or have caused such a reaction (e.g., "You mentioned your being angry with your husband and also that you completely forgot your luncheon engagement with him. Do you think these are related?"). The therapist then carefully attends to the patient's response. Dewald (1965) suggested the therapist consider the following questions when assessing patient response to interpretation: (1) How capable is the patient of recognizing the connection or pattern of functioning? (2) Does the patient offer further elaboration? (3) Is the patient incapable of recognizing the proposed relationship? (4) Is the intervention disregarded? (5) Is the interpretation immediately accepted in an uncritical fashion with no personal contribution to furthering the understanding?

The depth, degree, and type of interpretation used during the assessment interview depends on the actual clinical situation (Davanloo 1978). The interviewer is not always able to use interpretations in every initial assessment interview. In his assessment interviews, Davanloo (1980) favored interpretations that link patient behavior with the therapist to similar behavior patterns with contemporary and past significant others. Davanloo called this a T-C-P (transference/current/past) interpretation. To make a T-C-P interpretation, the interviewer gathers data with respect to the patient's pattern of behavior in significant contemporary relationships, as well as genetic patterns of relating to significant people in early life. The pattern of the patient's behavior during the interview (the transference situation) is also noted. Having some information and hypotheses regarding the development and continuation of behavioral reactions, the interviewer is in position to link these various patterns together. A high correlation was found between a positive response to the T-C-P interpretation and successful outcome (Davanloo 1978).

Interpretations may be used effectively during assessment to deal with patient resistance and to increase motivation for further therapeutic interchange. Offering a new understanding of a pattern of behavior is often responded to by elaboration and increased interaction. Many previously resistant patients, upon experiencing the empathy, concern, and understanding indicative of a correct intervention, develop increased motivation for treatment.

> TF was a 32-year-old dental student who sought therapy for vague feelings of unhappiness and lack of fulfillment in his interpersonal relationships. TF had an engaging manner and articulately discussed a variety of subjects and experiences during the interview. As the session progressed, however, the interviewer experienced mild irritation and difficulty in attending to TF. TF seemed to control the content of the session through rapid, almost forced, discussion of places he had been and things he had done. He tended to deflect questions and, when pressed, became increasingly anxious and verbose. At the end of the hour, the interviewer found that he had learned very little about TF. In addition, he felt a detachment and lack of emotional contact.
>
> TF came to the second session in a discouraged state. He reported that he had almost cancelled the session because therapy was not what he had hoped. The therapist, through consultation, had gained a better understanding of his reaction to TF. He shared his perception of their first meeting, as well as his reactions to TF's style. He noted feeling controlled and being kept at a distance. He suggested that perhaps TF's style, while engaging and entertaining, also had the effect of keeping people away. TF responded with apology, then anger, and finally with silence as he considered the therapist's comments. He went on to explain that he also felt a superficialness and lack of contact in their first meeting and that he tended to respond to such feelings with increased talking. TF discussed similar difficulties in talking to fellow students. He related that while his classmates found him witty and the "life of the party," no real friendships seemed to develop, resulting in a sense of emptiness in his life. TF spent the remainder of his this hour productively exploring his conflictual means of relating to others. The ability to identify and begin examination of a basic source of distress in TF's life led to his increased interest and commitment to treatment.

At the other extreme, there are patients who respond to inter-pretative intervention by withdrawal and unwillingness to partici-pate. In such a case both therapist and patient are saved the time and effort involved in further attempts at using interpretative tech-nique. Alternative treatment strategies may be more productively considered. The patient's response to interpretation must be care-fully monitored. Interpretations are powerful therapeutic tools and may have side effects. Many of these side effects are not productive in an initial interview. Early interpretation may increase personal disturbance, raise strong and unrealistic hopes that help will be available from an omniscient figure, and/or produce an intense and immediate attachment to the interviewer. The interviewer must not produce these side effects and then leave the patient "high and dry." Malan (1980) recommended that trial interpretations be no deeper than the moment-to-moment situation requires and that they be constantly regulated by the degree to which the required informa-tion has been obtained, the view of the patient that is emerging, and the ability of the assessing agency to provide appropriate treatment.

Davanloo's Trial Model of Assessment

Davanloo (1980) developed the concept of using trial interpreta-tions in a format that may be called the "trial therapy" model of as-sessment. A period of trial therapy to assess a patient's suitability for treatment is not new. Freud (1913), in discussing how to begin psychoanalytic treatment, recommended provisionally seeing a pa-tient in daily therapy for a period of one to two weeks. Freud felt this to be the best way to assess a patient's suitability for analytic therapy. "No other kind of preliminary examination but this proce-dure is at our disposal; the most lengthy discussions and question-ings in ordinary consultations offer no substitute" (Freud 1913, p. 124). Freud used this trial period to observe how the patient functioned in the treatment setting. During this time he attempted to develop a clearer diagnostic picture of the individual. Freud was most specifically concerned with identifying those seriously disturbed patients for whom psychoanalysis was contraindicated but did not present strong evidence of their disturbance in the initial interview. Additionally, Freud preferred the gradual development of transference that a period of trial therapy allowed. He saw a question-and-answer assessment interview as unduly influencing the type of transference developed.

It was for similar reasons that Davanloo developed his trial therapy model of assessment. Davanloo viewed initial assessment as entailing more than a careful assessment of the patient's history and current situation. To properly determine how a patient will respond to short-term therapy, Davanloo initiated certain aspects of the therapeutic process in the initial interview. Davanloo considered the trial therapy model of assessment to be the only way to accurately determine if a patient could withstand the impact of unconscious material and be responsive to uncovering treatment.

Davanloo often was able to conduct his trial therapy in one interview of an hour's duration. Davanloo would first exclude patients presenting contraindications to brief treatment, such as previous psychotic decompensation, paranoid conditions, poor impulse control, and serious suicide attempts. Once this had been done, the major part of the interview contained comparable interventions used in the main body of therapy. Davanloo consistently challenged the patient's neurotic defenses while paying meticulous attention to responses. A technique of gentle but relentless questioning and confrontation of unexpressed feelings was used. Davanloo persistently inquired about patient feelings rather than interpreting them. As he was faced with vagueness, avoidance, and passivity, he persistently confronted the patient with this in the therapeutic interaction and attempted to link it to the patient's behavior with significant people in current life. This technique often mobilized anger and the patient's typical defenses against anger. Davanloo attempted to bring this into focus the moment it occurred. Very often anger towards the interviewer had links with unexpressed anger in the past (e.g., controlling mother, authoritarian father). This in turn could be linked with the patient's mal-adaptive way of handling anger in current life situations. As noted earlier, Davanloo referred to this intervention strategy as a T-C-P interpretation. Each T-C-P interpretation attempts to link aspects of the patient's emotional reaction in the transference situation to similar reactions in the patient's current and past relationships.

Use of interpretations during assessment requires the inter-viewer to pay careful attention to the patient's moment-to-moment responses. This provides direct evidence of the patient's ability to respond to the confrontational, uncovering technique used in short-term psychodynamic psychotherapy. An important aspect of this feedback consists of monitoring fluctuations in motivation. A great majority of patients respond with relief at being understood and having the burden of their neurotic defenses temporarily lifted. At such times their motivation for further therapeutic work shows marked increase. At the other end of the spectrum of responses, a patient may give evidence of being too fragile to withstand the im-pact of unconscious material by behaving in an increasingly regres-sive manner (e.g., cognitive disorganization, intense projective and denying defenses, helpless withdrawal). In these cases it is necessary for the interviewer to adopt a more supportive approach and accept a more modest goal.

Davanloo (1980) stressed that the trial therapy model of as-sessment should allow the interviewer to answer the following questions:

1. What is the central neurotic structure of the patient's prob-lems?
2. Does the patient relate in a meaningful way?
3. Were there meaningful relationships in the past?
4. Does the patient have the capacity to form a therapeutic alliance?
5. Does the patient's history suggest ego resources to accept un-covering therapy without severe regression?

6. Does the patient have some potential for motivation to work in treatment?
7. How does the patient react to trial interpretation?
8. Has it been possible to make links between the present and past?
9. Can the patient recognize and elaborate these connections?

When assessing a patient's capacity for uncovering therapy, it is best if the therapeutic trial is not explicitly presented as such to the patient. Dewald (1965) presented the following rationale for this strategy. (1) For some patients a therapeutic trial represents a test that must be passed to be accepted for treatment. The patient may work harder and more effectively with the immediate goal of passing the test. When accepted for treatment, a letdown may occur with the patient no longer feeling the need to work so hard. (2) Since it is a therapeutic trial with no commitment by the therapist, the patient may be reluctant to enter into the treatment relationship and to work actively in this therapeutic situation, anticipating that it may be a temporary one. Therefore, the patient might ask, "Why should I get involved if I am not sure that it is going to continue?"

The use of the assessment interview to engage the patient in the therapeutic procedures that make up short-term therapy is essential in determining the patient's ability to benefit from an interpretative, interactional treatment. It is important, however, to balance this task with that of gaining background information about the prospective patient. A problem to be avoided in assessment is initiating a therapeutic process without an adequate understanding of patient dynamics or available treatment resources. Before formulating an interpretation, the interviewer must have gained some understanding of the patient's character structure. In addition, the interviewer must be aware of the treatment resources that are available. Can the interviewer offer the patient immediate treatment? Is the patient being evaluated for referral? The interviewer should avoid excessive disturbance of the patient's current adaptation when considerable uncertainty exists regarding what underlies this adaptation, or when appropriate treatment cannot be offered.

Establishment of a Treatment Focus

The ability to establish a treatment focus is another crucial selection criterion. Based on information from the patient and the patient–therapist interaction, the therapist must arrive at a dynamic understanding and a therapeutic focus that crystallizes the specific conflicts to be resolved during treatment. This focus is communicated to the patient with efforts being made to obtain cooperation and agreement. The focus becomes the central point of the treatment.

Establishing a treatment focus is used diagnostically in the assessment process. Sifneos (1972) placed special emphasis on the ability of the patient to identify and agree to work on one chief complaint. The patient's ability to develop a circumscribed complaint denotes a capacity to choose one out of a variety of problems and assign it priority for resolution. The ability to make such a choice, realizing that all problems won't disappear, indicates ego strength, ability to tolerate a certain degree of anxiety, and potential to withstand stress. These assets are used in short-term therapy, since this treatment constantly necessitates making choices and reaching decisions. An example follows of a patient with the capacity to productively accept a limited focus to treatment.

GN was a 42-year-old male who sought treatment for low self-esteem, lack of assertiveness, and dissatisfaction with his present level of achievement at work. GN's wife was a university professor with numerous publications and a strong national reputation. He found himself jealous and resentful of her success. GN wanted therapy to help increase his self-esteem and assertiveness in order to achieve at a greater level. GN stated that he enjoyed his work and was comfortable with its demands and level of responsibility, but a higher position was essential to make him feel more like a man and to increase his wife's respect for him. As his relationship to his wife was explored, GN related that while deeply caring for her, he felt she controlled their marriage. He found it difficult to express his feelings and confront her when they disagreed. A history taking revealed significant parallels with his relationship to his mother, who was described as benevolent, strong-willed, and domineering. GN was assessed as an appropriate candidate for short-term psychodynamic psychotherapy. He was motivated, possessed strong evidence of ego strength, and responded well to mild interpretations. The interviewer's main concern was whether GN would accept a limited focus for therapy in that he had many expectations for therapy including obtaining a better job, greater self-assertion and esteem, and more satisfaction with his life. The interview worked to delineate a basic issue in GN's life that could be productively focused on. He suggested to GN that perhaps the most helpful focus for their work was his relationship with his wife and, less directly, with his mother. The interviewer explained that in these relationships many of the issues GN was most concerned with found expression, most specifically feelings of passivity and inability to express feelings. Initially, GN balked at treatment that didn't include direct focus on increasing his achievement potential and getting him a better job. With further discussion, however, GN agreed that working on one problem at a time would give him some direction and that his feelings about having to be a good son and agreeable spouse were troubling issues. GN's experience in short-term therapy was highly successful. He was pleasantly surprised that work on issues with his wife and mother significantly affected other aspects of his life. Short-term therapy was successful in part because GN possessed the ego strength to delay gratification and tolerate the frustration inherent in the realization that all concerns could not be addressed at once. This allowed for a persistent focus on a basic conflict area.

Patients who present a variety of complaints in a diffuse manner and persist in wanting relief of all problems are inappropriate for short-term psychodynamic psychotherapy. Such patients frequently suffer from a chronic, diffuse anxiety and experience strong needs to establish dependent relationships that provide support for an ego that lacks cohesion and stability. If a patient does not present with a specific complaint, and if in preliminary interviews it is still not possible to arrive at one, this in itself may be taken as a contraindication. In such instances, this may be a clue to the presence of a borderline or narcissistic disorder in which motivation for change is compromised by intense longings for (or defenses against) a dependent relationship with a parental figure. An example of such a patient follows.

> SY was a 22-year-old college student who had recently transferred from a home town junior college. SY sought treatment for insomnia, depression, and fear of open spaces. During the interview SY behaved in a tense, anxious fashion. She hadn't slept for two days, was unable to study, and was worrying about upcoming exams. In addition, she felt alienated by her roommates and mistrustful and afraid of people she met. SY had been in family treatment previously. Her most important relationship was with her mother, who she described in highly ambivalent terms: she would feel lost without her yet often engaged in violent arguments. SY lived at home while attending junior college. As the therapist attempted to help SY gain a better understanding of her situation, SY consistently disagreed, qualified, or would "yes, but" his observations. When the therapist commented on this, SY replied that people found it difficult to talk to her and that her mother was the only one who could understand her. The therapist sensed a desperation and aloneness about SY. He assessed that she needed a stable, long-term relationship in which she could develop increased ego strength while working through preoedipal issues of separation-individuation. An open-ended treatment was offered.

In addition to being used diagnostically for identifying suitable patients for short-term psychodynamic psychotherapy, establishing a focus for therapy is an essential aspect of the treatment process. Clear delineation of the focus and goals of therapy serves a number of purposes. (1) A specific treatment focus helps avoid what Malan (1963) termed the "quest for therapeutic perfectionism." A manageable task must be identified that fits the time constraints of the treatment. (2) Establishing and maintaining a focus on the therapeutic work limits the tendency of the patient to develop a highly involved attachment to the therapist (i.e., transference neurosis), the development of which prolongs the treatment time. (3) Rapid establishment of a focus for therapy provides direction for interpretative efforts and for the patient's observing ego and its integrative abilities. (4) A treatment focus reduces the probability of involvement in unstructured treatment of a variety of issues.

The ability to establish and concentrate on focal conflicts counteracts the tendency in many interpretive therapies of increasing diffusion and ambiguity of goals. Such treatment often becomes stalemated but may continue to serve dependent and/or masochistic needs of the patient. In an open-ended, unfocused therapy, the patient may relinquish growth-oriented goals and develop a transference attachment to the therapist that primarily gratifies primitive needs for nurturance and support. Desires for emotional growth and regressive wishes exist side by side in the unconscious. Patients are ambivalent about their wish for growth and autonomy. The stance taken by the therapist strongly influences the attitudes and behaviors of the patient.

Crystallization of a focus usually occurs within the first two interviews. To develop a focus the interviewer explores and explicates the patient's emotional difficulties and repetitive, self-punishing, self-defeating patterns. From the overall complaints brought to treatment, the interviewer delineates a problem or problem area that would be useful for the patient to work on. Malan (1976) suggested that the interviewer project him/herself into an imaginary therapy and say, for example, "I think it might be valuable to work through this patient's latent hostility with father. This might help overcome the problems being presently discussed." Interpretations based on the emerging focus are given during the assessment. It is important that the patient respond positively to interpretations based on this focus. Positive responses by the patient may include: (1) overt agreement as to the significance of the issues highlighted by the therapist, (2) attempts to further elaborate on these issues, and (3) increases in patient enthusiasm and motivation for therapy.

The ability to define a therapeutic focus is dependent on the interviewer's ability to identify ongoing, repetitive life problems and to make sense of the psychodynamics that underlie them. Wolberg (1965) contended that a therapeutic focus is most effectively generated by attending to the immediate concerns and distressing symptoms of the patient and that focus on underlying aspects of a patient's mental life—before they are shown to be significant causatory factors of emotional stress—is usually unproductive. He recommended that the presenting concern be explored thoroughly in the context of the question, "How is the symptom related to the patient's personality structure as a whole?"

Immediate concerns may be but a tip of the iceberg in terms of the patient's intrapsychic problems. They do, however, consume the patient's attention. A skilled therapist is able to relate present difficulties and complaints to more basic issues. Only when a continuity between the immediate stresses and basic ongoing conflicts within the personality has been demonstrated will the patient be able to work on more substantial issues. New and experienced therapists must constantly practice formulating complaints and presenting problems into more basic psychological conflicts. The human dramas expressed and highlighted in literature, plays, and movies may provide different settings to practice this skill.

Patient Agreement on Treatment Focus

The conclusion as to what problems are to be focused on is not the decision of the interviewer, or the patient, but rather a mutual agreement. Although the interviewer attempts to identify and define an area of functioning that may be worked upon in therapy, it is essential to involve the patient as much as possible in this process. The goal of dynamic uncovering treatment is to enable the patient to gain freedom from emotional conflicts that impede autonomous functioning. The selection of treatment goals solely by the therapist is contrary to the development of autonomy and sense of responsibility for personal action that must ultimately be fostered in the patient. In addition, the greater the degree the patient involvement with selection of treatment goals, the greater will be the patient's investment in their accomplishment. A vignette follows that illustrates the development of a treatment focus.

> LB was a 22-year-old college senior entering the final semester of college. He presented for treatment with multiple complaints including panic attacks, study and concentration problems, difficulties in making decisions, assertion issues, and fears of the future. Although presenting numerous complaints, LB appeared to be an appropriate short-term psychodynamic psychotherapy candidate. He was highly motivated, possessed strong evidence of ego strength, interacted flexibly with the therapist, and responded well to trial interpretations. LB's eligibility for therapy was limited to the duration of the semester. This provided a built-in termination date. After gaining confidence of LB's appropriateness for short-term therapy, the interviewer worked to establish a treatment goal. He first briefly summarized what had been discussed, including any new understandings and insights that had been developed. LB's panic attacks, for instance, were found to occur after discussing upcoming job interviews with his friends. Finishing school was a frightening prospect for LB. He was considering becoming engaged, even though he had only briefly known his girlfriend and was unsure of his true feelings for her. To help crystallize a treatment goal and to include LB in this process, the interviewer posed questions such as: What was meaningful in the discussion that day? What had struck a chord? What could they do in the brief time they had together that would make a difference in his life? What seemed important to talk about? LB replied that he didn't know. Everything seemed important. He needed to sort out his feelings about his girlfriend, he wanted to feel less anxious and to be able to study. The therapist cautioned LB that it would not be possible to directly address all of his concerns, and then he made the observation that LB's feelings about finishing school and leaving the university seemed to be related to many of his concerns. LB was silent and then reported feeling anxious with the interviewer's comments. Further exploration of this feeling resulted

in an agreement to focus on LB's fears of being on his own and of becoming independent.

Treatment helped LB confront and modify conflict-laden issues around growing up and becoming an adult. It is important to note that LB was assessed as primarily struggling with oedipally-derived conflicts around achievement, self-assertion, and becoming an adult male rival of his father as opposed to the pre-oedipal issue of separation from the mothering object. The therapist, therefore, felt comfortable in working with such a focus in a brief, time-limited manner.

Mutual agreement on treatment focus is often a relatively straightforward procedure. It can, however, become a therapeutic issue. For example, patients highly conflicted around control issues may be unwilling to allow the therapist much input on what they feel they need to work on. It is probably best not to pursue short-term psychotherapy if the therapist does not sense some degree of cooperation from the onset. Conversely, many individuals seeking treatment demand that the therapist tell them what needs to be discussed and worked on. Such patients often fear assuming responsibility for themselves and are acting out dependency conflicts. Only when the therapist is willing to make abdication of responsibility the focus of treatment should the therapist define the problem. In a sense, the therapist is saying, "I will define the problem, but that is the problem: I defined it and not you."

Adjuncts to Traditional Interview Format

The achievement of a focus may be facilitated by the use of a joint diagnostic effort. This may be accomplished in a variety of ways.

1. Individual members of the treatment team may assess the prospective patient. Specialists on the team could use their individual expertise to facilitate the diagnostic process, i.e., psychological testing, history gathering.

2. Prospective candidates for therapy may interact with two or more members of the assessment unit in a group interview.
3. The patient is seen by one therapist and the data of their interaction is presented to the treatment team for discussion. Information gleaned from such contact may then be reviewed by the treatment team with therapeutic recommendations as to type of therapy and focal issues being the result. Such procedures, though time-consuming, have much to offer in terms of developing increased clarity of the patient's life problems and psychodynamics.

Personality measures may aid in the establishment of a treatment focus. Such measures tap areas that cannot be reached in an interview and provide additional information about psychodynamics, ego strength, and severity of disturbance. It has been noted (e.g., Small 1979) that psychological testing is not always a part of the evaluation for brief therapy because of the press to initiate and complete treatment. This is often a mistake. Brief therapy is rooted in a theory and value that treatment is most effective when an accurate and in-depth assessment has been made and clear goals developed. This requires a thorough evaluation. Brief therapy is less effective if the diagnostic phase (e.g., psychological testing, history taking) is sacrificed in order to begin the treatment.

Treatment Brevity

During the development of the treatment focus, patients are informed that treatment is to be brief in duration and that as much will be accomplished in as short a period of time as possible. Agreement between patient and interviewer as to the focus and brevity of treatment becomes the contract of therapy. This contract establishes the limits to therapeutic work and lays the foundation for the therapeutic alliance. Short-term psychodynamic psychotherapy should not be undertaken without the establishment of such a contract at the outset of treatment.

In agreement with Malan (1963) and Mann (1973), we suggest setting a definite time limit to treatment. A definite time limit facilitates short-term therapy in the following ways:

1. A helpful incentive is provided for both participants to focus their work on the agreed upon task.
2. Treatment is prevented from becoming diffuse, aimless, and drifting into long-term involvement.
3. A definite beginning, middle, and end is established. This structure forces the patient to confront whatever illusions may be harbored regarding immortality, finiteness, and the sense that there is plenty of time in the future for change. Mann (1973) described this as facilitating the patient's movement from "child" to "adult" time.
4. A time limit brings into clearer perspective patient conflicts regarding separation, autonomy, and loss, thus making them available for therapeutic attention.

Determining the time limit for treatment is a difficult task for the less experienced therapist, and often for the experienced one. At times it may feel arbitrary, but in actuality it is based on an overall assessment of the patient and available treatment resources. Skill in evaluating the length of time needed to work on the psychological problems presented by various patients is developed with experience and training. We suggest that treatment length be determined by evaluating the patient's ego strength and resources, level of motivation, severity and nature of focal conflict, and environmental constraints. Fifteen sessions, for example, may be used with a highly motivated patient possessing good ego strengths, psychological mindedness, and a clearly delineated focal issue. Thirty sessions may be used with a patient presenting characteristics that make an early establishment of a productive therapeutic alliance more difficult (e.g., less clear motivation, more rigid intrapsychic and inter-personal defenses, greater environmental stress).

It is helpful to set a time limit to treatment in terms of a date rather than a number of sessions. The advantage to this strategy is twofold: (1) it is easier to keep track of a date versus counting sessions, and (2) the patient is offered a firm limit that is easily discernible and more easily defended if the patient resists termination. For example, if a ten-session limit is contracted, the patient may avoid dealing with termination issues by missing sessions, thus complicating the process and prolonging the length of treatment. If possible, the termination date should be correlated to the patient's natural life cycle of beginnings, endings, and separations (e.g., birthdays, seasons, semesters). For example, an appropriate termination date for a college student is often the semester break. Such a time limit is clearly identifiable, less arbitrarily perceived, and fits the treatment into the natural cycle of the patient. This provides a ready format to discuss the process of attachment, separation, and the finiteness of time.

The termination date should be adhered to if at all possible. Although the patient may be informed that later sessions are available to reinforce insights or to reevaluate the patient's condition, the patient is encouraged to cope with life affairs as independently as possible. Alexander (1956) felt that such a stance provides a mixture of limit-setting encouragement and emotional support that is effective in countering possible panic reactions and regressions encountered around termination.

Treatment Planning

The therapist practicing short-term psychodynamic psychotherapy assumes an active role in the treatment process. Therapist passivity has been discussed as the most important factor in lengthening analytic treatment (Malan 1963). The area of greatest agreement in the brief therapy literature is that passivity must be replaced by activity in various forms. This activity begins with the active, strategic planning of a circumscribed therapeutic goal and a means of reaching this goal (i.e., the treatment plan). For treatment to be brief, yet effective, an early development of a plan for therapy is imperative. Alexander and French (1946), strong proponents of an in-depth establishment of a treatment plan, emphasized that the therapist worked most effectively from a well-developed information base including a sound grasp of psychodynamic theory and an understanding of the particular dynamics of the individual patient. From this base, primary therapeutic goals and strategies to accomplish these goals are crystallized.

Lacking accurate assessment, identification of meaningful and workable goals, and development of therapeutic strategies to reach these goals, the therapist runs the risk of drifting into an aimless, reactive treatment. The therapist does not have the time to settle back and let a patient meander through the "lush jungles of the psyche" (Wolberg 1965). Such a stance often results in interminable therapy. Active development and implementation of a treatment plan helps therapists counteract the common therapist tendency of assuming a passive, nondirective stance and merely reacting to whatever material the patient chooses to present. While such a stance benefits certain patients, it runs the risk of reinforcing patient resistance to confronting anxiety-provoking issues. Short-term therapy is contraindicated for patients needing prolonged experience in therapy before developing sufficient security and trust to meaningfully confront their conflictual issues.

Environmental Support

When designing a course of treatment, it is crucial to assess what support is available in the patient's environment for emotional growth and behavioral change. During the course of treatment, intrapsychic and interpersonal conflict will be mobilized, often eliciting considerable anxiety and uncertainty within the patient. At these points, the patient may require additional support, understanding, or encouragement from significant others. Lack of support, or perhaps hostility towards the therapeutic process, will make it difficult for therapy to proceed. In addition, it is important to assess how supportive significant others will be of improvements in the patient's emotional functioning. Any changes an individual makes in patterns of responding and reacting to others will place pressure on these individuals to also behave differently. If significant others feel threatened by such occurrence, they may sabotage (consciously or unconsciously) the patient's use of treatment. It is perhaps this dynamic that led Freud (1912) to discuss the "natural opposition" of relatives to a patient's treatment (p. 120).

The possibility of introducing changes in the patient's present life situation must be evaluated. A patient may present qualities suggestive of good potential for treatment but have such extenuating circumstances in his/her life that change may be impossible. Such life situations may include irreversible physical illness, a large number of children or other dependents, or the inability to separate from a neurotic or psychotic spouse due to economic reasons. In such situations, a more supportive treatment is often more suitable in helping patients more successfully adapt to environmental constraints.

The level of current instability and stress in the patient's environment also must be considered. Involvement in an unstable, chaotic, and disruptive environment (e.g., hostile separation and divorce) often ties up psychic energy to such a degree that treatment becomes difficult. The more one's energy is tied up in current conflict, the less one's energy is available to uncover therapeutic work. Preoccupation with the struggle to cope with the stress of immediate problems limits patient capacity and inclination to observe and examine intrapsychic processes. Thus, current involvement in major emotional conflict and preoccupation with present crisis may make it difficult for a patient to be sufficiently introspective and reflective to permit an intense, uncovering therapy such as short-term psychodynamic psychotherapy. In such cases it may first be necessary for the patient to attain a degree of stability through ego-supportive, problem-solving therapy in order to free up psychic attention and interest, which then can be invested in an uncovering treatment. Dewald (1965) observed that this introduces something of a paradox. For such a patient, the chaotic and disruptive external environmental situation may result from preexisting unconscious intrapsychic conflicts; hence the patient will be unable to settle these problems without having resolved the inner conflicts to some extent.

SELECTION CRITERIA: A SUMMARY

An integration of the above discussion of selection criteria suggests that the following qualities are of importance in short-term psychodynamic psychotherapy assessment.

1. *Motivation for change.* Not to be confused with a wish for symptom relief, motivation for change implies an acceptance of the need to change maladaptive coping strategies and an inclination to become actively involved in the change process. Short-term psychodynamic psychotherapy is emotionally taxing and requires significant expenditure of psychic energy. The patient who does not possess a strong desire to identify and master problems in living is a risk for premature termination. Skillful interventions by the interviewer in the assessment phase of treatment may facilitate patient motivation.

2. *Psychological Mindedness.* Such a patient is able to attend to and verbally communicate thoughts, feelings, and fantasies. There exists a curiosity regarding emotional reactions and a willingness to reflect on the functioning of inner psychic processes. The ability to introspect and think in psychological terms facilitates understanding and acceptance of psychological insight.

3. *Ego Strength.* A patient's ego strength is assessed by attending to such characteristics as intelligence, academic and vocational achievements, satisfaction and stability of interpersonal relationships, and other noteworthy creative endeavors. Evidence of persistent and successful activity in a goal-directed manner indicates a strong capacity to productively integrate life experiences. It may be expected that such a patient possess the ability to tolerate frustration and painful affects through the flexible use of a variety of ego defenses and coping strategies. This ability allows the patient to tolerate the stresses of therapy and to constructively use this experience towards further growth.

4. *Object Relations/Ability to Interact with the Therapist.* The relationship developed between patient and therapist repeats aspects of the patient's previous interpersonal relationships. Minimally satisfying previous relationships allows for development of basic trust and a sense of the basic benevolence of others. These qualities are essential for the development and maintenance of the therapeutic alliance. Sifneos (1979) recommended that the patient have developed at least one meaningful relationship.

5. *Response to Trial Interpretations/Trial Therapy.* Davanloo (1980) felt that the only way to ascertain if a patient can work with short-term psychodynamic psychotherapy is to attempt it. A good candidate shows evidence of being able to work with early interpretations. The patient must be able to withstand the emotional stress resulting from the impact of uncovering unconscious material and to collaborate with the therapist in examining thoughts, feelings, and reactions, even though such work elicits painful affect (i.e., guilt, anxiety, dysphoria). An appropriate patient demonstrates a willingness to look at oneself and to consider the therapist's viewpoints. Evidence is shown of the ability to accept and elaborate on therapist interpretation. This does not mean a total lack of defensiveness and resistant behavior, but rather a will-

ingness to attempt exploration and understanding. Patient response to early uncovering work is considered the best indicator for future success in short-term therapy.

6. *Establishment of Treatment Focus.* Successful short-term therapy requires identification of a central area of conflict to be focused on in treatment. The short-term therapy patient is able to actively assist in developing a treatment focus and to accept its limits. Active involvement in focus development suggests ability to collaborate with the therapist. Acceptance of limited goals suggests the patient is realistic, able to tolerate frustration, and capable of giving up the wish for "perfect happiness" or "complete gratification."

SHORT-TERM PSYCHODYNAMIC PSYCHOTHERAPY ASSESSMENT PHASE: A SUMMARY

Selection tasks, crucial to successful short-term psychodynamic psychotherapy, have been highlighted. These tasks are complex and often cannot be fulfilled in a predetermined sequence. More than one meeting may be required to satisfactorily complete them. It is often helpful to think of assessment as a phase of treatment encompassing, for example, the first three sessions, rather than attempting to accomplish all tasks in the initial session. Malan (1980) outlined the assessment phase of short-term therapy in the following manner:

1. Take a full psychiatric history to acquire a picture of the patient's difficulties and level of crisis. Check on features that may constitute dangers to an uncovering therapy. Such dangers may include potential psychosis, poor impulse control and anxiety tolerance, serious suicidal tendencies, and extreme environmental crisis.
2. Attempt a tentative formulation of patient psychodynamics. Strive to understand the patient and his/her difficulties as deeply as possible.

3. Decide whether the patient is suitable for an attempt at trial therapy by evaluating the patient–therapist interaction, evidences of ego strength, and motivation level.

4. If patient is suitable for trial therapy, test out his/her response to uncovering interventions. Assess psychological mindedness and willingness to work with confrontations and interpretations.

5. In light of patient's response to such interventions, decide whether the patient is suitable for uncovering therapy, and if so, could it be short-term therapy. Assess patient's capacity to rapidly enter into a therapeutic alliance and work collaboratively with the therapist.

6. If the patient is thought to be suitable for short-term psychodynamic psychotherapy, formulate a therapeutic focus and treatment plan. Assess the patient's capacity to accept a limited treatment goal and work with the therapist in delineating such a goal.

7. Be alert for early manifestations of resistance to treatment (e.g., difficulties in arranging future sessions, over-under-compliance, vascillating motivation level). Explore resistances and underlying anxieties, and attempt to resolve them. Look for increase in motivation as resistances are confronted and worked through.

8. Carefully attend to the consequences of the assessment for the patient; avoid leaving the patient psychologically vulnerable and attempting to cope with a constellation of unresolved feelings.

INDICATIONS FOR
SHORT-TERM PSYCHODYNAMIC PSYCHOTHERAPY

The Patients

Short-term psychodynamic psychotherapy requires a patient who has average intelligence, is psychologically minded, and able to experience, express, and tolerate at least a moderate range of feelings. The patient must possess the ego strength and basic trust to work with the therapist in a situation that alternates frustration with gratification without exhibiting massive resistances or primitive regressive behavior. The patient must be capable of working with a barrier imposed onto the therapy (Tarachow 1963). This therapist-imposed barrier opposes the patient's attempt to view reactions to the therapy situation as totally justified by here-and-now reality. The transference component of the patient-therapist relationship is heavily focused upon. The "real" situation is transformed into an "as if" situation demanding attention and comprehension. The total spectrum of patient thoughts, feelings, and actions become grist for the therapeutic mill. The therapeutic task is the examination of interpersonal and intrapsychic functioning.

The qualities that identify candidates for short-term psychodynamic psychotherapy also identify candidates for psychoanalysis or long-term dynamic therapy. With the exception of the existence of focal conflict and strong motivation for change, the essential selection criteria for short-term therapy are similar to selection criteria for any form of dynamic, uncovering therapy (Marmor 1979). Freud (1905b) wrote that to undergo psychoanalysis the patient must: (1) suffer from a chronic neurotic syndrome, (2) have passed adolescence but not yet reached 50 years of age, (3) possess a good intelligence, and (4) show a reliable character. If such a patient possessed strong motivation for change, and if a focal conflict could be identified, s/he would in all likelihood be a good candidate for short-term therapy. We suggest that a substantial number of individuals presenting for treatment who may ordinarily be deemed appropriate for long-term analytic techniques may be equally appropriate for short-term psychodynamic psychotherapy. Individuals of all ages beyond adolescence may be candidates for brief therapy. People in middle age and beyond are evaluated by the same criteria of ego strength, character structure, and focal conflict. Individuals dealing with a changing family constellation, loss of parents and/or children, facing remarriage and career change, or sharpening their world view or philosophy of life will profit from a brief dynamic therapy.

The Problems

Short-term therapy is best suited for patients suffering from neurotic and transient situational problems in living. Such patients have successfully engaged in such developmental tasks as: (1) attachment to a mothering object, (2) development of a basic trust in people, (3) establishment of a stable, cohesive, and independent sense of self, and (4) the ability to see others as whole, complex individuals with their own thoughts and feelings as opposed to objects who frustrate or gratify. They have established a basic sense of who they are and are able to live in moderately independent, cooperative, and productive fashion (or exhibit strong potential to do so). The interpersonal difficulties and circumscribed symptoms presented by these patients tend to relate to anxiety, guilt, and dysphoric affect stemming from unresolved oedipal conflict.

Unresolved oedipal conflict may be reflected in such interpersonal difficulties as: (1) compulsive need to compete and achieve, or conversely, inhibition of competitive strivings, (2) dissatisfaction and inhibition in opposite-sex relationships stemming from anxiety and guilt, (3) jealousy and envy regarding the possessions of others (such possessions may be material or relationships), (4) chronic patterns of conflictual involvement in triangular, three-party relationships (e.g., affairs with married individuals, "stealing" a best friend's boy/girl friend, (5) difficulties with authority figures, expressed in feelings of fear, hostility, and rebellion towards authorities or more subtly, in terms of choosing a marital partner/lover who is significantly older or younger, or who possesses significantly more or less power (social/economic) than does the patient. The patient with unresolved oedipal conflicts typically complains of unhappy relationships with parents, peers, members of the opposite sex, children, teachers, or superiors at work. Inability to work, to enjoy work, and uncertainty regarding professional and personal goals may also be part of the picture. Also evident may be circumscribed neurotic symptoms such as anxiety (free-floating or panic attacks), moderate phobias and depressive episodes, and mild obsessive-compulsive symptoms of sudden onset.

Patients presenting difficulties that center on interpersonal problems tend to respond better to short-term therapy than those presenting crystallized symptoms (Sifneos 1972). The formation of a neurotic symptom (e.g., phobia, obsession) offers the patient a compromise solution for intrapsychic conflict. As such, it provides a derivative expression of forbidden drives/wishes, as well as defenses against it. This state of affairs represents a stable means of adapting to internal and external realities, as well as means to bind anxiety. Patients presenting difficulties primarily interpersonal in nature tend not to have developed as stable a neurotic solution as those with crystallized symptoms. They experience greater anxiety and uncertainty in their ways of relating and are more amenable to considering change. In addition, the highly interactive technique of short-term psychotherapy emphasizes the analysis and working through of conflicted patterns of emotional reaction. Short-term therapy is most effective with problems that readily express themselves in the patient–therapist interaction (e.g., conflicts with authority figures).

Davanloo (1980), in addition to applying short-term therapy to patients having a predominantly oedipal focus, also applied this treatment to patients having: (1) difficulty coping with object loss, (2) severe phobias and obsessional neurosis, and (3) long standing, neurotic characterological problems. In similar fashion, Malan (1963) extended the application of short-term therapy by stating that nature of the psychopathology and symptom duration are of less importance than patient motivation and ability to develop a treatment focus. Although Malan felt short-term therapy was not appropriate for patients presenting evidence of latent thought disorder, severe depression, and addiction, he felt it could be effective with certain more disturbed or complex patients, provided a carefully chosen focus is identified, agreed upon, and adhered to. In selecting such candidates, a thorough and careful assessment was seen as critical. When evaluating a patient with a previous psychiatric history or history of severe disturbance, Malan (1980) felt it imperative to assess the following:

1. The maximum severity of the past disturbance. The question, "What have you been like when you have been at your worst?" is one that very frequently needs to be asked.
2. The patient's strength, as shown by inner resources and interests, the history of relationships, and capacity to bear stress and disturbing feelings in the past without breaking down.
3. The degree of support available in the environment.
4. The capacity of any potential therapist to cope with the degree of disturbance that is likely to occur.

Davanloo and Malan have been successful in applying a highly focused technique with patients presenting more severe disturbances. This has provided impetus to expand the boundaries of brief, dynamic treatment beyond the traditional criterion of "acute and recent" onset. With careful selection, relatively disturbed patients can be helped towards permanent change by an active technique containing the essential elements of analytic treatment. Successful use of short-term therapy technique with severely disturbed patients requires a high level of clinical experience and acumen. We urge beginning therapists to be cautious in the use of short-term psychodynamic psychotherapy with patients presenting severe emotional difficulties until a strong experience base is developed.

CHAPTER FIVE
Principles
of Technique

THERAPIST ACTIVITY LEVEL

Use of Free Association

An essential feature of short-term psychodynamic psychotherapy is an increased level of activity by the therapist. The degree of activity required in short-term therapy is greater than in traditional psychodynamic psychotherapy. This more active stance may at times feel somewhat new, different, or foreign to the therapist trained in a more traditional psychodynamic format. While grounded in analytic theory, short-term psychodynamic therapy reverses the trend toward therapist inactivity initiated by Freud. Freud's establishment of free association as an essential component of analytic technique has been cited as a primary force behind the development of therapist passivity (Flegenheimer 1985). The free associative technique has considerable value in circumventing resistance and in learning about patient functioning. It is an antidote to social convention and internal assumptions patients maintain regarding appropriate behavior. It does, however, decrease verbal interaction.

An active therapist is incompatible with a free-associating patient. The more the therapist talks, the more the patient's associations are interrupted.

It is interesting to note that while Freud's writings on technique generally encouraged a passive analytic stance (Freud 1913), his case studies suggested an active, vigorous involvement with his patients (e.g., Freud 1909). Freud may have had some ambivalence as to the appropriate analytic stance. This stance was perhaps dependent on what was to be accomplished by the treatment. One of Freud's major commitments was to deepen and enrich his theory of personality development and his understanding of the functioning of the human mind. The analyst's stance of evenly hovering attention, quiet listening, and few interruptions into the patient's free association provided considerable material for developing psychoanalytic theory. Such intervention strategy was not accepted unequivocally. As early as 1925, Rank and Ferenczi questioned the continued need for using treatment to investigate analytic theory. Such procedures were seen as neglecting the actual therapeutic task for the sake of psychological interest.

Short-term psychodynamic psychotherapy requires a complex and demanding use of free association. A requisite aspect of short-term therapy is free communication. The therapist must communicate, educate, and demonstrate that the patient will profit and learn by free and spontaneous expression of thoughts and feelings, especially reactions to the behavior and attitude of the therapist. In addition to encouraging a general attitude of spontaneous communication, free association may be used in a therapist-directed manner to explore specific, relevant clinical material. There are times, as the therapeutic work and relationship unfold, when the therapist requests the patient to discuss what comes to mind regarding specific topics or incidents in therapy. This use of free association requires the therapist to assume an active, involved, and goal-directed stance. In general, it is not helpful for the therapist using short-term therapy to take the role of passive interpreter of unfocused verbalizations.

Effects on Therapist Neutrality and Transference Reactions

The heightened activity level of the therapist has become a well-accepted short-term therapy principle. Intensified therapist activity is actualized throughout the process of therapy from assessment to termination. In brief treatment formats, the therapist cannot afford to comfortably position oneself alongside a slow-moving stream of associations and merely comment on what passes by. The effectiveness and utility of such technique with some patients is not questioned. However, with many other patients, such a stance may unnecessarily prolong treatment.

The increased activity in short-term therapy begins in the assessment phase of therapy as the interviewer vigorously seeks out information from the patient to determine the patient's capacity for successful treatment. The interviewing therapist actively establishes a dialogue with the patient. This transactional process is used to gain rapport and to obtain a first-hand experience of the patient's interpersonal style. Marmor (1979) contended that the active stance of the short-term therapy practitioner reflects the therapist's interest in and concern for the patient and the therapist's wish to be helpful, both important factors in successful treatment. Interest and concern for the patient helps develop a more active and responsible collaboration. Increased patient involvement in treatment allows a greater access to the patient's intrapsychic and interpersonal functioning, thus facilitating the prospects of therapeutic change.

Some therapists have criticized the active interventions of short-term therapy as endangering therapist neutrality and of contaminating the patient's transference reactions. Fenichel (1941) asserted that the therapist should strive to create an analytic atmosphere of tolerance that expressed the implicit message: "You will not be punished here, so give your thoughts free rein." He expressed concern that too much activity on the therapist's part would inhibit trust in the therapist and the patient's willingness to engage in therapeutic regression. Through active interventions, Fenichel saw the therapist as creating the possibility of becoming, in the unconscious of the patient, "a punisher, a repeater of childhood threats, or a magician waving away threats" (p. 86). The therapist's neutrality would be lost in the patient's eyes. The security of the therapeutic setting, so important in free-flowing communication, would be severely compromised. In addition to decreasing the security of the therapeutic environment, vigorous therapist interventions were thought to distort the natural development of transference, thus making these reactions to the therapist more difficult to resolve. Such reasoning often kept therapist interventions at a minimum, with many opportunities to elicit change being overlooked.

The need to establish a safe, secure atmosphere in therapy and the importance of understanding the nature of transference reactions are essential therapeutic tasks. However, inhibiting one's therapeutic involvement (e.g., interpretation, confrontation, clarification) with the patient out of fear of transference distortion does not make analysis and resolution of transference reactions easier. Such a stance may encourage the perception of the therapist as a cold, distant figure, regardless of the patient's transference predisposition. Gill (1982) encouraged the therapist to keep in mind that the patient responds to what the therapist does not do, as well as what s/he does. The patient reacts to inactivity or unresponsiveness in the therapist, as well as to more active interventions. The silent, emotionally unresponsive therapist who gathers data and emits interpretations does no more supply the psychological milieu for the most undistorted delineation of the normal and abnormal features of a person's psychological makeup than does an oxygen-free atmosphere supply the physical milieu for the most accurate measurement of one's psychological responses (Kohut 1977).

Lipton (1977) noted that traditional analytic technique seems to have validated silence. In theory, the therapist is silent so as not to behave in a fashion that stimulates patient fantasies. In reality, such a stance often stimulates fantasies that require as much interpretation and working through as any other action would.

Work with Patient Resistance

Short-term psychodynamic psychotherapy may be divided into four phases: (1) assessment, (2) uncovering, (3) working through, and (4) termination. The therapist is most active in the assessment stage and uncovering phases of treatment. In the assessment phase, the therapist actively seeks evidence of the patient's ability to work in therapy and prepares the patient (e.g., establishing treatment focus and contract) for later phases of treatment. The therapist activity continues into the uncovering phase, in which the patient's difficulties are increasingly identified and the patient's resistance to therapeutic work is confronted.

The short-term psychodynamic psychotherapy therapist points out resistance and defenses against feeling. The therapist does not wait for patients to gradually work through their own resistance to self-exploration and understanding but persistently confronts, clarifies, and interprets patient defenses. Davanloo (1978, 1980) has developed a particularly effective means of working with resistance, particularly with those patients presenting strong intellectualizing defenses. When a particular topic increases a patient's avoidance and defensiveness, rather than become passive and wait for further developments, Davanloo would challenge defenses more forcefully. The patient is not let off the hook. Challenging defenses inevitably arouses strong affect (especially anger) in the patient, as well as the patient's typical defenses against these feelings. Patient anger is brought into the open as it occurs. Davanloo found that by repeatedly confronting and working through patient defenses, underlying conflicts being defended against could be identified and worked on.

The therapist utilizing brief therapy actively encourages patients to collaborate in the investigation of resistance. This is initially facilitated by selecting patients who are able to collaborate, and later by establishing a strong therapeutic alliance. Use of short-term therapy requires pointing out how patients resist the therapeutic process of exploration and understanding and how they defend against a mature collaboration with the therapist. The therapist accentuates this activity in the earlier phases of treatment. As therapy proceeds, patients are increasingly taught to confront their own resistance. Through the experience of working through resistant behavior and its underlying meaning with the therapist, the patients gradually are able to do this for themselves. Such work, however, requires the therapist to both actively confront and educate regarding the purpose of resistance. To illustrate:

> AA was a 36-year-old male whose focal problem was fear of self-expression and dependency on others. AA would frequently fall silent during treatment. The therapist focused on the thoughts and feelings that accompanied these lapses into silence. AA was able to identify such lapses as moments when he felt his unexpressed thoughts would portray him unfavorably to the therapist. The persistent confrontation of these self-protective, yet constricting, silences helped AA to gradually realize how his fear of punishment and rejection led to verbal inhibitions. As treatment progressed, AA was increasingly able to identify and confront this resistance for himself, both in treatment and in his outside life.

Promotion of Optimal Anxiety

Effective short-term psychodynamic psychotherapy calls for the therapist to become a full partner in the therapeutic process. The therapist cannot wait for patients to gradually work through their own resistance to self-exploration and understanding; the therapist constantly confronts, clarifies, and interprets defenses. This stance requires a concerted effort by the therapist to become involved in an intensive interpersonal interchange. Short-term therapy is a highly interactive therapy. It makes liberal use of questions, confrontations, clarifications, and interpretations that lead to a high level of emotional involvement by *both* therapist and patient. Confrontation and anxiety-provoking questions are used to increase the emotional intensity of the session and to explore areas of difficulty the patients tend to avoid. A certain degree of anxiety is necessary during the interview. Optimum as opposed to maximum anxiety motivates the reluctant patient to understand the nature of emotional conflicts, to recognize defensive reactions utilized to deal with them, and to enable the patient to have a corrective emotional experience (Sifneos 1967). Therapist interventions frequently involve illogical conclusions, ineffectual responses, irrational wishes, and maladaptive behavior patterns. The anxiety-provoking quality of these tactics highlights the importance of a detailed assessment of ego strength in short-term therapy candidates.

Active Listening

Short-term therapy requires the therapist to actively listen for and examine the patient's conflicted patterns of emotional reaction. The therapist listens for what is being avoided or repressed and is alert for derivative or disguised expressions of the patient's underlying conflict. To illustrate:

> A patient (FE) was working on the focal problem of effectively expressing strong affect, particularly anger. FE began his session bitterly criticizing his work supervisor, an individual whom FE often spoke of in glowing terms. The therapist, in an attempt to understand these unusually intense feelings, remembered having ended the last session while FE was discussing a painful childhood incident. The therapist pointed out the possibility that FE might be displacing his anger regarding the therapist onto his supervisor. FE considered this hypothesis and gradually was able to own and express his hurt and anger towards the therapist for ending the previous session with FE in such a vulnerable state. FE was able to express these feelings without experiencing the dire consequences he had been conditioned to expect (i.e., rejection, retaliation). The therapist's alert listening, while taking into account FE's dynamic conflicts, facilitated the occurrence of a corrective emotional experience.

The therapist rapidly uses what is known or hypothesized regarding patient dynamics to further the process of treatment.

Rather than let opportunities for therapeutic work drift by, confident that real conflicts will show up again and again, an immediate investigation is initiated. If the therapist fails to actively intervene, opportunities will be missed, ambiguity as to both process and goals may develop, and what began as relevant treatment may become diffuse, indefinite, and vague.

The ability to intervene rapidly requires therapists to rely considerably on therapeutic acumen developed through study of psychotherapy principles, past experience with patients, and supervision. Horner (1985) emphasized that brief, dynamic treatment requires a reversal of the traditional process of building theory on the data of observation and experience. Instead brief, dynamic work entails a vigorous application of theory to the clinical situation. Such treatment requires therapists to trust their theories and themselves enough to help patients confront their issues and problems in living in a spontaneous and genuine manner. Due to the intense, fast-moving nature of treatment, it is recommended that therapists develop a supervision/consultation relationship in which their work is continually scrutinized. In discussing this issue, Goldin (1985) stated that the time needed in supervision is inversely proportionate to the length of therapy being done.

Analytic Activity

It is important to define the recommendation that practitioners of short-term psychotherapy actively intervene with their patients. The active participation does not mean that therapists, consciously or unconsciously, direct the conduct of patients' lives (Mann 1973). Short-term therapy essentially follows the nondirective model of traditional analytic treatment. When practical questions are raised, such as requests or demands for advice on outside problems or how to behave in the session, patients are encouraged to reflect on the nature, implications, or reasons for the request. Patients are asked to reflect on the feelings that accompany those requests, or the feelings of the therapist that the request seems designed to stir up or play upon. But in so doing, therapists remain flexible and do not attempt to play out in full the "incognito" of the traditional analyst (Schafer 1973). Rather than controlling the patients' lives, therapists actively attempt to establish an atmosphere of exploration and investigation. Activity in short-term therapy consists of questions, clarifications, confrontations, and interpretations. Persistent attempts are made to understand the problems in living and to spark patient curiosity as well.

MAINTENANCE OF THERAPEUTIC FOCUS

The active nature of short-term psychodynamic psychotherapy is clearly expressed in the concerted attempt throughout therapy to maintain a focus on a core conflict, as well as the refusal to permit defensive digressions from this central focus. This focus is developed with and agreed upon by the patient and may be conceptualized in numerous fashions: a circumscribed symptom, a specific intrapsychic conflict or developmental impasse, a maladaptive conviction about the self, an essential interpretive theme, or a persistent interpersonal dilemma or pattern of maladaptive activity (Schacht et al. 1984). The most appropriate foci for short-term therapy are those that are highly likely to be expressed in the patient–therapist relationship (e.g., inhibition with authorities, inability to accept responsibility or make decisions, conflicts around competition).

The focus of treatment should be clear, specific, and manageable. Symptoms resulting from personality disorders that are chronic, ingrained, and suggestive of severe underlying disturbance should be avoided. Such disorders include addictive and eating disorders, impulse disorders, and chronic feelings of emptiness, depression, and rage. Symptoms expressed in these disorders are not appropriate foci for short-term therapy in that they are suggestive of a patient who needs a significant amount of time in treatment to develop trust and to strengthen adaptive ego functions.

The focus chosen for therapeutic attention must be manageable within the treatment time frame. A need for perfectionism rooted in wanting to fix everything will be problematic for therapist and patient alike. Attention to too many issues or very complicated issues may lead to increasing diffusion with no particular issue being focused on, understood, and worked through. Both therapist and patient must be able to accept a limited aim in therapy. Both must deal with the fact that treatment will not lead to total change in behavior. This idea may be particularly intolerable to those individuals who have difficulties accepting personal limitations and who have underlying narcissistic problems.

Benefits of Focus Maintenance

Working with a clear focus helps the therapist avoid falling into a passive role in treatment. In order to help the patient keep working upon the agreed-upon focus and prevent defensive digression, the therapist assumes a more active stance than is traditionally taught in dynamic supervision. Adherence to the central focus and active discouragement of digressions maintains a high level of therapeutic tension and interaction throughout the therapy more effectively than the traditional patterns of abstinence in classical psychoanalysis (Marmor 1979).

Efforts to keep therapy focused promote a constructive task orientation to therapy that decreases its regressive pull. This is invaluable in preventing the development of a transference neurosis. In a transference neurosis the patient becomes extremely involved (preoccupied) with his/her relationship to the therapist. Real life issues often lose their sense of importance as more and more of the patient's energy becomes involved in what happens in therapy. Though valuable in many cases for understanding and working through conflicted past attachments, one cannot successfully accomplish this in a weekly treatment of brief duration. Keeping a clear focus helps the therapist and patient avoid overly complex involvements that interfere with brief analysis.

Focus Development

The focus of therapy is developed during the assessment phase. It is established by appraising the patient's current life situation and developmental history. The therapist constantly considers the question, "What are the important issues in this person's life, and what would be helpful to work through to enable further change and emotional growth?"

As the therapist identifies conflicted areas, their significance is explored with the patient. This may be done in terms of interpretive observations pointing out, for example, connections between various aspects of the patient's life (e.g., inhibited anger and a stomachache). The patient's response to these interpretations must be observed closely. You have the beginning of a therapeutic contract when the patient is able to consider the therapist's ideas and is able to acknowledge their importance. If not, then other hypotheses must be developed and presented.

Inability of the patient and therapist to agree on the patient's core issues can occur for a number of reasons:

1. The therapist may have an incorrect understanding of the patient and may need to gather further data. The therapist must be flexible in conceptualizing patient conflicts. This is important in the assessment phase when the preliminary focus is identified, as well as in later phases of treatment when the focus is further clarified and worked through. Schacht and colleagues (1984) noted that the treatment focus is always to be regarded as partial, preliminary, and subject to continued scrutiny and revision. No therapist ever achieves a complete and final understanding of a patient.

2. The patient feels threatened by the accuracy of the therapist's observations and may become defensive. The therapist may attempt to reframe interventions so that the patient is able to accept and work with them or confront the patient's resistance to looking at certain issues. To illustrate:

> While working to establish a treatment focus with WH, a 25-year-old man who sought treatment for social inhibitions, the therapist felt an appropriate focus would be WH's lack of self-reliance and his dependency on others. WH angrily rejected this focus, stating he would prefer to learn how to induce people to like him more. He further stated that there was nothing wrong with his self-esteem and that all he needed were some techniques to help him create a more favorable impression. The therapist pointed out the cost of WH's attempts to get others to like him (i.e., social inhibition), as well as how his dependency on others led him to behave in ways that made it difficult for him to like himself. Using information gathered over the session, the therapist further pointed out how WH's dependency conflicts affected their present relationship in that he was vascillating between deference and rebellion. Upon reflection and further discussion, WH agreed with the therapist's observations and was willing to accept his dependency conflicts as a treatment focus.

Whenever defensiveness occurs, the therapist should explore the defensiveness, as well as his/her own reactions. The goal is not to test the accuracy of the therapist's diagnostic acumen. The patient's defensiveness is likely to be sufficient data to confirm the hypothesis (i.e., "the truer the guess, the more violent the resistance," Freud 1913, p. 140). The more critical issue is the treatment relationship and whether the defensiveness is open to exploration. Free association in the form of free communication must be restored.

3. The patient may also disagree with the therapist about the focus because the patient is unable to delay gratification and accept the type of support an uncovering therapy offers (i.e., empathy, understanding, and an opportunity to develop increased autonomy). These patients demand immediate relief

of emotional pain resulting from a conflict and are unwilling to focus on understanding the underlying problem. To illustrate:

MX was a 32-year-old male who sought treatment for depression and loneliness. He presented a pattern of being attracted to women until they returned the attention. At that point he lost interest and broke off the relationship and began a frantic search for a new relationship. MX was adamant about his unwillingness to explore the dynamics underlying this pattern. Instead, he wanted the therapist to help him find other ways to meet women.

MX would find the frustrations involved in an uncovering therapy difficult and is a candidate for more supportive technique. He is an example of the patient who consciously disagrees with the focus, not because it is wrong, but because, in offering a treatment focus, the therapist is defining what treatment would offer; the patient rejects the proposed treatment, not the interpretation.

The initial development of the focus of treatment is done in the assessment phase of short-term psychodynamic psychotherapy. Establishment of a workable focus often takes more than one session. In fact, the entire course of treatment could be conceptualized as a continual formulation and deepening of the treatment focus. The identification, clarification, and understanding of the patient's focal conflict in all its various manifestations are integral components of the entire process of treatment and not a precursor to it (Strupp and Binder 1984).

In developing the focus to treatment, collaboration of the patient is essential. The autonomy and responsibility of the patient are fostered throughout treatment. Agreement as to the focus constitutes an important aspect of the therapeutic contract and is involved in establishing a strong alliance with the patient. The patient's agreement to a focus may be used later in therapy to confront resistive maneuvers. When the patient begins to resist and avoid the focal issue due to anxiety, the therapist may call this maneuver, as well as the initial agreement, to the patient's attention. The patient is confronted with avoidance tendencies, as well as the original agreement. This strategy facilitates the exploration of the patient's avoidance tendencies and forces more responsible behavior.

How to Maintain Focus

Once treatment focus has been developed, the issue becomes to maintain it. Malan (1976) noted that one of the most frequent questions he is asked regarding brief therapy is: "How on earth do you keep your interventions focused?" The answer involves patient selection, treatment planning, and technique. A focal patient can work at establishing a clear, manageable issue to work on in therapy and presents strong evidence of being able to work in short-term therapy (e.g., motivation, psychological mindedness, etc.).

If a correct treatment plan has been formulated and the selected focus is a significant issue for the patient, therapy will naturally unfold. The therapist's ability to identify a core issue of conflict with the patient facilitates the focused nature of treatment; the patient will talk about aspects of the core conflict, and the therapist will make progressively explorative and centralized interpretations (Malan 1976). An illustration is provided:

> A patient (SW) developed depressive symptoms following a camping trip on which he perceived his wife as expressing undue attentions towards another man. Looking into SW's past history, a pattern of self-depredation and blaming was identified, particularly in situations where SW had been disappointed by others. The therapist hypothesized that a core issue for SW was turning his anger inward and hurting himself when, in fact, he felt angry with others. This hypothesis was presented to SW. SW was able to elaborate on it and consider its implications. The issue was central to SW's functioning. Left to his own devices, this conflict would be continually reenacted. In therapy SW's basic drive towards growth and maturation was facilitated by focusing the psychic energy towards resolution of this conflict.

Proper patient selection and treatment planning facilitates establishing and maintaining a clear direction in treatment. However, even patients who are highly capable of confronting their conflicted feelings will engage in avoidance maneuvers that may be motivated by the desire to avoid psychic pain. They may also be motivated by the pull of other pressing issues in the patient's life that are not under the agreed auspices of treatment.

Malan (1963) suggested that focus may be maintained by selectively attending, neglecting, and interpreting.

> The therapist keeps in mind a focus in terms of an essential interpretation on which the therapy is to be based. This focus is pursued single-mindedly, guiding the patient by partial interpretations, selective attention, and selective neglect. If the material admits to more than one interpretation, that interpretation most consonant with the focus is used. The therapist refuses to be diverted by material irrelevant to the focus, however tempting this may be [p. 210].

When the patient's expressions, thoughts, feelings, and fantasies follow a path congruent with the agreed-upon theme of therapy, the therapist offers verbal (e.g., clarifications, interpretations) or nonverbal reinforcement (e.g., attention). When the patient discusses other issues, the therapist attempts to avoid reinforcing this discussion.

Malan's suggestion that the therapist selectively reinforce the patient's behavior in treatment is something that is done in most treatments, though perhaps not attended to. Schacht and colleagues (1984) cautioned that the principles of selective attention and selective neglect are not the same as arbitrarily ignoring material that appears unrelated to the focus. Ignoring what a patient says or does is unempathic and will generally lead to a weakening of the therapeutic alliance. What is critical here is that the therapist constantly attempts to help the patient work on the agreed-upon focal conflict. "The therapist's patterning of questions, the timing and shaping of the context for questions, the choices of what to name and what to leave nameless, should all create an associative atmosphere in which focally relevant material predominates because it seems most narratively natural" (Schacht et al. 1984, p. 108).

When listening to patient associations, the therapist attempts to conceptualize and relate the material to the selected theme. When material from the patient may be understood in more than one way, the therapist selects the mode of explanation that fits with the focus. For instance, the focus of therapy may be the patient's wish to rely on others and maintain dependent relationships even though he is capable of relative independence. Patient associations are listened to with this theme in mind. The therapist attempts to understand what the patient presents in light of the focus on dependency strivings. If material seems unrelated to dependency, the therapist may confront this by means of asking the patient to explain how it relates. The therapist avoids the temptation of working on distracting material, chooses interpretations that are relevant to the focus, and carefully avoids those that are not.

Horner (1985) recommended the intervention of "interpreting upward" in order to avoid undue patient regression. Such regression is seen to occur as a result of focusing on developmentally early (preoedipal) issues. What the patient decides to talk about in treatment is influenced by conflicts at all stages of development. Rather than be drawn into work on preoedipal issues, which are not as amenable to brief treatment, Horner suggested interpreting patient material upward to the oedipal conflict. The short-term therapy practitioner is thus encouraged to avoid any existing preoedipal implications of patient material (e.g., unresolved orality) and must attempt to understand and interpret patient material in the context of the oedipal conflict. For example, fear of punishment and loss of maternal love is interpreted as relating to competitive feelings regarding father's attention instead of relating to conflict regarding the early mother–infant bond. Horner (1985) noted that if the patient is unable to benefit from conceptualizing material in terms of the oedipal conflict, the patient's appropriateness for brief treatment must be reconsidered.

In addition to actively pursuing a focus by means of selective attention and selective neglect, Davanloo (1980) recommended a continuous confrontation of the patient's attempts to divert therapeutic attention to other issues. This is to be done with the goal of stimulating the patient's curiosity regarding present avoidant strategies. Such work must be accomplished with tact and as gentle a manner as possible. Little is gained by badgering the patient to talk about issues only the therapist is interested in. Schacht and co-authors (1984) cautioned against an overzealous approach to maintaining a focus lest this focal work transform a good therapeutic environment into one in which the patient acquiesces to a domineering professional. The skill of the therapist is tested in one's ability to maintain a therapeutic focus without neglecting to analyze the patient's resistance and without getting angry and punitive when the patient wanders. Patience, persistence, and fortitude are therapeutic prerequisites. In addition, the therapist must be able to tolerate emotional tension and pain elicited by an unrelenting focus at the heart of the patient's problem.

Additional adjuncts that may be instituted to help maintain focus include: (1) writing regular process notes summarizing how the focal material was generated in the meeting, (2) reminding oneself of the focal issue prior to entering the session, (3) recalling unfinished focal material from the previous session and bringing it into the current session, (4) being prepared to introduce focal material into the session, and (5) ending the session by commenting on how the focal issue was expressed, avoided, elaborated, or what new perspective the therapist had acquired of the focal issue during the meeting.

Continual difficulty in maintaining a relevant focus in treatment may require a reexamination of the treatment itself. This reassessment should evaluate: (1) the patient's capability to work in short-term psychodynamic psychotherapy, (2) the correctness and applicability of the chosen focus, and (3) the transference and/or countertransference impasses that may be significantly affecting the work.

THERAPEUTIC ALLIANCE

The therapeutic alliance is extremely important in short-term psychodynamic psychotherapy. Davanloo (1980) believed that the establishment of a working relationship was a prime objective of treatment and should be established very early. Sifneos (1972) recommended that the therapist attempt to establish good rapport with the patient as soon as possible in order to create a therapeutic alliance conducive to the problem-solving task at hand. A strong therapeutic alliance is seen as a prerequisite for motivating the patient to expose oneself in treatment and withstand the stresses created by an examination of conflicted intrapsychic and interpersonal processes. The positive attachment to the therapist and the commitment to the treatment process are used to induce the patient to do psychic work (Freud 1925). A strong relationship between patient and therapist must be established to learn about the patient's emotional conflicts and maladaptive strategies and to effect resolution of these issues in a short amount of time. In doing so, the relationship also serves as a source of support and encouragement for further psychic growth. This relationship is to be firmly established and should not be a constant source of concern during the treatment. When the therapeutic alliance is in a constant state of disruption, vital time is diverted from work on the therapeutic focus. In many longer-term treatments, the development of a productive, secure relationship may be the primary focus. This is particularly true with patients struggling with early trust and/or separation–individuation issues. Such work is a slow process requiring numerous repetitive corrective emotional experiences that go beyond the realm of short-term psychodynamic psychotherapy. The inability to establish a therapeutic alliance early in short-term therapy most often leads to a therapeutic impasse and treatment stalemate.

Definition and Importance

The concept of the therapeutic alliance has been extensively discussed in analytic circles. Zetzel (1956), Greenson (1965), and

Brenner (1980) discuss the therapeutic alliance; their works are comprehensive and highly recommended reading. The therapeutic alliance is essentially descriptive of the relatively nonneurotic, rational rapport the patient has with the therapist. The therapeutic alliance is not just a warm, friendly relationship between therapist and patient, but a mutually respectful and trusting forum for the treatment process.

Development of the therapeutic alliance enables patients to collaborate in therapy to examine their problematic intrapsychic and interpersonal functioning. A strong therapeutic alliance facilitates the ability of patients to transcend "an experiencing, subjective, irrational ego" in order to evaluate emotional reactions with "an observing, reasonable, analyzing ego" (Greenson 1965). During therapy patients will experience increased psychic stress and conflict. This leads to the use of their most tried and true means of dealing with conflict. Methods that were useful in the past, however, may be maladaptive and unrealistic in the present. In order for patients to explore and learn about themselves and their conflictual patterns of reaction and interaction, it is necessary that they view themselves in a reasonable, objective manner. A strong, trusting attachment to the therapist is used to sustain patients through the anxieties associated with this self-exploration. The development of a sense of trust in the competency and basic helpfulness of the therapist and treatment process enable the patients to risk an examination of their problems in living.

Contributions of the Patient

To establish an effective therapeutic alliance, patients must have the capacity to interact in a relatively flexible fashion. Patients must also be able to withstand increases in anxiety without resorting to use of rigid, primitive defenses (e.g., projection, denial, splitting). Such characteristics are strongly determined by past emotional conditioning. Those individuals who have had gratifying experiences with significant others in the past are able to face new situations with a willingness to trust, cooperate, and collaborate. They are able to stay with the therapist and the therapy even when it is painful and anxiety provoking. In ego developmental terms, these patients have completed the task of object constancy (Masterson 1976). Reasonable resolution of this task enables patients to tolerate ambivalent feelings towards another. When frustrated and angry with the therapist, these patients still realize that the therapist has redeeming qualities; they do not reject the therapist but attempt to cooperate so as to understand the impasse.

It is difficult to develop and sustain rapid and effective alliances with patients who suffer from significant impairment in ego development. The impairment may include lack of impulse control and frustration tolerance, or relative inability to distinguish internal wishes and fears from reality when under stress, resulting in tenuous and/or highly chaotic interpersonal relationships. Patients often show the capacity to become involved in the therapeutic relationship but are unable to step back and view the therapeutic interaction objectively. They have transference feelings but are too conflicted and threatened to work with the therapist to understand these reactions. The degree of threat and insecurity felt in their lives impels them to cling to a rigid manner of viewing the world and interacting with others. These patients are more effectively treated in long-term psychotherapy.

Contributions of the Analysts

Insight into the development of a therapeutic alliance is offered by psychoanalytic practitioners. Freud (1913) stated that prior to any effective exploration of transferential attitudes, a strong attachment/alliance between therapist and patient must be established. The first goal of analytic treatment is the formation of an attachment of the patient to the therapist. It is this bond that helps prevent "fresh flight" and prompts the patient face his/her defenses (Freud 1910). The friendly, trusting aspects of unobjectionable positive transference were seen as the "vehicle of success in psychoanalysis" (Freud 1912, p. 105). Freud (1913) felt this rapport/attachment was accomplished by: (1) exhibiting a serious interest in the patient, (2) clearing away any resistances that develop, (3) being nonjudgmental with the patient, and (4) being objective about the patient's concerns.

Sterba (1934) stressed helping the patient identify with the therapist as a fellow collaborator in treatment. From the beginning of treatment, the therapist should stress the work they have to accomplish together. The use of such terms as "let us look at this" or "we can see" promotes a cooperative working relationship. Sterba further noted that once a therapeutic alliance has been established, it must be maintained. Such maintenance calls for a constant scrutiny of how the patient and therapist are working together.

The therapeutic alliance, in addition to being influenced by the content of the therapist's interventions, is also influenced by the process of the therapist's intervention. This includes the therapist's attitude, mood, manner, and the atmosphere created. Fenichel (1941) believed that the therapeutic atmosphere was the most important factor in persuading the patient to risk self-exploration and behavior change. He emphasized that, above all, the therapist should be "human." Essentially, the humanness of the therapist is expressed in the compassion, concern, and therapeutic intent communicated to the patient. The therapist is genuinely concerned with how the patient fares and is not just an observer or a research worker. This concern is communicated by the therapist's attempt to create an atmosphere and environment where the patient can grow and change. Humanness is also expressed in the attitude that the patient is represented as an individual. While interpreting and intervening in the patient's psychic life, the therapist is also sensitive to the patient's sense of dignity and integrity as a human being. Rules and regulations are not imposed upon the patient without explanation. For a therapeutic alliance to develop, it is imperative that the therapist show consistent concern and respect for the integrity of the patient.

Greenson (1965) stressed that the therapeutic alliance is strengthened by the therapist's ability to be involved, yet unintrusive, with the patient. The therapist was encouraged not to take sides in any conflicts except in working against patient resistances, damaging neurotic behavior, and self-destructiveness. Greenson further noted that the therapeutic alliance is considerably facilitated by the analyst's constant emphasis on attempting to gain understanding of all that goes on in the patient. The therapist's constant search for comprehension tends to evoke in the patient the wish to know, to find answers, to find causes. Such work, although stirring up resistances to uncovering, stimulates the patient's curiosity and search for causality.

Freud (1913) felt that if the patient had the capacity to develop an attachment to the therapist (i.e., was capable of a transference neurosis rather than a narcissistic neurosis), rapport would be established with time and an attitude of sympathetic understanding. The therapeutic alliance was seen to develop almost imperceptibly, relatively silently, and seemingly independently of any special activity on the part of the therapist. Creation of a stable and consistent setting, adherence to ground rules (e.g., free association, abstinence, therapist neutrality), and an essentially interpretative approach directed at increasing understanding and awareness are used in long-term analytic work to establish and maintain the therapeutic alliance. Such technique, although sound in long-term strategy, needs to be addended for the rapid establishment of a therapeutic alliance needed in short-term therapy.

General Guidelines

It is difficult to compile a set of rules to be used in short-term psychodynamic psychotherapy for the rapid establishment of a therapeutic alliance. Factors apply in one situation that are not appropriate in another. We encourage the therapist to consider the following general principles.

Attention to the Therapeutic Alliance From the Onset of Treatment

Patients having potential to engage in a productive therapeutic alliance are identified during assessment. Once the decision is made to engage in short-term therapy, the therapist needs to work rapidly to do all that is possible to foster this alliance. Wolberg (1965) stressed that a solid working relationship may be developed with most patients within a few sessions. "If one tries to put oneself in the patient's position, attempts to empathize with feelings, and to define and reflect what must be immediate concerns, one has made an important beginning" (p. 146).

The development of a therapeutic alliance is facilitated by the therapist's ability to be sensitive to common reactions patients may have to entering treatment. There is great variety in the manner patients enter the preliminary interview. In part, this is determined by past history in regard to psychotherapists, physicians, and authority figures and strangers, as well as patient reactions to such conditions as feeling sick and needy and asking for help (Greenson 1965). Patients presenting for treatment have often suffered a breakdown in defenses and coping mechanisms. They may be experiencing or feel threatened with an imminent breakdown in adaptation. Such fears are often expressed by means of symptoms such as anxiety, depression, or psychophysiological reactions. Upon initial contact with the therapist, patients may feel confused and defeated. Their self-image is often deflated, and their sense of mastery is weakened. Patients may endeavor to compensate to save face. They may manifest defiance and externalize blame. Reduction in effective coping mechanisms increases dependency strivings. Patients may present dependency needs directly in the form of demands for help, answers, and support. Dependency needs may also be expressed in more disguised fashion such as masochistic behavior or counterdependent stances (e.g., denial of feelings of powerlessness through defensive competition with the therapist) (Wolberg 1965).

Patients' immediate feelings in treatment are also affected by the therapist and the treatment environment. Their reaction to early interviews are determined by their feelings about self-exposure, as well as their reactions to the therapist's personality and method of approach. This is a mixture of transference and realistic reactions. For example, talking about one's self is apt to stir up reverberations of past exposures in front of parents, doctors, or others, and is therefore likely to produce transference reactions. Knowledge or lack of it about procedures of psychotherapy and the reputation of the psychotherapist also influence initial responses.

Patients may harbor misconceptions about psychotherapy, gleaned from distortions from the press, television, or friends who know of people who have been in psychotherapy for years and are now worse off than when they started (Wolberg 1965). Feelings about needing treatment, fears, misgivings, and misconceptions of therapy should be identified and discussed as soon as possible. This is done to convey a sense of empathy and understanding and to foster resolution (however partial) of these attitudes. Such work is the beginning of the therapeutic alliance.

Utilize Naturally Occurring Positive Transference Feelings

The therapeutic alliance is dependent on the expectational set or predisposition that patients bring to therapy. Freud (1912) stated that the development of the therapeutic alliance was fostered by the "unobjectionable positive transference." He differentiated this transference reaction from two other types of transference, the negative (hostile) transference and a variant of the positive transference called the erotic transference. The unobjectionable positive transference was seen as the build-up of friendly, affectionate, and trusting feelings that are dependent on the transfer of similar feelings for significant early caretakers. Freud saw the unobjectionable positive transference as that portion of libidinal impulses that has "passed through the full process of psychic development, . . . is directed towards reality, is at the disposal of the conscious personality, and forms a part of it" (p. 100). Freud differentiated the unobjectionable positive transference from the erotic transference, which consisted of "impulses that have been held up in the course of development . . . kept away from the conscious personality and from reality, and have either been prevented from further expansion, except in phantasy, or have remained wholly in the unconscious" (p. 100). Freud viewed the unobjectionable positive transference as facilitating the joint work of treatment and excluded these feelings from the analysis, whereas hostile and erotic transference feelings were seen as fostering resistance to analytic exploration and were to be subjected to interpretation and resolution.

The use of positive transference to strengthen the therapeutic alliance is strongly encouraged by Sifneos (1968) and Davanloo (1980). The development of trusting, friendly feelings towards the therapist are to be used in furthering motivation for therapy. While positive transference feelings are fostered as long as they are realistic and helpful in accomplishing the goals of therapy, they must be examined if they obstruct the therapeutic process or create therapeutic misalliances. For example, perceiving the therapist to be trustworthy and respectful and feeling secure in the relationship is qualitatively different from perceiving the therapist to be a wonderful and ideal being who is to be pleased, ingratiated, and/or seduced. The former set of feelings forms part of the structure upon which treatment operates. The latter reactions to the therapist make it difficult to develop a realistic, working collaboration. Such reactions are often an expression of the patient's problem and are to be explored and understood.

Convey Unqualified Acceptance and Interest in the Patient

Sifneos (1972) recommended that the therapist convey acceptance and interest from the onset of the assessment. This is done through an active interest in the patient's past and current life. During the first few sessions the patient generally is very concerned with being accepted. A detached and passive attitude by the therapist in an attempt to be objective and nondirective is often unproductive, stimulating fears and resentments from which the patient may not recover within a brief treatment format. An interested, open, and warm attitude by the therapist is extremely helpful in increasing patient openness and comfort with treatment.

The therapeutic alliance significantly improves to the degree the therapist is able to care about the patient as a person and to be able to identify (at least temporarily) with the patient's experience (Strupp 1973). To the degree that a natural rapport is available between patient and therapist, the possibilities of a positive therapeutic experience are maximized. The ability of the therapist to significantly invest oneself in the treatment most often induces a similar reaction in the patient. Because of the emphasis on rapidly establishing a positive attachment in short-term psychotherapy, the selection of a proper therapist for each patient assumes great importance. The factors that may be involved include the therapist's age, sex, status, and cultural suitability (Bellack and Small 1978).

Actively Encourage Patient Verbalization

Patients are encouraged to discuss their problems and life situation as fully as possible. They are constantly drawn out to express their various thoughts, feelings, and reactions. The therapist attempts to phrase questions, clarifications, and interpretations in such a manner as to facilitate the flow of ideas and feelings. Prolonged periods of silence are actively interrupted. Such interruptions may first take the form of reestablishing the goal of free communication and continued exploration of relevant topics. If silences continue, their resistive aspects are examined. In exploring such inhibitions, it is productive to first explore the influence of the immediate therapy setting including the patient–therapist relationship. Comments such as, "Is there something that I do that gets in your way?" are often helpful in allowing patients to begin self-examination.

The goal is to help patients share thoughts and feelings as fully as possible. The more patients are able to open up and discuss issues that are of concern, the greater the possibility of developing a meaningful relationship. Sharing of important feelings deepens the relationship. Patient reaction to the therapist's active encouragement of verbalization must be closely monitored. For example, patients who are suspicious or fear being controlled may react with feelings of intrusion and threat and with withdrawal behavior. The therapist must flexibly adapt technique to patient needs.

Convey Your Understanding of the Patient as Soon as Possible

Empathy is critical in establishing contact. Feeling understood increases the patient's security. The sooner a patient feels secure with the therapist, the sooner s/he is able to begin collaborating on the therapeutic task. Accurate empathy and understanding increases the patient's confidence in the therapist. This leads to an increase in patient motivation. Davanloo (1980), in discussing his trial therapy model of assessment, noted that the ability of the therapist to help a patient gain some measure of self-understanding by means of successful exploration of conflict areas significantly increased the patient's motivation for further work.

Conveying empathy and increasing the security of the patient is a complex task. It is not merely an attempt, at any cost, to decrease the patient's anxiety. There are times during therapy when the therapist, by means of confronting patient defenses, increases the patient's anxiety. Increasing patient anxiety increases the patient's expression of conflictual patterns within the therapeutic hour. Eliciting patient conflict allows the therapist to assess how the patient's defenses cope with increased stress (to be used in gauging later treatment interventions), as well as furnishing the patient and therapist with an opportunity to begin to work on patient problems.

As discussed earlier, motivation for treatment is often significantly increased by initially raising patient anxiety in the examination and successfully handling problematic coping strategies as they present in therapy. To further illustrate:

A male patient (AC), though very successful in business pursuits, had problems getting along with his spouse and close friends.

Throughout the initial assessment, AC attempted to dominate the flow of conversation, to interrupt the therapist, and repeatedly rebut and argue the therapist's comments. The therapist hypothesized that such behavior served to increase AC's sense of control and thus his security. Not confronting such behavior would perhaps allow AC to feel less anxious in his interaction with the therapist but would also avoid his problem of compulsively needing to control and dominate others in order to feel safe. The therapist chose to point out AC's interactive style. This initially led to increased anxiety and defensiveness. Eventually, however, AC began to explore his underlying fears of insecurity and vulnerability. He stated that he was finally able to look at some things about himself that he had been aware of but had avoided for a long time. The therapist, by conveying an understanding of the patient's problems, and by confronting these issues as they developed in the therapeutic interaction, enabled AC to take an honest look at himself and in the process increase his confidence in the helpfulness of treatment and his motivation for further work.

The therapist does not foster undue anxiety within the treatment setting. At the same time, the therapeutic alliance is strengthened by the therapist's ability to help the patient deal with problems in living, even though such work will initially increase patient anxiety. The therapist both gauges and guides the patient towards an optimal working anxiety.

The therapeutic alliance is significantly improved to the degree that the patient is able to trust the therapeutic method. This trust is facilitated by successful explorations of patient conflict. It also is facilitated by trust in the therapist's own theory and method. A premium is thus placed on the therapist's commitment to carefully study theories of personality and psychotherapy, develop a considerable and varied experience base, and obtain supervision/consultation.

Interpret Negative Transferences Early

Davanloo (1980) considered early interpretation of negative transference essential for the establishment and maintenance of the therapeutic alliance. A predominately positive relationship between patient and therapist is necessary in short-term psychodynamic psychotherapy. Negative factors in the relationship should not be ignored or left unexamined, especially if they interfere with the therapy process or constitute an expression of the patient's problems in living. To develop an effective working relationship with the patient, the therapist must explore the patient's feelings regarding how they work together, including fears and dissatisfactions with the therapist. The therapist must be alert for possible distortions by the patient that may lead their relationship to be perceived in a threatening, punitive, authoritarian (i.e., negative transference) fashion. Fear and anxiety regarding the therapist will inhibit the establishment of a working bond. If these feelings exist, it is important to identify them, determine how they operate in the therapy, discover what purpose they have, and eventually come to understand them in terms of their origin.

It is of key importance to confront and work through anxiety in the therapy relationship rather than avoid or deny it. If the patient and therapist are to develop an effective collaboration, issues that inhibit such work must be explored. In supportive psychotherapy, it is sometimes helpful to avoid confronting a patient with negative transference unless it significantly impedes the therapeutic relationship. Premature confrontation of negative feelings may endanger the patient's tenuous ability to relate to the therapist. This may be especially true with certain patients who have suffered early and severe emotional trauma. However, the properly selected patient for short-term therapy should possess sufficient levels of ego strength and basic trust to be able to work out relationship conflicts in a relatively straightforward manner. Such patients are seen as able to view their interaction with the therapist in a relatively objective manner while under the stress of significant affective involvement.

Negative transference reactions (e.g., feelings of hostility, fear, threat, being controlled) may be seen as attempts to fit the therapist into a predetermined neurotic pattern, which, while unsatisfying, offers some safety. Patients persistently fall back on judgments developed in relation to significant people in earlier life and apply them later in almost rote fashion in an effort to maintain security (Fromm-Reichman 1950). To help them become able to realistically and authentically encounter others, previously learned patterns of anxiety avoidance need to be confronted, explored, and worked through.

While we recommend that therapists identify, discuss, and attempt to resolve negative transference as a means of increasing the therapeutic alliance, the therapist is cautioned to avoid arguments, quarrels, or competitive power struggles. Negative feelings are examined to establish an honest and solid basis for interaction. Arguing and quarreling, no matter how provocative the patient may be, suggests that the therapist has temporarily given up an attempt to establish emotional contact and an investigative attitude, and is involved in a battle to establish/reestablish personal security or esteem. Such struggles may be used defensively by both therapist and patient to avoid authentic and meaningful interaction.

Convey a Sense of Hopeful Optimism

In undertaking a time-limited psychotherapy, the therapist begins with a sense of confidence about the helpfulness of this format, as well as the patient's capacity to profit from it (Mann 1973). The therapist conveys the conviction that the patient has the capacity for emotional growth and development. While confident and optimistic, the therapist avoids promising a cure. An attempt is made to instill a sense of enthusiasm tempered with cautious optimism. Such an attitude encourages the patient to actively work with the therapist at understanding and resolving conflictual issues.

Educate Patients About Their Role in Therapy

In short-term psychodynamic psychotherapy, the therapist actively discusses the therapeutic process in order to increase the bond with the mature aspect of the patient's ego and to provide the patient with a model of examining and exploring feelings that can be used during and after treatment. From the onset of treatment, the therapist aims to secure cooperation with the therapeutic task. Early in treatment, patients are told that getting better depends on their willingness to cooperate in working on problems. Patients are educated as to the process of therapy, as well as their role in this process. In short-term psychodynamic psychotherapy a major aim is to help patients become aware of how conflicted thoughts and feelings lead to problems in living. To help the patients understand personal emotional conflicts and motives in irrational behavior, an appeal is made to their good judgment. People are able to collaborate more easily on tasks they understand and comprehend. To this end, the therapist strives to explain the therapeutic process and patient responsibilities in this process.

An attempt is made to assess and modify (if need be) initial expectations of therapy. For some patients, therapy is mysterious and scary. For others, it is challenging. It is important to help patients appreciate that the patient–therapist relationship is different from other relationships between doctors and patients. In other situations, patients expect to (1) present symptoms, (2) be told what to do, and (3) receive a cure in return for doing what s/he is told to do. Psychotherapy patients must be taught to play a more active, responsible, and collaborative role in treatment. The responsibility (burden) of therapy is equally divided between the patient and therapist. Assumption of the "expert doctor" role by the therapist sets up the expectation that the therapist can provide a cure, a magic answer, or a key to happiness. In such instances, the patient gives information, expects the therapist to solve the problems, and becomes a spectator of therapy.

In educating patients regarding the therapeutic process, the therapist strives to convey a method of dealing with emotional conflict. Patients are taught about defenses, anxiety, and repressed feelings. The concept of transference is explicated. Immediate, here-and-now interchanges between patient and therapist are used to illustrate the concepts involved in uncovering therapy. The aim here is twofold: (1) to treat patients as active, responsible partners on an investigative venture, and (2) to help patients learn a mode of resolving emotional conflict. This problem-solving component is a critical aspect of short-term therapy and will be discussed more fully in a later section.

The therapist provides information, explanation, and guidance about how therapy works. The therapist also conveys, by manner and attitude, a spirit of collaboration and shared interaction. Education into the therapy role is a complex task. The therapist must be sensitive to the patient's knowledge base and interpersonal style. Demonstration and observation regarding the initial therapeutic interactions are most useful. The therapist avoids an intellectual discussion of therapy and theoretical concepts with the patient. Insight, to be valuable, must be firmly grounded in experience.

Transference and the Therapeutic Alliance

In short-term psychodynamic psychotherapy, it is critical to rapidly establish a relationship that enables the patient and therapist to work in partnership on the patient's problems. This relationship may be conceptualized as an agreement between therapist and the conflict-free part of the patient's ego. There is a tendency among therapists to consider the therapeutic alliance only in terms of an agreement with the rational, objective part of the patient and to disregard the transference component of the relationship. Brenner (1980) contended that the transference component of the therapeutic alliance cannot be distinctly separated from the nontransference component. Failure to attend to the fact that every relationship, including the therapeutic alliance, is a mixture of transference and reality may result in surface-oriented (versus depth-oriented) thinking and noninterpretive, nonanalytic interventions (Langs 1981). To ensure the continued viability of the alliance, it is essential for the therapist to be aware of its transferential component and to explore with the patient transferential attitudes that are disruptive to the alliance. For example, a patient has agreed to work on a particular problem and seems willing to work with the therapist and his uncovering method. An alliance has been formed. This alliance, however, is continually being affected by experiences with the therapist in treatment. These experiences may serve as catalysts for new reactions to the therapist that have as their basis unresolved past conflicts with significant others. Such reactions continually influence the nature of the therapeutic alliance. The therapeutic alliance, then, fluctuates throughout treatment. These variations are significantly affected by the transference component of the patient–therapist relationship. The therapist cannot assume that, once having established an agreement to work with the patient, this agreement will sustain itself. Careful attention must be given to maintaining this alliance amidst the emotional struggles of treatment. If transference or other factors interfere with this alliance between patient and therapist, immediate intervention is necessary to reestablish this working bond.

ANALYSIS OF RESISTANCE

For many therapists, the term resistance elicits negative reactions. Resistance to some implies an irresponsible patient who is avoiding therapeutic work. Resistance is best thought of as a complex defensive organization that can be helpful or nonhelpful. The therapist is encouraged to view resistance, not as opposition to treatment, but as a critical part of the unfolding of the treatment process.

The short-term therapy practitioner strives to examine how the patient resists the therapeutic process and actively confronts the patient, helping the patient work through resistance. Manifestations of resistance are not interpreted as a decline in the therapeutic alliance but rather as an invitation for working through of defenses through active interpretation.

The Concept of Resistance

Resistance has various definitions within the psychotherapy literature, depending on the therapist's theoretical orientation as well as of individual philosophical views. We define resistance as any behavior in therapy that interferes with the process of uncovering, affective expression, and working through of patient conflicts. Resistive behavior is an impediment to an effective therapist–patient collaboration on resolving patient problems.

Resistance typically refers to thoughts, feelings, and behaviors that are determined by the intrapsychic make-up of the patient. There are some external events over which the patient has no control, such as the death of a loved one, that may significantly interfere with the treatment. Such events should not be called resistance, although patients may use external events to rationalize resistive needs. To illustrate:

> A patient (NL) justified missing a session due to a flat tire on the freeway. However, further study of his reactions, including his defensive manner, resulted in the revelation: (1) the flat tire occurred at a time that would have allowed sufficient time to fix the tire, and (2) failure to come to therapy was, in part, determined by fear of exploring some disturbing feelings he had the previous week. In this case, NL had used an external situation to rationalize avoidance of treatment.

Resistance is an integral part of the therapy experience. Freud (1912) stated that resistance accompanies the treatment step by step. "Every single association, every act of the person under treatment must reckon with resistance and represents a compromise between the forces that are striving towards recovery and the opposing ones" (p. 103). Although patients come to therapy asking for, pleading for, or demanding help, they repeatedly have problems forming an alliance and working in psychotherapy (Schafer 1983). Patients experience difficulty in developing alliances and working on their concerns because they bring their neurotic conflicts into the patient–therapist interaction. Defenses that impede open, direct, and meaningful interaction in the patient's outside life are also enacted in therapy to resist a collaborative therapeutic alliance and an examination of psychological conflict. Patients may rationalize and intellectualize with the therapist, they may act seductively, or provoke fights. Analysis of resistance in therapy is essentially the analysis of the patient's conflicted means of reacting to and working with other people. Keeping this idea firmly in hand helps reduce therapist frustration with patient resistance. Working with resistance is not just an unpleasant task to be completed in order to get on to more interesting and gratifying aspects of therapy, but it is a natural part of the therapy process.

Manifestations of resistance are varied. There are untold opportunities for obstructing the therapeutic process. Patients use a variety of conscious and unconscious methods to carry it out: relevant material may be avoided through obsessional ruminations, sessions may be forgotten or attended late, the patient may engage in conscious censoring of material. Other ways of resistance that may manifest themselves in therapy include: difficulty in freely expressing oneself characterized by silence or by complaining of having nothing to say, talking about the past to avoid the present or vice versa, producing confusing thoughts or dreams, externalizing blame for one's difficulties, questioning the value of therapy or the integrity of the therapist to avoid focusing on painful feelings regarding oneself, creating a crisis situation outside of the therapy, overtalkativeness, avoiding specific subjects, and being remote or unclear. Resistance may even take the guise of the patient trying very hard to be a good, conscientious patient. Such patients may report all thoughts and feelings and sincerely attend to everything the therapist says while simultaneously avoiding work on real problems, such as the need to ingratiate authority figures in order to feel secure. Just about any thought, feeling, or behavior can have a defensive or resistive component.

Resistance and Defense

To work effectively with resistance, it is important to consider the relationship between defense and resistance. Freud (1936) noted that the manner in which a patient resists mirrors the defensive organization of the patient's ego. A defense is a measure utilized by the ego to master anxiety and resolve intrapsychic and interpersonal conflict. In the course of growing up, people learn to fear the development of various thoughts or feelings (e.g., anger with parents) that occur naturally during the process of emotional maturation. They learn that expression of these various feelings may lead to physical or emotional consequences: abandonment, loss of love, physical punishment, moral condemnation. Discharge of these feelings is seen as threatening their security. The pressure of these naturally occurring, but threatening, feelings and the prospect of expressing them leads to anxiety, and after sufficient conscience development, guilt. People can't escape their thoughts and feelings as they can a storm or dangerous animal. Therefore, they rely on intrapsychic mechanisms that maneuver to block awareness and expression of threatening feelings. These mechanisms are an intrapsychic means of adapting to internal needs and perceived external demands and are referred to most succinctly with terms such as repression, denial, projection, and isolation. Such operations allow individuals to reduce anxiety by means of an intrapsychic rearrangement of feelings. This may be a selective forgetting or blocking of some feelings as in repression, or it may be separating a thought from its feeling counterpart as in isolation. Defenses have an interpersonal component. People learn ways of interacting that afford an avoidance of punishment and maintain emotional security (Sullivan 1953). Through their experience with significant others, individuals learn certain patterns of behaving that protect their sense of security in their environment. These may be called defensive patterns, character styles, or coping strategies. They are an attempt at adapting most effectively to the particular life situation the individual has experienced. A problem develops when a person's methods of intrapsychic and interpersonal coping, although once valuable for psychological survival, are maladaptive in present life.

When we discuss defenses, we are referring to: (1) intrapsychic operations used to avoid threatening thoughts and feelings and (2) interpersonal strategies (character patterns) used to protect security and self-esteem. Defenses may be adaptive or maladaptive, conscious or unconscious, used by the patient in daily life or in therapy. Defenses become resistance when they impede the process of self-exploration and authentic interaction with the therapist. Resistances tend to be problematic in that they are supportive of the patient's present mode of adaptation and of maintaining outdated strategies of relating to self and others.

Resistive maneuvers obstruct the therapeutic process of self-exploration and honest interaction with the therapist. They are a means of defending the patient from anxiety. This anxiety may be kindled by honest exploration of oneself. In the process of therapeutic examination, a patient must face aspects of personal functioning that are painful or that take away one's emotional crutches (e.g., the realization that one has responsibility for one's life and can't continue to blame others). This anxiety may also be kindled by being progressively forced to interact with the therapist in a more mature, reality-oriented (i.e., nonneurotic) manner. Such interaction threatens the patient's previously learned, albeit neurotic and maladaptive, means of relating. For instance, open and honest interchange between therapist and patient is anxiety provoking for the patient who has learned through previous life experiences to be cautious and to withhold one's opinions.

Sources of Resistance

It is generally agreed that resistance is engendered by a sense of danger or anxiety. Resistance may be viewed as opposition to uncovering anxiety-provoking material or acting in ways that have previously threatened one's security and esteem. It is an expression of the patient's conviction that a way has been found, no matter how painful, to minimize anxiety and maintain some semblance of self-esteem and dignity. Resistive behavior reflects the patient's inability to perceive an alternate way of life. Paradoxically, therapy may be viewed as a threat to the most effective means of psychological survival yet developed.

The understanding of resistance is further complicated by the observation that patients prove to be attached to the very things that seem to cause them much grief and psychic pain. They cling to their problems and often display a strong reluctance to relinquish them. There are a number of sources for this inclination to hold on to ways of being that seemingly are painful. It may be the patient's preferred way to continue an early emotional tie (Schafer 1983). The patient may not want to give up this tie or this identification because, however consciously painful it is, it once was the whole world and the matrix of a developing sense of self. Thus, it serves as a guarantee of survival and a sense of continuity. Frequently, there is also the factor of relief from unconscious guilt or of gratification of the patient's wish to be punished (Freud 1923). The patient may also hold on to problems as a means of defeating the therapist. In the patient's unconscious, such an act may symbolize taking revenge on, or successfully competing with, father or mother. Resistance is an overdetermined behavior serving multiple functions in the patient's psychic life.

Transference as Resistance

Freud (1914) wrote that the transference developed by a patient towards the therapist is a form of resistance. Transference was seen as an acted-out repetition of memories that the patient wishes not to consciously remember; the patient relives rather than remembers. The patient resists remembering by insisting that all feeling towards the therapist, positive and negative, are fully justified or explained by the here and now of the therapeutic situation and relationship. The felt conclusion of the patient is that there simply is no blind repeating of past patterns of relationship to be understood (Schafer 1983). Transference may be understood as a resistance to viewing current interpersonal dilemmas as having a historical component. This reluctance or inability to entertain the possibility that one's reactions toward people are to some extent determined by previous learning is a major impediment to interpersonal learning. It can be very difficult to explore the possibility that one plays a role in creating personal problems. Holding on to transferential reactions may be seen as the patient's escape from facing oneself, the present moment, and one's responsibility in bringing it about.

Resistance Analysis: General Principles

Effective handling of resistance calls for the therapist to be able to identify its occurrence and how it interferes with therapy. The therapist must determine the nature of the resistance: what the patient does, when the patient does it and what effect it has on the therapeutic process. Resistive behavior is then brought to the attention of the patient. For example, the therapist may point out that the patient is ruminating, blocking, or being overagreeable. Therapists need to develop personal strategies for bringing the resistance into the awareness of the patient. Techniques for demonstrating the style and form of the resistance must be cultivated. Use of metaphor or humor, for example, may be of benefit in pointing out resistance and its style. Effective portrayal of resistance requires that the context be offered — for example, "You always talk softly when you think I am angry with you." Presenting the general context is helpful in that it conveys empathy, as well as helping the patient begin to identify defensive operations.

The therapist helps the patient explore the meaning and purpose of this behavior. What feelings are being avoided or acted out by the resistive maneuvers? What are the implications of this behavior in terms of the present relationship with the therapist, other current relationships, as well as past relationships. For instance, a "good" patient may resist by always agreeing with the therapist and working "hard" with what the therapist brings up, never expressing any angry or frustrated feelings towards the therapist for fear of rejection and loss. This behavior may be understood in terms of its meaning with the therapist, current friends, and past significant others. The patient can understand ongoing defenses and ways in which anxiety is dealt with and can consider the possibility of replacing ineffective interpersonal strategies and destructive defenses with more effective and appropriate ones.

When exploring patient resistance, it is helpful to point out to the patient the cost of such adaptation. Examples of such intervention include: (1) "When you come late, valuable therapy time is lost." (2) "When you avoid people, you lose the opportunity of new friends." (3) "You assume that anger will end relationships. You are losing the chance to see that anger is related to closeness and may improve a relationship." When pointing out the cost of patient behavior, it is important to avoid inducing guilt or the impression that the patient is "bad" and can't do anything right. Eliciting such reactions will decrease the patient's self-esteem and sense of security, increasing the need for defensive operations and further resistance.

Pointing out the cost of resistive behavior may be softened by acknowledging and exploring with the patient what has been *gained* by such behavior. For instance, coming late allows the patient to avoid and put off for a little while longer the anxiety engendered in therapy. The therapist knows the patient has lost valuable exploration time but the patient feels pain has been avoided. Attending to the intrapsychic gains as well as costs of resistance increases the patient's sense of being understood and, in turn, strengthens the therapeutic alliance.

The contributions of ego psychology and interpersonal theory have enriched the view of resistance. Resistance was initially seen as something to be broken through (i.e., eliminated) in order to understand the unconscious complexes of the mind that were causing conflict. Change was seen to occur through insight into such complexes. Dynamic theory has evolved to a point where the task regarding resistive behaviors is not to eliminate them but to understand their role in the patient's life and in the maintenance of problems in living. Resistance may be most productively viewed, not as an obstacle to be removed as prelude to change, but as behavior to be examined and understood in its own right (Strupp and Binder 1984). To be worked with most effectively, resistance is not to be viewed as patient opposition to therapy or the therapist, but rather as a natural and crucial aspect of the process of uncovering therapy. The therapist's failure to cultivate such a view of resistance increases the likelihood of developing an adversarial therapist-patient relationship.

The therapist should strive to deal with the defense/resistance before taking up that which is being defended against. Analysis of the process of resisting and its implications often yields considerably more therapeutic movement than a focus on underlying content. Schafer (1983) stressed that it is an error to try to elicit directly some thought or feeling that one senses is close to being expressed but is being warded off by the patient. In such situations it is more productive for the patient to learn why it is that this thought or feeling is being warded off. "Suppose the analysand is evidently struggling not to cry: Why the struggle? The analyst interested in resistant strategies will first want to know the answer to this question, for that answer will do more for the analysis than the crying itself" (Schafer 1983, p. 75). The therapist's task is not to force certain affects or demand certain behaviors from the patient, but rather to help the patient learn about one's strategies of reacting to others and to oneself. The issue is not what secrets the patient has, but how they became secrets, as well as how and why they remain secret.

Resistance Analysis in Short-Term Psychodynamic Psychotherapy

The previously discussed principles regarding working with resistance are consonant with the strategies of traditional, open-ended treatment. In open-ended treatment the therapist patiently points out patient defenses and encourages reflection but does not force reflection. Over time the patient gradually becomes acquainted with one's defensive style and begins its exploration and working through. Such work requires many repetitions of the sequence: defense, confrontation, reflection. Such work facilitates understanding and gaining control/mastery over resistive strategies. It also takes time. In short-term therapy the process of working through resistance and analyzing patient defenses is facilitated by a more active, confrontive stance by the therapist.

Resistive behavior is more quickly confronted in short-term psychodynamic psychotherapy. The therapist more actively focuses energy into helping the patient overcome defenses against exploring painful feelings and maladaptive modes of interaction. Strong emphasis is placed on helping the patient to work through defenses and to examine the conflicted feelings that lead to their construction. Relying on careful assessment, the patient is seen as capable of examining behavior, tracing its origins, and seeing how conflicting feelings give rise to present difficulties.

In an attempt to deal with patient resistance, Davanloo (1980) recommended the technique of gentle but relentless questioning and confrontation of unexpressed feelings. Strategies used by the patient to avoid self-exploration and realistic interaction with the therapist are focused on and confronted. Rather than interpreting patient behavior, the therapist persistently inquires about the feelings of the patient. A most powerful technique to help a patient overcome defenses is to ask about feelings. Questions such as: "How do you feel about it?", "What do you feel?", "What are you feeling right now?", or "How do you feel about what I just said?" may be used productively to deepen the patient's awareness of feelings.

A persistent focus on feelings increases the emotional meaningfulness of the sessions. A situation to be avoided is an intellectual understanding of the patient's problems, defenses, and interactive style and failure to make the experience emotionally meaningful. Effective therapy increases cognitive understanding in the medium of emotionally meaningful experiences. Attitudes or personal constructs of an individual are too hardened to bend without being heated in the fires of emotional involvement. Unless the fire is hot (i.e., emotions are high), the metal (attitudes, ways of viewing the world) is not receptive to change in shape. Getting at the patient's feelings is a way of stoking the fire. Short-term therapy helps the patient to: (1) become involved with feelings, (2) identify what is most prominently being experienced at any given point, and (3) experience, understand, and integrate feeling. The therapist should strive to help patients experience as much of their true feelings as they can handle.

Davanloo (1980) noted that the therapist's inquiry of "How do you feel?" is an opening move into the patient's unconscious. By such technique patients are invited to do something they may have been avoiding all their lives — being honest about what they actually feel. This is, in fact, the core of all psychoanalytic psychotherapies. A focus on patient feelings inevitably mobilizes resistance. Resistances are essentially the complex of defenses used throughout life to avoid anxiety and maintain security. Focusing on feelings leads patients to present their typical mechanisms of dealing with emotions and conflicted issues. By focusing on feelings, the therapist is in the position to help patients examine habitual patterns used to avoid an authentic and honest interaction with themselves and others.

The therapist persistently confronts vagueness, avoidance, and passivity. By confront, we do not mean an aggressive assault. The word confront means that the therapist observes interpersonal and intrapersonal conflict, especially in the form of defensive resistance, and assumes responsibility for bringing the issue into the open. Confrontation implies openness, willingness to deal with difficulties, and sensitivity on the part of the therapist to follow up and pursue the feelings and reactions of the patient.

The patient is invited to examine the purpose and meaning of resistive behavior. In inviting the patient to examine a resistance, the therapist implicitly challenges a rigid mode of relatedness

(Strupp and Binder 1984). The patient is offered the opportunity to interact with the therapist in a manner that differs from present coping strategies. Such an opportunity is often met with ambivalence; giving up ingrained modes of reaction and interaction are threatening to the patient's sense of equilibrium and security.

Negative Transference and Realistic Anger

The frequent and continued focus of the therapist on painful, unexpressed feelings frequently leads to the development of angry, resentful feelings towards the therapist, as well as defenses against such feelings. It is essential to focus on this anger. The therapist should watch for subtle indications of the emergence of anger, however minor, in the therapy relationship. When such feelings are sensed, the therapist's task is to help these feelings surface and be acknowledged by the patient. Davanloo (1980) suggested that questions such as "What do you feel right now?" and "How do you feel inside?" may be used productively to help the patient more accurately clarify and examine negative feelings towards the therapist. Careful focus on the patient's angry feelings allows the patient the opportunity to explore his/her mode of dealing with negative affect.

Very often anger towards the therapist has a strong transference component. For example, the therapist's intervention strategy may stimulate unresolved feelings regarding an intrusive mother or a domineering father. The patient's manner of dealing with angry feelings, learned in relation to parents, may in turn be linked with the patient's maladaptive way of handling anger in current life situations. This pattern is identified and explained to the patient. Davnaloo, as discussed earlier, referred to this as a transference/current/past interpretation. Davanloo (1980) found that patient improvement often became evident after they were able to openly acknowledge and examine angry feelings towards the therapist and to begin to look at their typical means of dealing with negative affect. Similarly, Malan (1963) stressed that it is essential for the patient to experience and understand angry feelings towards the therapist in order to learn to tolerate such feelings towards others.

Helping the patient see how threatening feelings (e.g., anger) are defended against in the patient–therapist relationship, as well as in other current and past relationships, is a powerful therapeutic tool frequently leading to the expression of further repressed feelings involving love, hate, loss, and forbidden childhood wishes. With the uncovering and reexperiencing of these conflicts, therapeutic effects begin to occur. Active confrontation in the form of pointing out defenses requires the patient to experience repressed feelings. This results in core problems being uncovered and more fully experienced. Davanloo (1980) believed the intense experience of this highly interactional treatment significantly decreased the amount of time needed to complete the working through process of therapy. In addition, he felt that the persistent challenging of defenses makes short-term therapy an increasingly viable treatment even with very resistant patients suffering from chronic symptomatic and character problems.

It is critical that the therapist deal with the patient's anger stimulated by the persistent, active nature of therapeutic investigation. Failure to focus on such feelings will affect the patient's trust in the therapist. The patient may perceive the therapist as unable/unwilling to deal with negative confrontation and may become increasingly frightened of the prospect him/herself. The inability of the therapist to deal with negative affect elicited in therapy additionally compromises the therapeutic alliance in that an angry, resentful patient will find it difficult to collaborate with the therapist.

Inquiry into negative affect may include such comments as: "What do you feel about what we are doing?" "You answered my question but seemed resentful toward me." "Do you wonder what you have gotten into when your emotions come to the surface?" "Let's talk about what some of your reactions toward me have been. It will be hard for us to work together if you politely put aside your irritation with me and just say I'm doing my job." These and similar comments can be useful in exploring the client's anger.

Short-term psychodynamic psychotherapy places great importance on the therapist's ability to deal with his/her own hostility, as well as the hostility of the patient. The therapist must avoid intimidating and being intimidated by the patient. Either situation conveys to the patient that anger is dangerous and must stay repressed.

It is important to note that the strong affect stimulated during this therapy has *both* a transference and realistic component. The therapist's active confrontation of resistance and search for unexpressed feelings furnishes fertile soil for the development of frustration, resentment, and anger. Such activity by the therapist may threaten the patient's preferred strategies of dealing with conflict-laden feelings. Angry, resentful reactions towards the therapist, however, tend to have an unrealistic component in that the therapist is basically trying to help the patient and has the patient's ultimate benefit in mind. The therapist's actions will often trigger reactions the patient experienced in past interactions that raised anxiety and threatened security. To illustrate:

> A patient (PB) had unresolved issues regarding control and dominance. The therapist's attempt to maintain the therapeutic focus was experienced as an attempt to control and subjugate. The patient became threatened, frustrated, and angry with the therapist. He reacted in the manner he had learned to manage his angry feelings (i.e., increased passivity). Although angry with what he felt to be the therapist's controlling tactics, he was unable to express this. Rather, he became increasingly silent and withdrawn. Therapeutic attention to this behavior enabled patient and therapist to uncover the underlying feelings of being dominated and controlled along with the accompanying anger. Mutual discussion of what was to happen in therapy (i.e., work on the agreed-upon treatment focus) enabled the patient to begin to realize that a significant degree of his negative reaction to the therapist's attempts to focus were in fact related to past conflictual interactions with an authoritarian parent.

It is equally essential to acknowledge the realistic component of the negative affect stimulated by this therapy. The patient's negative reaction, while containing a transference component, is often a rather realistic reaction to certain attributes of treatment. The therapist must stay in touch with some of the realities of the therapy to which the patient may be reacting. Treatment is intense and fast-paced, often creating a high level of anxiety. It is hard work in which the patient is asked to take an honest look at oneself and to relate in a fashion that is at variance with well-developed, albeit maladaptive, coping strategies. Such an environment offers a fertile soil for realistic anxiety, pain, and resentment. Realistic negative emotions are to be identified and acknowledged. Treatment in short-term therapy is facilitated considerably by the therapist conveying to the patient recognition of the intensiveness of the treatment, of how hard the patient is working, and of how difficult it is to give up maladaptive reaction patterns. The therapist needs to offer realistic support for the anxiety and pain the patient experiences in treatment. Such support allows the patient to go on, to continue to work, as well as undermining neurotic avoidance patterns. Inability to ventilate and discuss negative feelings leads them to be acted out with the therapist in therapy (e.g., withholding, termination) or to be displaced to other relationships (e.g., rage reactions to one's spouse).

The question is raised at this point as to how to differentiate transference from nontransference feelings. Such a differentiation is often difficult. Thompson (1964) observed that therapists all too often include all attitudes that a patient has toward the therapist as transference. Lipton (1977) discussed the difficulty in separating the realistic aspects of the therapeutic relationship from the part that is unrealistic and subject to interpretation and understanding. He concluded that this issue is most effectively resolved through collaborative discussion.

Importance of Feelings

The therapist's attention to patient affect in short-term therapy has a number of consequences:

1. It supplies a means of highlighting defenses against self-exploration. Character resistances such as passivity and intellectualization may be highlighted when the therapist focuses therapeutic attention on such responses as "I don't know what I feel" or "I don't feel anything."

2. Strong emphasis on inquiring into feelings and confronting resistance significantly increases the emotional involvement of the patient in therapy. Davanloo (1978) found a positive correlation between a high level of emotional involvement and successful outcome.

3. Helping a patient tune into feelings allows for an abreactive effect. Abreaction makes it possible for the patient to relieve tension through the discharge of emotion. In addition, a degree of psychic energy is tied up in repressing feelings. Release of repressed feelings allows for psychic energy, formerly used in defending against awareness of these feelings, to be used in a more constructive fashion.

4. Discharge of emotion is of great value in validating for the patient what it is that troubles him/her (Bibring 1954). When a patient is able to see the intensity of feeling invested in certain people or situations, further motivation is provided to strive toward understanding, and problem resolution.

5. Helping a patient attend to feelings deepens one's sense of identity. Avoidant tendencies basic to all maladaptive defenses support lack of self-knowledge through a retreat from feelings and situations that cause anxiety. Learning how one feels, even when one isn't happy with it, decreases feelings of incompleteness and lack of rootedness (Singer 1965).

Attention to Patient Feedback

In short-term psychodynamic psychotherapy, resistive maneuvers are brought to the patient's attention as they occur. This rapid focus on resistance heightens the level of anxiety within the session. A "fight or flight" syndrome may be stimulated in some patients, especially early in treatment. It is critical that the therapist meticulously attend to the patient's moment-to-moment responses. The patient's reaction to interventions by the therapist provides direct feedback as to the patient's ability to respond to the technique used in short-term therapy. Malan (1980) believed that the essential nature of this feedback consists of changes in the level of rapport. The ability to evaluate level of rapport is one of the therapist's most essential tasks. Rapport is the universal indicator by which the therapist may be constantly guided. If rapport increases after an intervention, the intervention was appropriate and appropriately made; if rapport decreases, the intervention was inappropriate (not necessarily wrong), and the therapist must reconsider.

In short-term therapy initial feedback often consists of increased resistance. This most frequently is due to the emphasis placed on confronting patient defenses. In many patients, however, once defenses are challenged, and the underlying feeling reached, the patient experiences relief and hope. To illustrate:

> ET was a 25-year-old woman who sought treatment due to problems in interpersonal relationships. ET was conflicted around the expression of anger. Her inability to deal effectively with negative affect resulted in frustration and repressed anger. These feelings are expressed in derivative fashion (i.e., sarcasm and cynicism). As the therapist developed a clearer understanding of this pattern, he brought it to ET's attention and encouraged its examination. Although ET became threatened and uncomfortable when her accustomed means of expressing aggressive feelings was confronted, she responded with relief when the therapist was able to help her view a core problem (i.e., inability to express angry feelings).

Davanloo (1980) observed that the following pattern occurs repeatedly: (1) the patient's defensive patterns are challenged, (2) they initially become more rigid, but (3) when the therapist succeeds in penetrating the defenses, there is increasing rapport. The patient in one way or another is more in touch with previously defended-against feelings. The tension then drops within the therapeutic situation. The great majority of patients respond positively to increased awareness of repressed feelings, as well as to the therapist's understanding. This is reflected in an increased willingness to collaborate, i.e., an increase in motivation and therapeutic alliance. Such a response assures the therapist of the correctness of the approach.

At the other end of the spectrum of responses, the patient may present evidence of being too fragile to withstand the impact of uncovering repressed material. Challenging patient defenses and exploring underlying feelings may induce such anxiety that the patient regresses to more primitive coping strategies (e.g., massive denial, projection, withdrawal, impulsive acting out). Careful attention should be given to signs of extreme regression, fluidity of thought processes, and other symptoms of adverse patient reaction that suggest an intolerance of interpersonal and intrapsychic anxiety and a need for more supportive technique.

In general, patients who will have difficulty working in an uncovering treatment are identified during assessment. However, at all times the therapist needs to monitor patient reaction to interventions and evolving material, rapport, and therapeutic alliance. Questions for the therapist to consider may include: (1) Is the patient able to develop and maintain an observing ego and to objectively view what is occurring in therapy (i.e., is the patient able to take a realistic look at conflicted feelings and interactive patterns, even while experiencing threat and anxiety)? (2) Does the therapist feel an empathic connection with the patient? Inability to maintain feelings of "being with" the patient may point to a use of withdrawal and avoidance defenses by the patient. (3) With confrontation, do the patient's defenses become more primitive (e.g., patient gives up intellectualizing and begins to use massive projection or denial)? (4) When defenses are confronted, is the patient able to relinquish them momentarily to further explore oneself and relate in a less conflicted manner to the therapist?

A Caution

The discussion of handling resistance in short-term psychodynamic psychotherapy may convey an impression of the therapist as a gadfly who persistently torments the patient's defenses in an unrelenting fashion, or perhaps a military commander whose goal is to locate, attack, and overcome the defensive outposts of the opposition. In effective treatment the therapist does not attack defenses in an effort to break through, destroy them, and get at repressed feelings. The development of such an adversarial stance severely compromises the therapeutic alliance. It is unempathic, persecuting, and doomed to failure in most cases.

Short-term psychotherapy places emphasis on analysis of resistance and defense. This emphasis, however, first takes the form of identifying with the patient attitudes and behaviors that impede one's ability to use therapy and interact effectively with the therapist. Emphasis is then put on identifying the role of these defenses in the patient's life and finally on the purpose of these defenses (i.e., avoidance of underlying feelings). This is a large order in a brief treatment. It requires a patient who can quickly become a partner in this venture and who does not lose heart (i.e., motivation) when coping mechanisms are being questioned. It requires a therapist who is able to quickly identify the patient's defensive strategies and is able to help the patient take a look at them as well.

In short-term therapy the therapist actively focuses attention on patient resistance and attempts to help the patient understand how it is played out in therapy. Such a stance is empathic with the importance a patient's defensive strategies play in psychic functioning. An attempt to knock defenses aside without first studying them with the patient will lead to increasing rigidity as the patient gathers forces to protect against an unempathic assault on the most successful means of coping with problems that the patient has been able to develop.

Studying a patient's methods of coping with threat and anxiety is helpful in enabling a patient to learn new methods of dealing with stress elicited by psychic conflict. Short-term psychodynamic psychotherapy will not eliminate a patient's emotional conflicts, but it can give the patient the experience of effectively working on a number of issues. This topic will be expanded later.

CHAPTER SIX
Use of Transference

The analysis of transference reactions is generally acknowledged as the central feature of psychoanalytically oriented technique (Gill 1982). The understanding and interpretation of transference reactions was stressed by Freud (1912) as the vehicle of cure in psychoanalytic treatment. As Freud described it, transference played the central role of bringing to awareness repressed, hidden conflict, and of furnishing an arena in which resolution can be attempted.

Analysis of transference is an essential component of short-term psychodynamic psychotherapy. Malan (1976) reported a high positive correlation between successful outcome and the therapist's ability to identify and examine the patient's transference reactions. Davanloo and Sifneos concurred on the importance of working with transference reactions. Sifneos (1972) stated that transference feelings are to be explored in a vigorous and explicit manner. Transference reactions were seen as an opportunity to examine old family conflicts in the atmosphere of the developing patient–therapist relationship. Sifneos felt that the therapist should confront the patient with transference feelings and use them as the main therapeutic tool. Davanloo (1980) believed that transference reactions should be focused on very early in therapy. Rather than waiting for the transference to develop into a complex transference neurosis, it should be identified and discussed as soon as it appears.

Short-term therapy aids the patient in conflict resolution by examining behavior, tracing its origin, and seeing how conflicting feelings give rise to symptoms and character patterns that produce difficulties in the patient's life. The patient–therapist relationship offers a fertile ground for such work. This relationship provides an opportunity for the patient's difficulties in living to be expressed, clarified, and modified. Great importance is placed on examining how maladaptive patterns are reenacted with the therapist and recognizing the inefficient functioning that results from this repetition. Problems most amenable to treatment are those that allow themselves (or their derivatives) to be expressed within the therapist–patient relationship. Such issues as inhibited anger, competition, dependency, and fear of responsibility tend to be enacted in the patient–therapist interaction and are available for therapeutic attention.

THERAPIST ATTITUDES ABOUT TRANSFERENCE

To understand problems in living with others, the patient is first encouraged to consider and understand reactions to the therapist. To optimally facilitate this process, therapists may need to alter their own attitudes about transference. Transference reactions are most therapeutically viewed as normal and naturally occurring, an essential part of the treatment process. Therapy is likely to suffer when transference reactions are avoided and/or viewed as cumbersome impositions upon the therapy relationship.

The therapist is encouraged to consider the following general framework when conceptualizing transference feelings. Perception and interpretation of current experience requires using past learning to understand and organize experience. Patients organize their perceptions of the therapist around past experience. The process of dealing with perceptions can take the following sequential format: (1) The patient perceives the therapist in a certain manner (e.g., warm, aloof, reserved, fatherly). (2) the picture of the therapist is based on specific behavioral attributes of the therapist interacting with the psychological state of the patient. (3) The psychological state includes the patient's current need state and previous history. (4) The patient has developed a pattern of perceiving authority or parental figures as warm, aloof, reserved, or fatherly. (5) There is a genetic origin, typically in the family constellation, that generates these perceptions.

TRANSFERENCE DEFINED

A state of transference exists when the patient's thoughts and feelings regarding the therapist become strongly influenced by wishes, fears, and attitudes originally developed in past significant relationships. Saul (1967) explained the development of transference in the following manner. In the process of growing up, the child internalizes the parents through their attitudes and treatment and by identification with them. The parents form imagos in the child's mind. These imagos are introjected and become parts of the child's self-concept and value system. The child eventually reacts to these imagos as parents were previously reacted to. For example, the child whose actions are continually critiqued and constantly exhorted to greater efforts may internalize a critical, perfectionistic orientation towards oneself. In addition, the child projects these imagos onto other persons and reacts to these people in some part as one did with parents. The child expects others to be critically evaluative and therefore becomes very cautious about self-expression and risk taking. Of key importance is the child's projection of an internal intrapsychic experience onto the others and a reaction to others "as if" they were similar to internalized impressions of one's parents. (The term "parents" includes siblings and parental substitutes – all those responsible for and/or emotionally important to the child).

Although Freud was aware of the universality of transference, he generally discussed it in terms of analytic treatment. Freud (1905a) stated that transference feelings are revived during analytic treatment and are applied to the person of the therapist, but in reality, such feelings belong to a past relationship. He considered the concept of repetition compulsion to be important in understanding transference. In 1914 he stated that transference is a piece of repetition. The patient, in analytic treatment, was seen as repeating with the therapist attitudes and reactions originally developed in relationships with childhood figures. In applying the concept of transference to analytic therapy, Freud and other early analysts emphasized the intrapsychic component of transference characterized by projection upon the therapist of childhood wishes and fears stemming from relationships with important past objects. The therapist was felt to be a neutral, relatively opaque figure on whom the patient's conflicts were projected. Of late, there has been a significant trend among dynamically oriented therapists towards a growing appreciation of the interpersonal/interactional component of the transference relationship (Langs 1981). For example, in addition to attending to the patient's projection of certain qualities onto the therapist, increased study has shown how the patient interacts with the therapist in an attempt to induce the therapist to behave in correspondence to these attributes. The following example illustrates how therapeutic attention may be given to the interactional component of transference.

> A young man (CF) presented for therapy with complaints of depression and unsatisfactory relationships with women. As the initial session progressed, the therapist began to feel increasingly irritated and angry with CF. This feeling culminated in a confrontive and harsh interpretation that elicited considerable anxiety in the patient. In reviewing his feelings and behavior during consultation, the therapist was initially perplexed. Careful study of his interaction with CF, however, enabled the therapist to identify how he had influenced his feelings. CF, although presenting himself as very distressed and in need of help, effectively rebuked the therapist's attempts to help. The therapist recalled that the most common response to his inter-

ventions to be "Yes, but. . . ." The effect of this response was initially overlooked by the therapist as he continued to offer suggestions and interpretations to the patient. As the session progressed, however, the therapist began to experience considerable frustration. This frustration was finally expressed in a punitive comment. Work in consultation enabled the therapist to understand and gain control of his reactions to the patient. During the following session a historical review of CF's relationships with others indicated a strong masochistic trend, a discovery supported by the therapist's experience with him. During the course of treatment, CF's highly conflicted dependency needs were examined. Such feelings had led to an interactive style in which he asked for help but effectively impeded any attempt by others to do anything for him. The genesis of this conflict seemed rooted largely in the patient's relationship with his mother. His mother, while encouraging and supporting CF's dependency on her, was highly conflicted regarding her own dependency needs. This made it difficult for her to provide the understanding and affection that he required. The responses he received from his mother were unempathic and sometimes painful. This led CF to doubt the helpfulness of others. His compromise solution was to outwardly ask for help and inwardly reject it before it caused him distress. This allowed him to maintain a minimally functional relationship with a desperately needed maternal figure. This style, when played out with others, resulted in others becoming frustrated, angry, and ultimately rejecting him. Such rejection proved to CF that he was correct in never fully trusting others. And the cycle began anew. Work in consultation enabled the therapist to successfully explore how CF was eliciting anger and frustration in him and to use his feelings to increase CF's understanding of his problematic interpersonal strategies.

The interactional component of transference was given great attention by H. S. Sullivan. In his focus on transference, Sullivan emphasized how people develop behavior patterns that protect esteem and security in early childhood interactions. Sullivan (1953) saw anxiety engendered by disapproval as the most unbearable of human experiences. He thought that people learn methods of avoiding anxiety from the earliest days of life. Sullivan felt that people repetitively use anxiety-reduction maneuvers. Current situations that provoke anxiety and threaten personal security elicit previously learned devices. These coping mechanisms become part of the person's character style. To illustrate:

> As a young boy, NN learned to avoid anxiety and pain by passively submitting to his punitive father. NN subsequently developed a strong tendency to repeat this passivity in future interactions with authority figures because it offered him the best available adaptation in the past. NN's reaction to others was an expression of his defensive modes of avoiding anxiety. These general self-protective efforts were repeated with the therapist by assuming an attitude of polite acceptance and obsequiousness.

Fromm-Reichmann (1950) noted that individuals, in searching for a mode to interact and protect their security, often fall back mechanically and persistently on judgments developed in relation to significant people in earlier life. These judgments are applied in later life situations in almost rote fashion. The more severe the disturbance, the more mechanical and rote the application. The task of therapy becomes the clarification and reevaluation of these early judgments.

Transference attitudes result in the patient repeating a particular interaction pattern with the therapist. The purpose of this repetition may be to: (1) recreate a gratifying relationship from the past (e.g., mother's favorite son), (2) attempt mastery of a previously unsatisfactory relationship (e.g., gain father's love through obtaining love from father substitutes), or (3) avoid anxiety by relating to others in fashions that previously (albeit neurotically) led to some security (e.g., appeasement of a punitive father). It is likely that the transference reaction of a person is simultaneously determined by a number of needs operating within the individual (see Waelder's 1936 paper on the principle of multiple function and overdetermination).

All interpersonal interactions include some portion of repetition and transference. Transference reactions become neurotic and nonfunctional to the degree that the individual progressively involves others in the enactment of a conflict-laden intrapsychic drama. In such a situation, the individual relates to another in terms of a rigid set of predispositions and expectations. This allows little room to interact with others in a realistic, flexible, and emotionally spontaneous manner. Transference reactions are often disruptive to effective communication and the development of mature relationships.

In psychotherapy, transference has the somewhat paradoxical role of facilitating and impeding treatment. It facilitates treatment in that it allows the therapist and patient an immediate view of the patient's reaction patterns and protective strategies. Yet it is also an impediment to the therapeutic endeavor if the patient is unable to resolve transferential attitudes. Until transferential attitudes are solved, the patient remains susceptible to a mode of relating that impedes the realistic encounter of others. Reality is comprehended through glasses tinted by the past. Past distortions obstruct learning and make further growth difficult.

A SHIFT OF EMPHASIS

An essential task of the therapist in an uncovering dynamic therapy is to help the patient gain a cognitive and emotionally meaningful understanding of oneself through studying current emotional reactions and interactive strategies. Insight and understanding is gained as the patient relates current thoughts, feelings, and behaviors towards the therapist to past formative experiences. The process in which this work is accomplished varies with the therapist and with the evolution of dynamic technique. Abrams and Shengold (1978) observed a shift from a traditional to a neotraditional model of intervention in dynamic therapy. The traditional model emphasized the primacy of interpretation, recovery of repressed memories, and conscious insight, with transference being the chief source of data. The newer model was seen as emphasizing investigation of the interactional process between patient and therapist and the interpersonal experience of the patient–therapist relationship.

A shift may be seen in dynamic work from a focus on instincts and drives to an investigation of interpersonal and intrapsychic defenses. As early as 1959, Fromm-Reichmann noted that therapeutic interest shifted from a focus on the content of what has been repressed to an investigation of the anxiety aroused by the process of uncovering repressed material and the anxiety operating in the relationship with the therapist. The interpersonal theory of Sullivan (1953) and developments in ego psychology (e.g., Hartmann 1958) have facilitated this change of emphasis.

This shift in emphasis has strong implications for short-term psychodynamic psychotherapy technique. Davanloo (1980) emphasized that the role of the therapist is not to analyze, but rather to examine the nature of the reciprocal interaction between therapist and patient. The therapist is not a neutral, impersonal conveyor of interpretation, but an active human participant in a verbal and nonverbal, affective and cognitive, reciprocal interaction.

HOW TO WORK WITH TRANSFERENCE

The therapist has two sequential tasks in working with transference reactions. The therapist's first task is to help the patient attend to and express reactions and perceptions of the therapist as a form of therapeutic interchange. Patients are often reluctant to do this. This work may be termed the "analysis of resistance to transference." The second task of the therapist is to focus on clarifying, working through, and effectively modifying transference reactions in order to reduce their effect on present and future interactions. This may be termed the "analysis of transference as resistance to remembering and mature, realistic interchange." In practice, these tasks blend together and are difficult to separate. For the sake of discussion, however, we will deal with them in sequential fashion.

Analysis of Resistance to the Awareness of Transference

To analyze transference reactions, it is first necessary to help the patient become aware of possible transferential components of the patient–therapist relationship. The therapist aims to facilitate the patient's awareness of reactions to the therapist. The psychotherapy patient is often resistant to viewing reactions to the therapy and the therapist as being an important aspect of therapy. The patient may deny having feelings about the therapist or may discount their importance. For transference to be effectively analyzed, however, it must be attended to. The therapist is advised to focus not only on the nature of the interaction occurring with the patient, but also on the devices used by the patient to avoid working with these feelings. This may be a difficult part of therapy. Therapist and client fears of a direct, immediate interchange may collude to encourage the avoidance of expression of potentially powerful feelings between two people.

Resistance to awareness of transference is initially managed by the therapist's explanation of the patient's task in therapy. The importance of openness, honesty, and free expression of thoughts and feelings is highlighted. In addition, the therapist emphasizes the crucial patient–therapist dialogue regarding their interaction and relationship. This preparation may take the form of such statements as: "Please speak as openly and freely as possible about what goes on in your mind during our sessions." "You need to talk about whatever occurs to you: what you think about me, how you feel about coming, how you react to things that I say. I'll try to be direct as well. In the process of trying to understand what goes on between us, we'll be able to figure out your problems with others." Such remarks encourage the person to observe the patient–therapist interaction and to present these observations for joint examination.

Even with initial explanation and encouragement, the therapist will often find that patients are reluctant to discuss thoughts and feelings toward the therapist, to accept the concept of transference, and to entertain the possibility that transference may influence their relationships. Patients tend to be reluctant to consider how their internal representations of the world influence their perceptions and reactions to the therapist. This resistance has a number of sources. Some patients resist attention and examination of the patient–therapist relationship because they are unwilling to accept its "as if" nature (Tarachow 1963). They are unable to give up the therapist as a potential gratifier of frustrated childhood wishes. Acceptance of the "as if" nature of the therapy relationship (and subsequent resolution of transference reactions) requires the patient to explore reactions and feelings for the therapist. These reactions are to be clarified and understood rather than acted upon (Freud 1912). Such a task requires frustration of the patient's need to have the therapist as a real, need-satisfying object. Setting aside the therapist as a real object creates tension and a sense of aloneness. Patients strongly conflicted around dependency are often unable to tolerate using the therapy relationship as a means to learn about themselves. They want/demand some type of gratification, be it advice, prohibitions, or love.

No patient can totally set aside the therapist as a need satisfier (nor would that be helpful). However, those patients who demand a more direct and a literal form of need satisfaction (e.g., literal love, sympathy, or guidance of their life) are relatively unwilling to tolerate the loss of immediate tension–relief in return for accomplishment of longer-term goals (e.g., insight into intrapsychic conflicts, understanding of neurotic coping behaviors). These patients will resist the conceptualization of treatment relationship as a vehicle to be used to learn about their reactions and interactions with people. Such individuals tend to be inappropriate candidates for short-term psychodynamic psychotherapy.

Attending to and discussing feelings about the therapist may be avoided by some patients because they are a source of embarrassment and shame. For example, sexual feelings for the therapist may be difficult for the patient to admit or talk about, particularly if sex has been a conflictual topic. This dynamic may be illustrated by discussing the case of a woman working on conflicts regarding achievement, success, and academic pursuits.

> GS entered treatment highly motivated to work on her inhibitions towards school and attaining a more successful position in life than either of her parents. She worked enthusiastically for a time, presenting and attempting to understand her various thoughts and feelings about her life. After about ten sessions, GS began to feel she had nothing to say and that there wasn't anything important left to talk about. This feeling persisted for a number of sessions. In an attempt to understand this impasse, the therapist encouraged a more intensive discussion about their relationship. In the past GS had been reluctant to discuss this relationship. Since she was working hard, and with some success at uncovering and understanding her feelings in other aspects of her life, the therapist did not force the issue. The therapist now pointed out how therapy had reached an impasse and that they needed to try to understand what was happening. GS had no ideas. She felt that perhaps they should end since she was doing better than when she started treatment. She also stated that therapy had become progressively uncomfortable. The therapist asked GS if there was something about their relationship that was getting in the way of their working together. GS said no but became increasingly uncomfortable. No headway was made in exploring her reaction in the present session, but in future sessions GS gradually began to discuss her feelings for the therapist. GS stated that their relationship was unfair: the therapist knew so much about her, and she knew so little about him. Continued discussion led GS to disclose sexual feelings for the therapist and of wanting to have a different type of relationship than patient–therapist. GS continued to discuss her feelings for the therapist: she felt secure and warm when the therapist listened to her and showed respect for her opinions. This was different than her relationship with her boyfriend, and with her father, whom she felt was close to her when she was little but became distant as she matured. The therapeutic exploration continued.

What is important to note here is that GS's erotic feelings for the therapist impeded her ability to continue working on herself in therapy. This, in part, stemmed from the difficulty and uncomfortableness GS experienced in expressing these feelings. She felt like a little girl. She was afraid her therapist might reject her as a patient if she acknowledged having something other than professional feelings for him. Such feelings made it very difficult for her to focus on the patient–therapist relationship and its transference components. These feelings were so uncomfortable to GS that she attempted to avoid being even aware of them by becoming vague and superficial with the therapist and by perceiving that there was nothing left to talk about in therapy. Work with such reactions consists of sensitive, gentle, yet persistent interpetative exploration.

Resistance to awareness of transference is met by the therapist's curious, investigative attitude and attempts to facilitate a similar attitude in the patient. The therapist is curious as to how and why the patient thinks, feels, and reacts to the therapist as s/he does and attempts to stimulate the curiosity of the patient as well. The therapist questions the patient's viewing of reactions to the therapist as totally determined by the present interaction and as not having any relationship to habitual modes of perception and attitude. To illustrate:

> LB was a 22-year-old male who sought treatment for feelings of inadequacy and depression. During the interview LB expressed almost total and enthusiastic agreement with all the therapist's observations. LB's agreement with the therapist was understood, not only in terms of the appropriateness of the therapist's interpretation, but also in terms of premises LB had developed to guide his relations to authority figures. These premises had a developmental history. LB had learned that the least painful way of interacting with his father was to suppress his own thoughts and feelings and to feign wholehearted agreement with his father. Helping understand these reactions as an interaction between predisposed attitudes and a realistic response to the present situation was of crucial importance in facilitating insight and further growth.

Unless the therapist focuses interest on understanding the patient–therapist interaction as a means of identifying and resolving the patient's problems, it is highly unlikely that the patient will initiate such work. Patients most often come to therapy concerned with the resolution of a particular problem or problem con-stellation. The idea of reflecting on the process of how thoughts, feelings, or behaviors are manifested in therapy may not make sense to many initially. Patients need to be educated on the impor-tance of discussing their reactions to the interpersonal transactions that occur between patient and therapist. The patient's natural re-luctance and perhaps unwillingness to observe and attempt under-standing of this interaction pattern is pointed out and discussed. Though the therapist must take the initiative in recognizing and working through transference reactions, it is imperative that the therapist involve the patient in a collaborative understanding of the nature of the patient–therapist relationship.

Examination of patient resistance to exploring reactions to the therapist is often slighted in clinical practice. Such underemphasis is a significant reason why transference interpretations often lack significant emotional impact. Interpretation of the transference may have little meaning (other than increasing intellectual defenses) if the patient has not been sensitized to the importance and possible meaning of such feelings and is to some degree willing to consider the possibility of transference. Without proper preparation it is easy for the patient to distort and reject allusions to the therapeutic relationship as the therapist's idiosyncratic style.

Identifying Transference

The therapist identifies transference feelings by carefully listening for how the patient perceives the therapy and the individual session, and, most specifically, for references to the person and activities of the therapist. The patient is aided in becoming more aware of transference by exploring allusions to transference in statements not manifestly related to the therapy relationship. Transference feelings may be disguised and/or symbolized in various fashions. One way they are expressed is through displacement; a patient, experiencing the therapist as critical, may discuss an overly evaluative supervisor. Transference feelings may be expressed through identification; the patient may become critical and demeaning of oneself. It is helpful for the therapist to consider that all communications in therapy contain some relevance or relationship to the transference situation. Freud (1925), for example, taught that everything that occurs to the patient during the therapy hour is partially determined by the patient's perception of the therapist and the therapy. The therapist's task is to develop latent transference material into manifest material for investigation.

Identifying and discussing transference feelings must be done with sensitivity. Wording of the therapist's comments is important. Lipton (1977) stated that although the therapist may feel reasonably certain that the patient's discussion is an allusion to latent transference feelings, telling a patient what "really" is being discussed will be met with resistance. A better approach to identifying and clarifying transference feelings would be to begin with such statements as "A possible meaning of what you are saying, in so far as our therapy is concerned, may be. . ." or "An implication of what you are saying for our relationship is. . . ."

Telling a patient what is "really" meant is incorrect for other reasons. To speak of real meaning disregards the principle of overdetermination (see Waelder 1936). Briefly, this principle suggests that several factors operate concurrently to create a specific behavior or reaction pattern. For example, the content and sequence of patient material during the therapy session is a reaction to a complex of motives, only one of which is influenced by feelings towards the therapist. The fact that the therapist has discerned further meaning, more disturbing meaning, or more carefully disguised meaning does not justify the claim that the therapist has discovered the ultimate truth that lies behind the world of appearances—the "real" world. A sounder claim would be that a point has been reached where reality must be formulated in a more subtle and complex manner than before (Schafer 1983).

The therapist often resists sensitizing patients to the importance of identifying transference reactions and frequently avoids discussing patient feelings about the therapist, fearing that such discussion may impede the establishment of a therapeutic alliance. Attention to transference feelings, especially negative transference, is essential to the establishment of a sound treatment alliance. Avoidance of transference issues results in a problem-solving, externally directed (as opposed to intrapsychically directed) treatment; such a treatment aids in problem resolution but often effects little personality change. A generalizable coping strategy for similar problems is not learned.

Therapist resistance to focusing on transference issues may also be related to the fear that such attention slights the patient's reality concerns. It is helpful for a therapist with this dilemma to consider that interpretive, dynamic treatment is not a method of direct intervention into the patient's life. Rather, patients are given the opportunity to explore and learn about themselves, including the various means in which their thoughts and feelings and reactions play a part in bringing about their problems in living. This learning and understanding is then carried over into their life situation. Gill (1982) contended that most patients are greatly relieved and feel support for their autonomy when the therapist doesn't tell them how to live their lives.

Analysis of Transference as Resistance

In short-term psychodynamic psychotherapy, the therapist encourages the patient to attend to and discuss one's reactions to the therapist and to their interaction. This is done through education, modeling, and interpretation of patient resistance. As the patient is progressively more able to focus on the patient–therapist interaction, therapeutic attention is directed towards understanding and working through the transference components of this relationship. The therapist helps the patient identify how aspects of one's reactions are related to, and stem from, previously learned attitudes and security operations. Transference behavior is viewed as resistance to: (1) remembering and reexperiencing painful events of the past and (2) relating to the therapist in a more mature but, because of past learning, more anxiety-provoking manner. Transference may be viewed as resistance to genuine, authentic encounters with other people due to the anxiety entailed by such interaction. This resistance to realistic, mature interaction is partly conscious and partly unconscious. Effective therapy helps the patient realize the extent to which relationships are constructed by means of rigid application of outdated attitudes and coping behaviors.

Transference is a preexisting perceptual and emotional bias. Working on transference reactions in therapy helps the patient (and therapist) become increasingly able to develop genuine collaboration concerning the patient's problems. Often the patient's predisposition to transferring conflicted feelings and interaction patterns from the past onto present interaction *is* the person's problem; once these reactions are modified, the patient is able to interact with others in a more effective fashion.

In sum, the tasks of the therapist regarding transference are: (1) to help the patient attend to the patient–therapist interaction and to its possible transference components (i.e., analyze resistance to transference) and (2) to focus on understanding and modifying the effect that previous learning and predetermined attitudes have had on effective communication and mature collaboration (i.e., analyze the transference as resistance).

ANALYSIS OF THE TRIANGLE OF INSIGHT

The traditional interpretation of transference material involves relating aspects of the current patient–therapist interaction to its development in the patient's past history of relationships (in particular with significant childhood figures). Malan (1976) found interpretation of the link between present behavior with the therapist and past behavior with parents to be an essential component of successful treatment. Concurring, Sifneos (1979) stressed that the therapist repeatedly attempt to link patient reactions to the therapist with past reactions to parents. Sifneos felt that the therapist–patient interpretation brought repressed oedipal issues and feelings associated with them into the therapeutic relationship. The displacement of feelings, attitudes, and behavior patterns that the patient experienced towards parental figures could be examined and analyzed; the possibility of new learning was thus made available to the patient. To illustrate:

> A woman (AD), working on the focal issue of dissatisfaction with romantic relationships, related a humorous incident to her therapist. The therapist reacted to AD's story with laughter. Following his laughter, the woman became silent for a long period, finally breaking the silence with a statement about ending therapy. Exploration of this thought led her to express discomfort, anger, and resentment towards the therapist. She felt the therapist was laughing at and making fun of her. She added that she had similar reactions to the therapist in the past and that this was the "straw that broke the camel's back." Upon reviewing his reactions to the patient, the therapist felt comfortable in telling her that although it may have been an error for him to laugh when he did, to the best of his knowledge he had meant no harm and was not laughing at her. Rather he was attempting to share a warm moment. The therapist pointed out that to believe he was making fun of her was only one of a number of possible interpretations that she could have made to his laughter. He asked her to consider how she decided upon that particular interpretation. Further discussion resulted in sharing some feelings about her father. Her father had no respect for women and never took her seriously. She then related a memory of an incident that occurred at ten years of age: when explaining to her father her career plans of being an astronaut, he broke into a fit of laughter, leading her to feel embarrassed, ashamed, and unsupported. Discussion of this event led to tears and the uncovering of much hurt and anger toward her father and men in general, whom she felt were all alike. Patient and therapist carefully explored these feelings and the impact they had had on her attitudes towards others. They also explored conclusions she had made regarding the intentions of her father, as well as her therapist. Such work enabled AD to consider the possibility that her interpretation of her therapist's laughter may not have been completely accurate. AD was then able to consider other alternative

modes of reacting to her therapist. Work on the therapist–patient link had opened up the possibility of learning that her therapist may not have had the same motive as her father and could perhaps be responded to in a different manner.

In addition to clarifying how patient reactions to the therapist are influenced by past relationships, the therapist helps the patient see that reactions to the therapist may be similar to reactions the patient has to other people in current life situations. Interpretations linking behavior patterns with the *therapist* to behaviors in *current* and *past* life relationships are called therapist/current/past (T-C-P) interpretations (Davanloo 1978). The T-C-P interpretation requires attention to three interrelated situations: (1) the *therapeutic situation*, involving clarification of the here-and-now patient–therapist relationship, (2) the *current life situation* involving parallels between the patient–therapist interaction and interactions in present life, and (3) the *childhood situation* involving the carry-over of the childhood past to the patient–therapist interaction. Davanloo (1980) found early and frequent use of T-C-P interpretations to correlate positively with successful outcome.

The T-C-P interpretation is not new. Alexander (1956) discussed a "total" interpretation that connects the patient's current life situation with experience in the transference and in past life. Menninger (1958) suggested the phrase "triangle of insight" to describe interpretive interventions connecting the patient's pattern of behavior in therapy to current and past situations. The therapist's task, according to Menninger, was to help the patient recognize the following: (1) There is a pattern to the patient's feelings, attitudes, behavior techniques, and roles in which people are cast. (2) This pattern originated long ago and stamps itself on every step of the patient's life journey. It is present in contemporary relationships, and it is present in the therapy relationship. (3) This pattern, which originated for a valid reason, persisted, despite changes in some of the original circumstances. (4) This pattern contains elements that are injurious to others, as well as expensive and troublesome to the patient. Application of the triangle of insight may be illustrated by expanding the previous vignette.

> AD felt her therapist was making fun of her and was not respecting her feelings. She reacted with hurt, anger, withdrawal, and an impulse to leave therapy. Careful study of her reactions led to her identifying a similar reaction pattern in her childhood relationship to her father, a relationship in which she felt unloved and insignificant. AD reported that after initially trying to please her father and gain his affection, she finally found herself putting increasing distance between her father and herself. Her withdrawal from her father may have been adaptive at the time in that it protected her vulnerable sense of self from her father's put-downs. However, such learning resulted in a tendency to read critical meanings and motives into other people's behavior as well.
>
> AD's readiness to view her therapist's behavior as critical and derisive resulted in defensiveness and distancing behavior. These reactions increased her sense of security (superficially) but made her feel lonelier. Discussion of her relationships with other men in her life yielded a pattern similar to that experienced with her therapist. She was guarded, mistrustful, and sensitive to rejection. By examining her reaction to her therapist, AD was able to begin a therapeutic examination of a conflicted relationship pattern. She developed insight into how conflicted relationships in her past encouraged continuation of childhood attitudes and expectations in her present life. This was a valuable beginning to helping AD give up some ingrained and constricting behaviors.

The development of insight is not an intellectual exercise in which something in the therapy situation is identified as something in childhood, or a childhood problem is reflected in contemporary life. Menninger (1958) stated that insight is the "simultaneous identification of the characteristic behavior pattern in all three of these situations, together with an understanding of why they were and are used" (p. 148). To be effective, insight must be experienced in an emotionally meaningful way. Insight may be facilitated by close attention to the therapeutic interaction and use of this interaction to give the patient an in vivo look at currently active behavior patterns. AD's experience and exploration of her intense feelings of anger towards the therapist allowed her to realize the importance of her need to feel respected. An intellectual discussion about not being taken seriously or feeling belittled would not have had as much influence.

Gaining an emotionally meaningful understanding of a behavior is not all that is needed for change; it is only the beginning. Momentary insight increases self-awareness; in all likelihood, the patient would still be caught in a web of repetition compulsion. Still needed is repetitive confrontation of the patient's conflicts in order to develop ever-deepening insight and understanding into oneself. The repetitive experience of abreaction, and insight into the experience, leads to decreased anxiety when doing something new, as well as increasing awareness that other options are available.

Early and active interpretive work involving the triangle of insight characterizes short-term psychodynamic psychotherapy. Links are developed between current behavior patterns, past behavior with parents or parent-substitutes, and behavior in the therapy relationship. The therapist uses transference interpretations as soon as transference reactions are observed. Davanloo (1980) recommended the use of T-C-P interpretations early in therapy, even in the assessment interview. Patient responses to such interventions are assessed to gauge their ability to effectively use the therapy. Patients who are unable to work with and elaborate on the intrapsychic conflicts and interpersonal patterns highlighted by the therapist are inappropriate candidates.

Summary

A T-C-P interpretation is preceded by gathering evidence of the individual's patterns of behavior with significant people in present life (a patient, FG, avoids expression of angry feelings with his wife, consequently feeling frustrated and depressed). Further exploration brings data regarding a pattern of behavior with significant people in early life (FG was reared by a domineering stepmother who threatened to send him away if he wasn't a "good" boy). The patient's pattern of behavior with the therapist is then viewed in light of this information (FG is overly compliant and never expresses disappointment with the therapist). The therapist is now in a position to make a connective link between the patient's reaction and interaction with the therapist and his behavior with past significant figures — the T-P link ("You never disagree. This seems similar to how you described it with your stepmother.") The therapist next develops the link between the patient's behavior towards the therapist and the patient's current pattern of behavior with significant people in his/her life — the T-C link. ("It seems that expressing disagreeable feelings is hard for you with your wife as well as me.") The final step is to help the patient develop a comprehensive picture of his/her characteristic style of interaction by connecting all points of the triangle of insight — the T-C-P interpretation. ("We've got a pattern here: first with your stepmother, then your wife, and now with me. You seem afraid to express yourself.")

The process of making a successful T-C-P interpretation varies as to: (1) how information about the patient's dynamics is gathered (the therapist may base early interpretations more on the patient–therapist interaction than to the patient's discussion of past history and current problems), (2) what links are made first (it may be easier to help FG see a similarity in how he relates to his wife and how he previously interacted with his stepmother than to relate either interaction to the therapy interchange), and (3) how much time is needed to clarify each link (patients vary as to their ability to accept and work with various types of insights). It may be easier and more meaningful for a patient to explore a relationship pattern that is currently problematic (e.g., a spouse) than to explore the past.

The patient's resistance to exploration, due to the underlying rigidity of one's defenses, plays a major role in determining how quickly the therapist can aid the patient in identifying and working through the current interplay of conflicted childhood emotional patterns. In some instances, the therapist can present a complete and emotionally meaningful T-C-P interpretation early in treatment with a particularly motivated and psychologically minded patient, provided that the interpretation is not too distant from the patient's experience and is presented palatably. Once the pattern is identified and deemed meaningful, the patient is in the position to struggle with motivations, fears, and underlying feelings keeping the particular pattern alive after reasons for its development no longer apply. In other instances, therapists need more time to get a patient to attend to reactions to the therapist and to make meaningful links to other contemporary and past experiences.

We recommend that the therapist formulate the patient's material according to the triangle of insight and consider the T-C-P interpretation as a basic and crucial intervention. We encourage the therapist to be flexible in determining the sequence and timing of intervention.

ANALYSIS OF THE TRIANGLE OF CONFLICT

The triangle of conflict is used to help the patient explore and understand problematic reactions to others at each point of the triangle of insight. The triangle of conflict describes the intrapsychic relationship between repressed or hidden feelings, the anxiety and/or guilt generated as these feelings become conscious (or threaten to do so), and the defenses used to bind the anxiety and avoid awareness and expression of threatening feelings. An illustration follows:

> Mary is a teenaged girl. One day, Mary's sister brought home Bill, her boyfriend. Mary found herself experiencing an intense dislike for Bill. When Bill visited, Mary found herself arguing with him, making it difficult for Bill to converse with her sister. It is noteworthy that as much as Mary professed dislike for Bill, she found him constantly on her mind and frequently talked about him with friends. Comments by friends suggesting that there was more to her feelings were met with bristling indignation. Mary found herself increasingly distressed by this situation. Her daydreams became pre-

occupied with ruminations about Bill and her sister, and her sister was becoming angry with Mary's treatment of her boyfriend. Mary decided to talk to a counselor at school.

The counselor helped Mary sort out her feelings. Mary revealed that she had little experience with boyfriends and was afraid that her sister would get married and leave her. Mary felt her dislike for Bill resulted from being uncomfortable with boys and of being afraid of losing her sister. These revelations, however, did not relieve Mary's feelings of distress. More work was needed to further clarify her feelings. Something was missing in explaining her dreams about Bill and her high level of contact with him when he was visiting. The counselor was particularly interested in a remark Mary made in discussing Bill. In relating how Bill preferred to sit home watching TV rather than go out, Mary exclaimed that she would "love to have him herself." When the counselor brought this to Mary's attention, she immediately corrected herself, stating that she meant to say she would "love to let him have it herself." By this she meant that she would not let a guy "mooch" off her parents and that her sister couldn't seem to prevent it. This errant phrase, however, set the counselor thinking. She began to piece together Mary's situation a bit differently. Slowly, patiently, she helped Mary continue to search her feelings about Bill, including her contradictory reactions (e.g., she disliked Bill, yet spent much time interacting with him). The counselor planted a seed of doubt in Mary's determined negative stance to Bill. Over the course of treatment and with much anxiety and embarrassment, Mary gradually uncovered strong feelings of attraction and longing. At first, these feelings caused anxiety concerning competition with her sister and her own insecurities about being attractive and desirable to men. In addition, she found herself feeling guilty over wanting her sister's boyfriend because she loved her sister and didn't want to hurt her.

The counselor and Mary clarified Mary's situation in the following fashion. Mary's sexual feelings for Bill created anxiety and guilt. This resulted in Mary repressing these feelings and defending against their awareness by developing reactions (i.e., intense dislike) that kept the feared, yet desired, action (i.e., competing for and winning Bill) firmly out of the picture. This defense allowed Mary to avoid the conflict of simultaneously experiencing two dissonant goals (i.e., winning Bill and remaining a loyal and "innocent" sister). Upon uncovering and talking about these feelings, Mary felt less distressed and was able to attain a position where she could decide how she wanted to relate to Bill, this time with greater understanding and awareness of her true feelings toward him.

The triangle of conflict may be applied to Mary's experience. (1) Various thoughts and feelings cause anxiety and/or guilt due to one's past learning and present intrapsychic state (Mary's attraction to Bill resulted in anxiety and guilt). (2) People learn to avoid expression of these feelings. This is done through the establishment of defensive strategies (e.g., symptoms, character traits) that protect the individual's security by keeping feelings out of awareness and not acting on them. Mary's feelings of attraction and the possible actualization of these feelings were avoided by her attending closely to Bill's faults; at a conscious level she developed a negative impression of him. (3) These defensive strategies often allow the expression of repressed feelings in a derivative fashion (Mary's conscious irritation and dislike of Bill resulted in frequent arguments with him; such behavior allowed her to interact quite intimately with him, thus gratifying an unconscious wish for closeness).

Work with the triangle of conflict involves: (1) identifying patient defenses (or defensive strategies solidified into character traits), (2) helping the patient grasp the purpose of these tactics (e.g., avoidance of anxiety and threat), and (3) clarifying the feelings being defended against and avoided. Active interpretive work facilitates an emotional understanding of the relationship between the patient's defensive pattern (e.g., conscious dislike and criticism), the wish/feeling defended against (e.g., sexual attraction), and the anxiety experienced at the threatened breakthrough of the feeling. Of key importance is the uncovering of personally threatening feelings, reexposing the patient's ego to unresolved conflict for further mastery and integration. The patient's more mature ego is offered the opportunity to confront these feelings, and to learn new means of coping with situations that formerly elicited anxiety and new strategies of defense and avoidance. To illustrate working with the triangle of conflict:

BW, a male patient, was working on the focal issue of assertion. BW related to the therapist in a passive, inhibited manner. BW's passiveness intensified in situations where BW experienced frustration and anger (e.g., when the therapist confronted BW's chronic lateness to sessions). The therapist recognized BW's anger and displeasure by careful analysis of his own reactions while working with BW. When they discussed certain issues such as BW's lateness, or his tendency to blame others for his difficulties, BW became passive and withholding of his feelings. This behavior elicited frustration and helplessness in the therapist. It also stirred up feelings that the therapist was bad and that he was being punished. These reactions led the therapist to hypothesize that BW was angry with him and was dealing with his anger in a defensive yet expressive fashion (i.e., although BW denied any angry feelings for the therapist, the therapist felt as if he was being punished). The therapist presented his reactions to BW. He wondered aloud if BW was aware of the effects he had on him (and perhaps on others). BW was able to relate two feelings: first, anxiety at the prospect of confronting his therapist; and second, satisfaction that he was able to affect the therapist. The therapist encouraged further discussion of the anxiety about confrontation. BW related fears of being overwhelmed, losing control, and of hurting the therapist with things he might say. When asked, "What kinds of things," BW initially blocked, but gradually discussed, his complaints about the therapist (e.g., he provided no definite answers, he made BW uncomfortable with certain questions, he was picky about meeting times). Further discussion of BW's reactions to the therapist resulted in a strong expression of resentment toward the therapist, followed by guilt and apology. The therapist noted that BW seemed so afraid of his strong feelings that sometimes he didn't even allow himself to be aware of them.

Work such as this helped BW to identify the process he used to deal with feelings he was conflicted about expressing openly. BW had not learned healthy, nondestructive ways of being angry. When he felt angry, he wanted to punish others, but he also wanted to protect his relationships from what he feared would be the consequences of such action (e.g., devastating others, or being devastated). He dealt with the anxiety elicited by this conflict through intrapsychic and interpersonal defenses that enabled BW to avoid awareness and open, direct expression of anger. Repressed feelings, however, continue to seek expression. BW, although consciously dissatisfied with his tendency to withhold his feelings from others, gained a degree of satisfaction (gratification) from his ability to make others feel as thwarted and helpless as he often did.

This process of examining BW's defenses to reveal underlying anxieties and unexpressed feelings may be done at each point of the triangle of insight. For example, BW's difficulties and resultant defenses against expressing anger were examined in the therapist–patient relationship, then in relationships with friends and loved ones, and in his relationship with early parental figures. Identification of this pattern of dealing with his angry feelings gave BW the opportunity to begin confronting a developmental task in an adaptive fashion.

ANALYSIS OF TRANSFERENCE IN THE HERE AND NOW

There has been increased interest in the use of the interpersonal relationship between patient and therapist as a vehicle for modification of maladaptive coping strategies displaced onto the therapy situation. This mode of work has been termed the "analysis of transference in the here and now" (Gill 1979, 1982) and deals with the interpersonal and interactional component of treatment. Early trends in psychoanalytic intervention emphasized understanding and reconstructing the genetic development of psychic conflict; the therapist–patient relationship was used as a way of gaining access to repressed material of the past. Such work, though effective in deepening self-understanding and identity, frequently resulted in strengthening intellectual defenses and causing less than optimal behavioral change. As early as 1925, Rank and Ferenczi emphasized using the current, here-and-now relationship to clarify, examine, and modify interpersonal conflict, rather than using this relationship as a springboard for discussing the past history of a patient. Such work was seen as intensifying the level of affect within the session, creating the possibility of a corrective emotional experience, and increasing the efficacy of treatment. Working on patient defenses and transference reactions in the immediate therapy relationship, thus deemphasizing genetic insight, was felt to heighten the emotional immediacy and relevance of feelings and behaviors. Such intervention strategy generated a greater degree of emotional involvement than the exploration of "the conflicts of the remote past, which are concerned with dead circumstances and mummified personalities, whose outcome is already determined" (Strachey 1934, p. 120).

Focus on the current interaction between patient and therapist has become a critical component of brief dynamic treatment (Strupp and Binder 1984). This emphasis is reflected in Davanloo's description (1980) of modern dynamic treatment as an attempt to identify, understand, and resolve the reciprocal interactive process occurring between patient and therapist, rather than an analysis of the psychic contents of the mind as presented through free association. The immediate patient–therapist relationship is used to examine the patient's various patterns of reaction and interaction with others. Although identifying similar patterns of behavior in past and current functioning are important in transference resolution, the critical focus is on the use of the patient–therapist relationship for modification of conflictual patterns of relating. The immediate interpersonal relationship between patient and therapist is utilized to correct persistent maladaptive coping strategies created by an interpersonal relationship of the past (Strupp 1977).

In the analysis of transference in the here and now, great importance is placed on helping the patient identify and reevaluate characteristic patterns of interacting. Therapist and patient work to clarify what is occurring between them and how effective their interaction is in meeting mature needs (e.g., clear communication, honest expressions). When such interaction is problematic, efforts are made to develop a relationship that is less conflictual. This work is facilitated by helping the patient look at how the transfer or displacement of previously learned coping strategies to the present relationship has constricting, distorting, and generally unsatisfactory effects.

Early strategies learned with parents, siblings, and other significant figures tend to be resistant to later remediation. Interaction patterns that protected security and reduced anxiety tend to be used and reused in new relationships, often to the detriment of the individual. To illustrate:

> A patient (FG) learned to interact with his mother in a dependent, submissive fashion in order to avoid the threat of abandonment. Holding on to such a behavior pattern compromised the development of peer, colleague, and mature love relationships. In treatment, his therapist worked with these repetitive (transferred) reactions to help FG more realistically adapt responses to present life circumstances. This is done through helping FG examine his interaction with the therapist, evaluate its utility and effectiveness, and collaborate with his therapist in the evolution of a relationship that is mature, adaptive, and relatively nonconflictual.

Short-term psychodynamic psychotherapy is characterized by an active patient–therapist dialogue regarding the appropriateness and utility of their immediate interaction. The here-and-now quality of this dialogue heightens the degree of emotional involvement by both patient and therapist and facilitates the development of a meaningful, change-inducing experience.

A Posture of Certainty

Psychotherapy requires the therapist to communicate trust in one's method and oneself. The manner in which the therapist communicates confidence and trust in his/her observations needs consideration. The effective analysis of transference requires an atmosphere that facilitates examination of the patient's assumptions when reacting to and interacting with the therapist in his particular style. Patients are often reluctant to have their views about the world and attitudes toward others questioned. They can also be defensive about examining the role they play in causing their own problems. It is important for the therapist to be sensitive to defensive feelings when helping a person examine these reactions to interpretation of transference in the therapist–patient relationship.

To effectively uncover, identify, and discuss transference, a posture of certainty by the therapist regarding what "actually" occurs in the relationship must be avoided. To illustrate:

> FR was a 38-year-old male who sought treatment for his depression and who possessed strong narcissistic character traits. After an intervention by the therapist, FR withdrew into a cold, icy silence. Upon explaining his behavior, he stated that the therapist was insensitive and unempathic. The therapeutic task was to understand and explain FR's reaction. Was the therapist bored and impatient, and out of his impatience, intervening unempathically and punitively? Did FR possess such strong needs for accurate mirroring and confirmation that the therapist was bound to disappoint him? A dialogue was developed to examine FR's reaction and their ongoing relationship. The therapist paid careful attention to how FR perceived what had happened between them and also shared his own views. Through this mutual exploration and discussion a more mature collaboration was developed that ultimately resulted in a clearer understanding of this incident, their relationship, and FR's problems in living.

It is always helpful to intervene in a way that continually elucidates the patient's view of the therapy situation. A therapist's posture of absolute certainty as to occurrences in the patient–therapist interaction makes it difficult for the patient to thoughtfully consider feelings in a nondefensive, explorative manner. To tell FR that he is oversensitive and that his reaction to the therapist is *his* problem would, in all likelihood, encourage a resistant, defensive stand by the patient. Therapy is facilitated by viewing patient ideas regarding what is happening in the interaction as viable hypotheses and not as distortions of reality. The therapist also has only a working hypothesis regarding reality. Reality may only be approximated by both the patient *and* the therapist. To approach the patient–therapist dialogue in any other spirit compromises the development of an ongoing sense of investigative collaboration needed to help the patient struggle with problems in living (Schafer 1983).

Dealing with Attempts at Engagement

During the examination of the patient's intrapsychic and interpersonal styles of relatedness, the therapist provides an environment in which the patient is encouraged to behave in a more mature and collaborative fashion. In addition to understanding the genetic basis of the patient's emotional conflicts, the therapist grapples with the impact of these conflicts on their relationship. Neurotic modes of interaction are identified and discussed as they occur in the interaction. Rather than engage in an interaction in which the patient and therapist act out the patient's (or the therapist's) neurosis, the therapist attempts to identify and examine problem areas and facilitate development of an interaction that is more open, mature, and less constricting than the patient's present adaptation. An illustration:

> SM was a 29-year-old man who sought treatment for numerous self-defeating and masochistic behaviors. SM expected and, it seemed, elicited punishment (i.e., rejection, hostility) from others. Rather than engage in a sadomasochistic interaction, the therapist helped SM examine his style of relating, the reactions it elicited, and the repressed feelings, unconscious fears, or irrational beliefs that motivated such interpersonal strategy. The therapist experienced and observed the patient's intrapsychic struggle (eg., masochism as a disguised plea for love) but worked to avoid being pulled into behaving in a punitive fashion. The patient was given the experience of having his neurotic ploys fall short of their expected impact and was encouraged to explore more constructive means of gaining attention and care.

While avoiding being engaged by the patient's neurotic attempts to act out intrapsychic conflict, the therapist participates nonneurotically in the patient's constructive attempts to grow, to master irrational feelings and attitudes, and to come to grips with the significant problems in his/her life (Strupp 1973). Relating with empathy, acceptance, and concern, the therapist refuses to be pulled into the neurotic interactions. For example, a dependent patient often attempts to elicit advice and guidance from the therapist, often to avoid the responsibility for personal decisions and the risk involved. The ability to find and elicit such guidance from others keeps the patient involved in a neurotic parent–child interaction. Rather than advisement and guidance, the dependent patient is offered: (1) empathic identification of the need for guidance, (2) examination of how this need is played out, and (3) the opportunity to relate in a fashion that supports the patient's own autonomy. The therapist relates to the healthy, more mature aspects of the ego and conveys understanding of the fear of self-determination but also an expectation that the patient can and will take more responsibility.

The extent to which the therapist frustrates the patient's neurotic needs, and how quickly the patient is able to confront feared situations, is dependent on the patient's inner resources and ego integrative abilities. Through careful assessment, the short-term therapy practitioner selects patients who are able to withstand the frustration of having maladaptive coping strategies confronted and examined without withdrawing from the relationship. The therapist avoids gratifying neurotic coping mechanisms in order to keep the patient in treatment. The emphasis is on pointing out maladaptive transference reactions and attempting to provide the patient with an experience of relating to someone in a manner in which problematic defense mechanisms are neither needed, nor, for that matter, effective.

Goals of Here-and-Now Analysis

The therapist and patient attempt to work out a relationship that is realistic, nonmanipulative, and void of the effect of constrictive security operations. The messages to be conveyed are that relationships are not conflict free and that the therapist is willing to proceed, with openness and purpose, towards interpersonal conflict resolution. To the extent that the patient learns to analyze and work through conflicts with a therapist, greater freedom is attained to do so with others. An illustration follows:

A patient (AW) entered therapy with an overt fear of authority and covert hostility to figures symbolizing authority. AW's conflicts with authority figures rapidly unfolded in his relationship to his therapist. AW expected the therapist to consistently agree with AW's perceptions of his problems at work (he was unable to complete work projects and attributed this to the tyranny of his supervisors). When the therapist questioned AW's conclusions, AW looked disheartened and expressed discouragement in therapy's helpfulness. Subsequent therapist comments were met with defensiveness and thinly veiled sarcasm. During such periods, the therapist's free associations were of a "hurt and spiteful" child. The therapist attempted to avoid engagement in AW's neurotic conflict. He neither took care of AW's hurt feelings, nor did he punish his spitefulness. Rather, he pointed out what he felt was occurring between them and encouraged AW to share his perceptions. These interventions provided the opportunity for AW and his therapist to begin a reworking of their relationship to reflect present realities rather than AW's conflictual past coping strategies. Once accomplished with the therapist, AW was in the position to transfer his learning to other situations in his life.

Past versus Present

Analysis of transference in the here and now focuses on using the patient–therapist relationship to help the patient learn about and resolve conflictual patterns of interaction. This should not be misconstrued as minimizing the importance of understanding the patient's developmental history. Attention to how conflictual patterns have developed offers the patient a chance to understand and to connect across time the events of one's life. This strengthens the patient's identity. It also creates confidence that the patient's way of reacting may be understood and that one isn't involved in confused meandering through unrelated situations. The therapist, however, must keep in mind that change rests on the reliving and modification of historically meaningful patterns within the therapeutic interaction and not on the elucidation of past events (Strupp 1973).

The primary value of exploration of genetic material is to facilitate the understanding and working through of the present relationship. Understanding the past is used to decrease its harmful effects on the present.

Summary

Problematic patterns of reacting to others are formed in relating to others (in particular, early significant others). Since these patterns essentially consist of feelings towards other people, they can be adequately corrected only by working them through as feelings towards the therapist (Saul 1967). Short-term psychodynamic psychotherapy is characterized by an active use of the patient's transference reactions to provide insight into intrapsychic conflicts and defensive functioning. Conflicted emotional reactions are progressively modified by means of analysis and working through within the patient–therapist relationship.

The triangles of insight and conflict are useful in guiding the therapist's interventions. The triangle of insight, grounded in the principle of repetition compulsion, provides a model to clarify: (1) conflictual patterns of emotional reaction, (2) current operation of these patterns in the patient's life, and (3) their development and history of use in early formative relationships. The T-C-P interpretation, which elucidates the triangle of insight, provides insight into and understanding of interpersonal functioning. The integration of past and present also has a stabilizing effect by identifying an underlying continuity in behavior. To facilitate these effects, the therapist continually observes and participates in the therapeutic interaction and attempts to identify conflictual patterns of behavior. These patterns are explained to the patient as the repetition of reactions learned through childhood experiences.

The triangle of conflict helps in the examination of conflictual patient behaviors representing a defensive adaptation to anxiety elicited by the prospect of becoming aware of and expressing repressed and hidden feelings. The sequence of hidden feelings→anxiety→defense is used to systematically examine patient reactions and behavior at each point of the triangle of insight. Questions for the therapist to consider when developing the triangle of conflict include: (1) How is this particular behavior being examined the result of an interplay between defense and defended-against feelings? (2) What does the behavior allow the patient to avoid and/or symbolically express? An illustration of how these triangles are used follows:

> BK, a male patient with histrionic character traits, was working on his dissatisfaction with romantic relationships. BK's relationships were intense, labile, and brief. He often felt alone and unloved. Insight into BK's problems was developed by examining BK's reactions to the therapist. BK enjoyed talking to the therapist about his life and experiences. However, he made little effort to examine his experiences and to identify themes and patterns that ran through his life. When the therapist pointed this out, BK stated that that was the therapist's job and that he was doing his part by free associating. The therapist pointed out the need to work together to understand BK's problems and BK's unwillingness to collaborate on this task. At this point, BK exploded in anger. He accused the therapist of calling him a bad client and of trying to make him feel guilty. He further felt that the therapist was lazy.
>
> The therapist's first reaction was to back off and to wait for another time to look at this issue. In addition, he sensed this to be just the reaction BK was trying to elicit by means of his emotional blow-up. The therapist experienced BK's outburst as faintly melodramatic and contrived. The therapist thus encouraged BK to think about his reaction to the therapist and to consider its effects on their interaction. The therapist noted that it seemed like BK wanted him to back off and that perhaps BK's outburst was a way of controlling the situation, perhaps to avoid something. This intervention was accepted in tentative fashion and served as an opening for further discussion and exploration.
>
> BK's reaction to the therapist, resulting in his blow-up, was closely examined. BK was able to identify feeling uncomfortable and nervous when the therapist pointed out how BK expected the thera-

pist to make all the connections and come up with all the insights. Although his immediate reaction to this interpretation was anger, BK was able to identify feeling helpless in meeting the therapist's demands. BK began to explore this area. He related feelings of inadequacy and a sense of being "a child in a world of adults." He further related an uneasy feeling of being unable to cope without somebody to look after him. He discussed feeling like a failure and being afraid to do much work in therapy because he would fail. It was safer to let someone more capable than he find answers to his problems. BK initially found self-exploration to be painful, scary, and embarrassing. How could he feel like this? After all, he viewed himself as very competent. He was successful at his job, a creative writer, and maintained a large circle of acquaintances. This didn't fit with the way he wanted to perceive himself.

The therapist pointed out how BK's feelings of helplessness and dependency conflicted with how BK wanted to be seen and how he perhaps avoided these feelings (i.e., kept them hidden) from himself and others so they wouldn't affect his life. One method of keeping them hidden was to respond in a dramatic, angry fashion to situations that threatened his superficial security, such as when the therapist requested BK's assistance in making sense of BK's life in terms of recurring emotional reactions and behavior patterns. BK's dramatic, exaggerated reaction was seen as a smoke screen to avoid dealing with feelings (i.e., inadequacy, helplessness) that caused anxiety and loss of self-esteem.

Understanding his reaction to the therapist enabled BK to deepen his understanding of his romantic relationships. BK tended to form relationships with older women who provided support, nurturance, and love. BK, in turn, provided the relationship with stimulation and entertainment through his charm and playfulness. Problems occurred when BK's lovers demanded more than entertainment with witty conversation (which usually focused upon himself). His lovers would eventually ask BK for the same support and nurturance he demanded from them. BK would react to such demands with anger and hurt. His blow-ups, intense, dramatic, but short lived, often worked in getting his lovers back in line. Eventually, however, they lost interest in the relationship, leaving BK depressed and lonely. BK began to realize how he set up relationships in which others became his caretakers. He was able to trace this pattern of relating back to his childhood, especially to his relationship with his mother. BK perceived his mother as loving but highly protective and discouraging of his autonomy.

Use of the triangles of conflict and insight helped BK explore a problematic pattern of emotional reaction (i.e., dramatic bouts of anger) and understand its purpose in his psychic economy (i.e., avoidance of feeling helpless and inadequate and unable to give). The therapist facilitated study of how BK's feelings of dependency and inadequacy were defended against and yet acted out in his patterns of living. This work allowed BK to develop increased understanding and mastery of his life and opened up the opportunity for new growth and maturation. The triangle of conflict was used to clarify BK's patterns of reaction at each point in the triangle of insight (therapist, romantic relationships, his mother).

By clarifying BK's intrapsychic experience and resultant interpersonal style, the stage was set for altering BK's neurotic problems. What must be emphasized, however, is the importance of using the patient–therapist relationship, not only to identify problems in living, but also to help the patient work through and modify his difficulties. If work stopped with identifying problematic patterns of relating, and tracing these problems back to formative experiences, BK would have left treatment with more understanding and a greater continuity to his sense of self; these are worthy gains frequently undervalued in modern therapy circles. Such gains, however, often convert to more overt manifestations of patient change only in the distant future and with some patients are never converted.

To more effectively facilitate emotional growth, the therapeutic relationship is used not only to identify and understand conflicted interpersonal styles; it is used as a catalyst for change. The therapist cannot force change. Growth occurs at its own pace and in its own time. One can water and fertilize a flower all one wants, and it will still bloom at its own pace (or be destroyed by its tending). However, effective watering, fertilizing, and the pulling of weeds (i.e., resistances to its growth) may allow a flower to mature at its optimal pace. The present, here-and-now therapy relationship is used for this purpose. The therapist actively fosters an environment and atmosphere that supports the patient's exploration of patterns of living and responses to others. In addition, the therapist continually works with the patient to modify and master these problematic reactions within the patient–therapist relationship, always with the goal of developing greater flexibility, collaboration, and realistic concern for each other in the relationship. In the above example with the patient BK, this was accomplished by helping BK explore his fears regarding being inadequate and failing at therapy, conveying empathy and concern for BK's dilemma, and gradually encouraging BK to confront these issues. The therapist provided patient, firm encouragement, steering a careful course between being intimidated by BK's defensive anger and responding to BK's dependency needs by directively parenting him.

The method we suggest to deal with transference reactions is perhaps familiar to many dynamically oriented therapists. Ferenczi (1921) noted long ago that most innovations in analytic technique are not new and are already part of the practitioner's repertoire. The difference is one of emphasis and attention. In an effort to increase the effectiveness and brevity of their treatment, therapists have increasingly emphasized the importance of active and intensive use of transference reactions as a means of facilitating insight and emotional growth. The active, persistent focus on the patient–therapist interaction allows a more rapid identification and working through of the patient's problems in living than does a more traditional stance. More rapid identification of issues and demonstration of how these emotional conflicts manifest themselves within the therapy allow the working through process to begin earlier. This crucial process of unlearning and relearning through repetitively experiencing and studying one's problems from different angles and perspectives is facilitated by the therapist's more active involvement in the interpretation of the transference component of the therapeutic interaction.

AVOIDANCE OF THE TRANSFERENCE NEUROSIS

Malan (1963) contended that one of the most important length-ening factors in psychoanalytic treatment was the analyst's need to develop and resolve a transference neurosis. The transference neu-rosis is the gradual transfer of unresolved intrapsychic conflicts onto the therapist–patient relationship by a patient with a relatively sound ego structure, a cohesive sense of self-identity, and firmly established boundaries between self and others. Short-term psycho-dynamic psychotherapy actively avoids the development of a trans-ference neurosis, as well as other complex and involved trans-ference reactions. Brief therapy involves: (1) rapid establishment of a patient–therapist collaboration, (2) intense, focused work on a carefully delineated and identified problem area, (3) careful, inter-pretive attention to the manifestations of this problem theme in the patient–therapist relationship, and (4) a productive and man-ageable termination. Development of an intensely involved and de-pendent relationship with the therapist impedes the treatment process.

Transference Neurosis Defined

A transference neurosis may be defined as the transfer onto the therapist of the attitudes and feelings the patient originally devel-oped toward early parental figures. The therapist becomes the person through whom the patient reexperiences the intrapsychic conflicts originally developed toward early caretakers. These intrapsychic conflicts represent unresolved libidinal and aggressive feelings that, although relegated to the unconscious, still affect be-havior. Freud (1912) noted that as these repressed, conflicted feel-ings resurface toward the person of the therapist, they may be identified, worked through, and resolved.

The intense, highly dependent involvement that characterizes the transference neurosis provides a forum for the analytic patient to relive infantile conflict and develop increasing maturity. A transference neurosis offers an opportunity to take a look at intrapsychic conflict within the confines of a safe, stable relationship. The safety engendered by a transference neurosis stems from the fact that it is partial imitation of past important relationships. These past relationships, although conflictual, contain strong elements of security and care. The development of the transference neurosis may serve as a safety net for the patient in analysis. Through the establishment of a strong, stable, albeit conflictual, relationship with the therapist, the patient is able to brave the danger and uncertainty of therapeutic examination. The establishment of a transference neurosis may thus offer the patient the security to face his/her problems in living. Long-term reconstructive therapies have as their most complex goal the working through of such involved transference attachments.

The transference neurosis differs from a transference reaction in that it is more intense, pervasive, and organized. It is a relatively stable mode of perceiving the therapist that is clung to by the patient in a tenacious fashion. The transference neurosis has been conceptualized as a specific clinical entity limited to the psychoanalytic therapeutic relationship, whereas transference occurs to some degree in all relationships (Palino 1981). The line of demarcation between transference and transference neurosis is not clear cut. For practical purposes, they differ in terms of degree.

Complications of the Transference Neurosis

In short-term psychodynamic psychotherapy, transference reactions of moderate intensity are profitably utilized to bring the patient's neurotic patterns into the open where they can be examined. There is universal agreement, however, that a full-blown transference neurosis should and can be avoided (Davanloo 1980, Malan 1963, Sifneos 1972). A transference neurosis presents a number of complications for treatment:

1. A transference neurosis affects the patient's reality testing and temporarily disturbs the therapeutic alliance. The development of a transference neurosis involves regression to a more infantile (immature) mode of perceiving and relating to the therapist. The transfer of infantile conflicts onto the therapist affects the patient's view of therapy. In order to help the patient develop self-understanding and consider new behavior in as rapid a manner as possible, the therapist must work in cooperation with the patient's ego. As soon as the patient's neurosis affects the patient's relationship to the therapist, the patient's judgment becomes temporarily impaired, and this cooperation becomes much more difficult (Alexander and French 1946).

2. The procedures of short-term psychodynamic psychotherapy do not lend themselves to effective resolution of a transference neurosis. With the establishment of a transference neurosis, the patient develops a preoccupation with therapy and the therapist. The therapist becomes one of the most important people in the patient's life. The patient's everyday thoughts and feelings are increasingly focused on the therapy. Energy is withdrawn from everyday life situations and invested into the therapy and therapist. The resolution of such an attachment requires an intensive involvement in treatment over a relatively long period of time. In a once-a-week, face-to-face interview of brief duration, the therapist does not have access to all the patient's unconscious fantasies and cannot analyze the transference neurosis as one does in analysis; thus the therapy may end in an impasse (Sifneos 1972).

3. A transference neurosis may lead to complications at termination. The transference neurosis (or any highly dependent transference relationship) is not easily given up by the patient at termination unless sufficient time has been spent helping the patient redirect one's attachments and psychic energy. The therapist does not have sufficient time to effectively analyze and work through a transference neurosis. The under-

standing, working through, and resolution of complex transference reactions is more suited for long-term treatment.

Symbiotic Transferences

The therapist attempts to forestall the development of an attachment to the therapist that does not avail itself to effective working
through in a brief, face-to-face, weekly treatment. In addition to
avoiding the transference neurosis, the therapist also attempts to
avoid the development of a symbiotic transference (Davanloo
1978). Symbiotic transference is a term used to describe a variety of
transference reactions that are experienced by patients presenting
preoedipal psychopathology. Such a transference attachment is resistant to resolution within the confines of brief therapy. Patients
highly susceptible to the development of symbiotic transferences include those presenting a borderline personality organization, as
well as severe passive-dependent and obsessional character types.

A symbiotic transference involves a complex, dependent, and
highly ambivalent attachment to the therapist. Patients developing
such attachments become intensely involved with the therapist in a
very rapid manner. Their reactions to the therapist are seen to be the
result of premature activation in the transference of very early
conflict-laden object relationships in contrast to the more gradual
unfolding of internalized object relationships as therapeutic regression occurs in the neurotic patient (Kernberg 1975). Such relationships are often characterized by attempts to control the therapist
and to gain literal gratification of wishes. Although ambivalent
about the therapist, the patient becomes highly dependent on treatment for maintenance of everyday functioning. Symbiotic transference reactions are most characteristic in patients who have ineffect-
ively resolved early developmental tasks involving self-regulation
of self-esteem, basic trust, separation, and autonomy. Although
such patients may benefit from short-term psychodynamic psychotherapy if a workable focus of treatment is carefully selected and

maintained, development of an overly dependent attachment will compromise the work.

How to Avoid Complex Transferences

To avoid the development of complex transference attachments, attention to the following may be helpful:

Initial Patient Selection

Patients chosen for short-term therapy must have an object-relation capacity that does not necessitate the therapist becoming all-important (Winston and Trujillo 1985). Individuals presenting evidence for developing highly conflictual, chaotic, and clinging attachments to the therapist (e.g., the borderline personality disorder) should be identified during assessment. Such patients tend to rely heavily on the defenses of projection and splitting, and they protect their security by rigid application of past coping strategies. These individuals are not appropriate for short-term psychodynamic psychotherapy and should be offered other modes of treatment.

Careful selection is highly important in avoiding development of attachments in therapy not amenable to short-term therapy. The type of transference developed by a patient, however, can never be forecasted in a completely accurate fashion. A patient may be initially assessed as possessing good treatment potential, but as defenses are increasingly challenged during treatment, the patient may cease partnership in the therapeutic venture and respond in an increasingly regressed (e.g., dependent or paranoid) manner. Such behavior is generally evidence that the patient is suffering from a preneurotic disturbance and is experiencing weakening of ego functioning due to treatment stress. The therapist must be continually vigilant in identifying such reactions, for a reevaluation of the treatment strategy may be indicated.

Decrease of Ambiguity of Treatment

Malan (1963) believed that a transference neurosis may be avoided by decreasing the sense of ambiguity and timelessness of the treatment. The patient must realize that the therapeutic contact is to be brief. From the onset of treatment, its ending is in sight. This clarity as to the brevity of treatment enables the patient to develop various coping and distancing mechanisms that help prevent a dependent regression (Winston and Trujillo 1985). In addition to a frank discussion of the time constraints of therapy, the therapist's ability to keep therapeutic attention focused on the agreed-upon treatment focus also forestalls development of the transference neurosis.

The ability of the patient to collaborate as a more or less equal partner in the treatment decreases the potential of a transference neurosis. Discussion of the brevity of treatment and the collaborative development and maintenance of a therapeutic focus provide the patient with orientation and direction. This serves to decrease the patient's sense of mystery regarding therapy. Alexander and French (1946) contended that the aura of mystery surrounding the therapeutic situation makes reality testing more difficult for the patient. If the patient does not have any idea of what to expect from the therapy and the therapist, it becomes easier to project onto the therapist and to develop fantasies, thus hindering the rapid establishment of an effective therapeutic alliance.

Early Interpretation of Transference Reactions

Complex, involved transference developments may be avoided by dealing with manifestations of transference as rapidly as possible (Sifneos 1972). During the course of psychotherapy most patients will develop strong transference reactions to the therapist. With patients who are optimal candidates for short-term therapy (i.e., moderate psychological disturbance, oedipally oriented problems), such transference reactions develop gradually over time. Sifneos encouraged the therapist to take advantage of the time lag in the development of an involved transference attachment in fairly healthy patients. Rather than reach the impasse of the transference neurosis, therapeutic work is initiated as soon as opportunity presents itself. The best way to do this is to respond to and work with transference feelings from their earliest manifestations in the therapy. Transference feelings are encouraged and discussed as soon as they are recognized.

Many therapists avoid early work with transference reactions in order to avoid alienating the patient. Such strategy may be sound with certain severely disturbed patients with strong avoidant tendencies. These patients must be met at the level of interaction they feel least threatened by. For instance, premature interpretation of a highly dependent patient's wish for an all-powerful parent figure may be felt as a painful assault to present coping strategies. The result may be a significant decrease in rapport and therapeutic alliance. In short-term psychodynamic psychotherapy, however, the patients are assessed to be capable of examining their reactions to others, tracing their development — both genetically and in the here and now — and gaining an understanding of how conflicting thoughts and feelings lead to their problems in living. Understanding reactions to the therapist is a productive place to begin.

The therapist is encouraged to avoid complex transference attachments by early and active intervention around the patient's transference reactions. Those transference manifestations that express patient wishes for gratification and dependency are to be quickly interpreted to prevent fixed fantasies and unreal expectations regarding the therapist (Winston and Trujillo 1985). The therapist works with transference as it presents in treatment and does not allow it to go unacknowledged and unquestioned. Lack of examination of the therapeutic relationship and its transference components encourages the transference neurosis to develop and deepen along lines predetermined by unresolved needs and conflict. The therapist becomes the figure around which the patient's intrapsychic drama is replayed. To an extent this is essential in that therapy is an arena for the examination of maladaptive coping mechanisms directed toward the therapist. However, in short-term therapy, the therapist attempts to work with transference patterns rather than a highly organized set of fantasies and attitudes displaced onto the therapist (transference neurosis). That is, the therapist works with the patient reactions to the therapist that have transferential components; the therapist avoids creating a situation where the patient, in a state of therapeutic regression, relives infantile conflicts around the person of the therapist.

The focus of short-term psychodynamic psychotherapy is on present problematic means of interacting that are transferentially based rather than on the intensive analysis of early infantile libidinal and aggressive wishes. The therapy relationship is used to identify, clarify, and work on specific problems rather than to mine the patient's unconscious of the gold of the infantile past. To accomplish this task, transference feelings are focused upon as soon as they occur.

Avoidance of Deep-Seated Characterological Issues

The short-term therapy practitioner is encouraged to avoid focusing on issues that cannot be adequately dealt with in a brief treatment, including material pertaining to preoedipal, characterological problems (Sifneos 1972). Such problems may include those related to early oral deprivation (e.g., severe dependency problems, addictive disorders, severe depression, alcoholism, eating disorders), severe compulsive symptoms, complex masochistic tendencies, gender identity issues, and symptoms related to the structural integrity of the ego (e.g., impulsivity, inability to tolerate frustration and anxiety, and ability to regulate self-esteem).

Focus on deep-seated characterological issues increases the potential that the treatment will be prolonged as the therapist and patient attempt to grapple with deeply ingrained problems in the patient's personality structure. Attention on such issues increases the probability of involving the therapist in an ever deepening transference attachment that will require an extended period of time for the patient to resolve and relinquish.

Patients may attempt to focus therapy attention on deep-seated character issues and resultant symptoms for a variety of reasons. It may be a reaction to a genuine need in a patient suffering the consequences of a failure to master early (preoedipal) developmental tasks. The patient, for instance, may have to struggle with difficulties in trusting and forming relationships before being able to work on anything else. Seeing such a patient in short-term therapy is generally inappropriate and is often the result of inadequate assessment. The desire to work on deeply ingrained character problems may also be seen in patients who, while possessing certain severe ego weaknesses, present numerous evidences of ego strength and ability to work in dynamic treatment. Malan (1963) found that certain patients presenting moderate to severe psychopathology may benefit from this treatment if they possess a certain complex of traits including high motivation, psychological mindedness, and the ability to focus on a single circumscribed issue. A case is presented for illustration.

> A patient (MB) presented for assessment with characteristics indicative of a higher-level (Masterson 1981) borderline personality disorder including highly conflicted interpersonal relationships, depressive loneliness, defensive clinging, multiple obsessions, and phobias. MB's present issue of concern was her relationship with her boyfriend. She felt stifled and constricted in this relationship, yet desperately alone (empty) without it. Such feelings led to a pattern of: intimacy — fear of losing herself — withdrawal (usually through provoking a fight) — loneliness — movement back towards boyfriend. MB's past therapies identified issues of dependency and separation-individuation and were supportive in nature. MB possessed a high degree of motivation to work on herself (her career aspirations were in jeopardy), was highly intelligent, and was often capable of introspection. MB was seen by the therapist as having the potential for making treatment a needed aspect of her everyday life, thus gratifying her dependency needs and separation fears. MB was offered short-term psychodynamic psychotherapy with the agreement that work would focus on her underlying fears of growing up, taking re-

sponsibility, and making decisions, and how she used her boyfriend to shield her from these tasks.

Therapeutic focus on these issues — while avoiding extensive discussion of other problems (e.g., her obsessions) — allowed her to productively examine these problems, and she began to see how they were played in her life and how they caused her distress. Treatment proceeded well, with MB developing the ability to separate from her boyfriend and increasingly cope with the decisions and tasks of her college career without relying unduly on others. Upon termination, MB's underlying character structure remained similar to what it had been before therapy. However, she had solved the problem she presented with and had increased her overall coping strategies. This brief treatment experience also modified her self-image as an inadequate little girl who needed constant therapeutic supervision (parenting) to function. MB had sufficient ego resources to put a brief treatment experience to good use. Her strong ego integrative abilities allowed her to take what she learned in therapy and put it to use in her outside life. The therapist facilitated this successful experience with a rather disturbed patient by keeping the treatment focused on the agreed-upon problem (e.g., relationship with boyfriend, taking responsibility for herself), with other issues in her life being avoided (e.g., multiple obsessions and phobias).

Attempts by a patient to discuss issues not amenable to brief treatment are often a defense against work on issues involving the agreed-upon treatment focus. The patient may avoid oedipal problems by expressing strong concern about other difficulties. For example, rather than discuss one's fear, resentment, and competitive feelings towards authorities (a problem being currently experienced in the therapy), a patient may wish to focus on alcohol abuse or perhaps a disturbing dream. Discussing one's dream, although perhaps significant, allows an avoidance of the anxiety concerning the reenactment of authority conflict with the therapist.

When the patient diverts the treatment focus and begins a discussion of complex, ingrained character issues, the therapist's tasks include: (1) attempting to understand the shift of focus in its therapy context, (2) pointing this shift out and encouraging the patient to explore it with the therapist, (3) establishing its purpose, and (4) reestablishing the treatment focus. Although care must be taken to help the patient understand resistive behavior, the agreed-upon focus needs to be reestablished.

Alexander and French (1946) noted that patients often seek to construct a safe, comfortable relationship with the therapist in the process of avoiding work on the anxiety-inducing issues that brought them into treatment. Such patients increasingly assume a passive, dependent stance towards the therapist with therapy becoming a permanent fixture in the patient's intrapsychic structure. There may be a repetitive discussion of issues that are of seeming importance but no conversion of this discussion into behavioral change. The patient becomes content to visit the therapist each week, with internal and external change being sacrificed in favor of sustaining the security involved in being in treatment. The therapy relationship becomes a source of various complex transference gratifications that are difficult to identify, yet difficult to give up.

Davanloo (1978) cautioned against development of such complex transference relationships, especially with passive-dependent and severe obsessional character types. He recommended that patient attempts to develop a passive-receptive, dependent orientation to treatment be counteracted by means of frequent confrontations. The patient is not allowed to settle into a comfortable, unexamined interaction with the therapist. Therapeutic attention is given to the patient's problem of adjusting to one's present reality and to one's relationships with others, including the therapist. The therapist focuses the patient on the agreed-upon problem and its manifestation in therapy. Attempts by the patient to repetitively discuss issues that sidetrack this endeavor are patiently but repeatedly confronted.

The therapist also counteracts the tendency to sink into a comfortable, yet unproductive therapy attachment by constantly working with the patient to apply what has been learned during therapy to current life situations. For example, a patient's ability to express angry feelings, examined and modified in the therapy relationship, must now be applied to the patient's everday life. The patient is continually pressed to take an active, progressive approach to converting treatment efforts into outside change. Such work creates a productive, problem-solving orientation that encourages focused work on the patient's concerns and discourages the regressive development of transference neurosis.

In short-term psychodynamic psychotherapy, transference relationships are kept at manageable limits within the confines of brief treatment. The selection process is used to eliminate those patients likely to develop intense, complex transferences. Once in therapy, highly dependent relationships are avoided through: (1) initial discussion of time limits and treatment focus, (2) encouragement of the patient to be collaborator, and not someone operated on, (3) active, early interpretation of and work on transference feelings, (4) avoidance of issues not manageable within a brief treatment format, (5) confrontation of patient attempts to establish a nonproductive, passive-receptive role and to avoid anxiety regarding the treatment focus.

PROBLEM SOLVING IN
SHORT-TERM PSYCHODYNAMIC PSYCHOTHERAPY

Short-term psychodynamic psychotherapy incorporates a teaching model demonstrating the exploration and investigation of various thoughts, feelings, and actions to increase the clarity of interpersonal and intrapsychic functioning. By focusing on a focal problem and its manifestations within the therapy, the therapist imparts to the patient the experience of examining oneself and one's reactions in a manner that reduces conflict and facilitates more adaptive behavior. Patient participation in this therapy experience sets the stage for the patient to apply the therapeutic method to future problems that may occur in life. Thus, the therapist has two goals in treatment: (1) resolving the agreed-upon focal issue and (2) teaching a patient a means of self-examination to be used in later situations.

The problem-solving component of short-term therapy was

particularly emphasized by Sifneos. In a paper written with M. McGuire (1970), Sifneos noted that brief treatment may be effectively used to teach the patient new ways of solving emotional problems, the learning of problem-solving techniques being an integral part of treatment. Patients learn to conceptualize their symptoms or behavior as problems to be solved. Of key importance is the premise that problematic behavior or symptoms are more than simply reactions to some external or unknown stimulus. Patients are taught to identify the signs and symptoms of intrapsychic conflict, as well as methods they can use to alter the existing balance of intrapsychic forces perpetuating these conflicts. Sifneos (1972) felt that the problem-solving, cognitive component of treatment was as important as the affective element; for that reason he placed emphasis on assessing the intellectual capacities of the patient. Sifneos (1979) later stated that the most significant long-term follow-up result of his method was that patients were able to learn a method of problem solving they could apply to future conflicts.

Learning about Dynamic Principles

The short-term psychodynamic psychotherapy practitioner educates the patient about the principles governing intrapsychic functioning. Patients are helped to develop an understanding of the principles of psychodynamics and how these principles apply to their individual situation. The therapist helps patients learn about their psychic functioning by paying close attention to its unfolding in the therapeutic situation. To illustrate:

> A patient (TG), after six sessions of therapy, was able to confront and deal with a disturbing and painful issue regarding her life situation; the patient felt a great sense of relief. This occurred within the context of intimate expression by TG and empathic understanding by the therapist. Following this moving session, TG became increasingly distant and uninvolved. This change of attitude was explored. Careful study of her feelings regarding therapy and the therapist, as well as other times in her life in which a similar pattern of behavior

occurred, suggested that TG's distancing behavior had a defensive aspect. Upon discussing the session in question, TG was increasingly able to remember feeling comfortable and secure with the therapist, as well as a fleeting wish for more closeness and intimacy. TG also noted that these latter feelings were anxiety provoking and quickly avoided. Upon reconstruction, it was hypothesized that the warmth and understanding of her therapist in that difficult sixth session had stimulated further wishes for intimacy and closeness that, due to past learning, evoked anxiety, resulting in distancing, withdrawing defenses. Through careful attention to the therapy process, the therapist was able to help TG learn how certain wishes and feelings (i.e., the desire for intimacy) may cause anxiety, which leads to constructing defenses (i.e., distancing, withdrawal behavior) against the recognition and expression of such feelings. This was demonstrated to TG as it occurred within the session.

In similar situations in the future, TG may use her therapeutic experience to productively examine if certain feelings and interactions are being avoided due to anxiety. The key is not to teach the terms (e.g., ego defense mechanisms) but to help the patient realize and appreciate the often subtle relationship between various thoughts, feelings, and subsequent behaviors and reactions. By helping TG learn how her psyche functions and how conflict develops and expresses itself, the therapist offered TG a tool to be used in resolution of future conflictual situations.

Becoming One's Own Therapist

The ultimate accomplishment of short-term therapy may not be total resolution of conflict as much as providing a patient with the tools to continue self-investigation. The therapist attempts to prepare the patient to become one's own therapist. Freud (1937) noted that therapy is never over. Throughout a person's entire life, one must engage in investigation and resolution of psychic and interpersonal conflict as it develops. The therapist, by explicitly teaching how to explore reactions/behaviors, gives the patient a tool to be used in future situations. Such work may be extremely helpful provided the patient is motivated towards further emotional growth and is not suffering from rigid and severe characterological and/or environmental constraints.

Handling Resistance

A significant value of short-term psychodynamic psychotherapy consists of the acquisition of a method of self-examination that may be used to resolve future problems. The therapist actively helps the patient learn to solve emotional conflict and promote further growth. Open-ended dynamic treatment also emphasizes the importance of helping the patient learn a method to examine and resolve emotional conflict. What is perhaps different is the manner in which resistance to the therapeutic process is handled.

The goal in open-ended therapy is the gradual development of understanding without undue interpretation by the therapist. The therapist constantly facilitates the patient's own interpretative efforts as a means of fostering patient autonomy and self-reliance. The patient is often allowed to sit with resistance until it can be "felt in one's bones" and the decision made to move beyond it. The patient is allowed the experience of struggling with oneself and one's defensive process at a pace determined largely by the patient. Patient resistance to change is often dealt with by the process of staying with the patient's repetitive discussion of problems until the patient has become thoroughly acquainted, perhaps even bored, with discussing the issues. The patient's problems in living, intrapsychic conflicts, and interpersonal conflicts, are repetitively experienced, confronted, and discussed until the patient progressively learns to master conflictual situations and the anxiety elicited by them. As anxiety is reduced, the patient is gradually able to leave behind old patterns. The patient becomes increasingly adventurous in trying out new behavior, perhaps initially with the therapist. This gradual and disciplined method of dealing with resistance to change has much to offer those patients who experience unproductive levels of anxiety during the course of therapy. Such patients tend to experience activity by the therapist as a painful intrusion upon a weak ego.

Short-term therapy is appropriate for patients who possess a greater degree of ego strength and integrative capacity. Such patients are able to work productively with a greater level of therapeutic tension and are able to put insights into more rapid use. Interpretation is offered early in treatment, not only to increase the patient's understanding, but to educate the patient in a method to be used in thinking about oneself and one's personal functioning. The therapist actively plans the treatment process, confronts resistances to therapeutic work, and offers a method to be used in exploring conflict.

Learning in Short-Term Psychodynamic Psychotherapy

The experience of working with the therapist towards resolution of the focal problem provides a significant learning experience for the patient. The successful patient gains an appreciation for the complex nature of the human psyche and psychic conflict (Schafer 1973). Through the experience of examining the focal problem, the patient develops a more comprehensive idea of the scope, multiplicity, and complexity of intrapsychic functioning. It is through this realization of the complexity of functioning that the patient is able to increasingly learn what one does to bring about and continue to support one's problems in living. Schafer (1973) believed that, especially in the examination of problems in the therapeutic relationship, the patient is able to develop an appreciation of the extent to which the patient is actively involved in bringing about the difficulties that were initially experienced as happening to him/her. Although such work does not make the problems go away, it does offer the patient a new way of looking at oneself and one's interactions, as well as the possibility of new solutions to old problems. To illustrate:

> RL was working on the focal problem of discomfort and fear of other males, particularly those whom he perceived as more physically powerful. This symptom was very constricting of RL's social and professional life, resulting in RL attempting various activities to protect himself from the perceived aggression of others (e.g., learning self-defense, avoiding social gatherings). Therapeutic efforts focused on helping RL look at what part he played in creating the situations where he felt anxious and fearful. The therapy relationship was used to examine his process of interacting, in particular the assumptions he made regarding how the therapist was feeling. The malevolence RL saw in others was gradually understood as his own disowned hostile feelings. The ability to take a look at his projective defenses in relation to the therapist facilitated his realization of how he created his own discomfort with others through projecting his consciously rejected aggressive feelings. Learning about his tendency to project enabled RL to approach previously feared situations with considerably less discomfort. Where he was previously held hostage by the dangerous intentions of other men, RL was now in a position to investigate how he held himself hostage by failure to acknowledge his own wishes and fears regarding male figures. The remainder of treatment focused on this theme, with RL developing considerable symptom relief and an increased understanding of and appreciation for how the conflict-laden relationship with his father affected his other relationships. This central conflict regarding RL's relationship with his father was not totally resolved in therapy. However, RL learned how to examine his reactions to people and to attempt to understand them in terms of his life experience. The patient is thus in the position to mediate how this problem affects future relationships, as well as using this method of self-examination to explore other issues in his life.

This ability to learn how one is involved in creating one's own problems, and the ability to begin accepting responsibility for these problems, are both threatening and liberating. Such realization requires relinquishing externalizing and projecting defenses and whatever self-esteem maintenance they offer. To honestly look at oneself can be painful. To accept responsibility also places one in a position of having ultimate control over personal destiny. This is a double-edged sword. It may be frightening because it requires giving up the fantasy of an omnipotent parent who will ultimately rescue and gratify. Conversely, it may also be liberating. The realization that one is not a passive victim of life circumstances offers the patient opportunity for change and further growth.

Identification with the Therapist

A crucial aspect of therapy has been accomplished when the patient begins to identify with the therapist, including the therapist's method of examining emotional conflict and the therapist's technique for analyzing information. Such identification helps the patient realize that old ways of handling problems are outmoded and that new patterns of behavior offer better opportunities for success (Sifneos 1972).

The therapist attempts to facilitate this identification by explicitly explaining the therapeutic process and what the patient must do to receive help. Providing some initial explanation of therapy helps take some of the mystery out of the therapy process. Alexander and French (1946) taught that such work increased the patient's conscious cooperation and strengthened the therapeutic alliance. The patient is taught to use psychotherapy to explore, understand, and resolve conflict. The therapist stresses certain guiding principles for treatment, such as the need to be open and honest, the importance of noting and sharing reactions to the therapy and therapist, awareness of when feelings are being avoided, and the need to grapple with the anxieties associated with taking an honest look at one's life and assuming responsibility for one's situation. The patient is educated as to the ground rules of therapy and to responsibilities within these ground rules.

It may sound untraditional, even manipulative, to attempt to facilitate the patient's identification with the therapist as a means of dealing with emotional conflict. After all, autonomy and freedom in making one's own decisions are essential goals of the analytic method. Marmor (1974) argued that although the therapist generally does not explicitly hold oneself forth as a model for the patient, this does not negate the fact that, in the presence of a positive transference, the therapist invariably tends to become a model the patient consciously or unconsciously attempts to emulate. As the therapist's implicit values and behavioral characteristics are gradually communicated, overtly or subtly, to the patient, they become part of a learning process in which the patient is involved. Throughout therapy the therapist serves as a model whose feelings, attitudes, values, and behavior (to the extent it can be observed in the therapeutic situation) the patient learns to accept, imitate, emulate, internalize, and respect. The therapist capitalizes on the patient's responsiveness to the therapist's attitudes in order to convey to the patient a method of dealing with intrapsychic and interpersonal conflict.

Depth of Change in Short-Term Psychodynamic Psychotherapy

Short-term psychodynamic psychotherapy attempts resolution of the agreed-upon focal issue. The prime arena of change is often the manifestations of this issue in the patient–therapist interaction. It is for this reason that treatment success is facilitated by selecting patients who present problems having a strong interpersonal flavor that can be expressed within the therapeutic relationship. Such difficulties include conflicts over competition and achievement, rivalry, jealousy, difficulties with authority figures, and inhibition, anxiety, and guilt in heterosexual relationships (not to be confused with gender identity, which is primarily a preoedipal issue).

What type and depth of change can be expected in short-term therapy? Will a patient struggling with an emotional conflict be completely free of this conflict after therapy? Suppose a patient has a conflict with those perceived as authority figures, feeling threatened when interacting with perceived authority figures. The reactions of authority figures to the patient are seen as commands and challenges to the patient's autonomy. Such feelings constrict the patient's ability to function optimally at work and to relate to peers. Will short-term psychodynamic psychotherapy resolve this patient's problem? The answer to this question is mixed. The recalcitrance of the patient's character defenses often combines with the time constraints of treatment to make it difficult for the therapist to facilitate an in-depth realignment of patient defenses. Therapy is unable to solve all the patient's problems and all aspects of a particular problem. The therapist is encouraged to reflect upon Malan's caution (1963) regarding the dangers of therapeutic perfectionism. An attempt to engage in a complete remodeling of the patient's character style is a difficult task, completion of which is questionable in any therapy. An attempt to do so most often results in an experience of failure for both patient and therapist.

Limited goals are an important aspect of short-term therapy. The results of treatment often include: (1) increased self-understanding, (2) improvement in self-esteem as a result of increased mastery, (3) resolution of the crisis that was instrumental in bringing the patient to therapy, (4) more flexible coping strategies, and (5) moderate resolution of focal problems (or at least a significant increase in the patient's ability to cope with this problem in life situations). The patient with authority conflicts may be reasonably expected to (1) gain understanding of conflicted feelings, (2) learn how underlying fears and anxieties may result in problematic interactions, (3) learn how one is involved in setting up or creating one's distress, and (4) gain some control over the expression of this conflict in personal and professional life. Such work allows for an increased sense of mastering one's own fate and, with this, an increase in self-esteem.

Short-term therapy, however, does not afford complete resolution of an emotional conflict. A more complete resolution of emotional conflict requires an extensive, as well as intensive, working through period. Short-term therapy provides an intense experience in which insight is conveyed. The patient is taught to observe one's reactions and develop as clear and as emotionally meaningful a picture of one's conflict as possible. Such work opens up the opportunity for in-depth character change. Character change, however, is a slow process; defensive strategies are laid down bit by bit, and they are changed in the same process. The working through period, in which the patient is repetitively alerted to the tenacity of one's maladaptive coping strategies, can only be *initiated* in short-term psychodynamic psychotherapy. An intensive therapeutic experience of learning how to look at oneself and one's problems through use of the focal problem and its manifestations in therapy sets the stage for a longer-term working through period that follows therapy and continues throughout life.

Upon completing brief therapy, some patients may opt for ongoing treatment as the opportunity presents itself. Experiencing some good therapy often leads to the wish for more. Others may avoid continuing to work their conflictual issues; resistance to ongoing examination of one's life is a potent force and must be recognized. As part of preparing patients to deal with their own conflicts as they develop in future situations, it is helpful to point out and discuss the tendency of patients to avoid working on themselves after their therapy is over.

The Ongoing Nature of Change

The benefits ultimately derived from short-term psychodynamic psychotherapy relate to the ongoing nature of growth and change. In discussing traditional theoretical objections to brief treatment, Marmor (1979) noted what he termed a closed-system model of psychiatric thought. The closed model posited that unless all aspects of the patient's libidinal fixations and unconscious conflicts were worked through, they would sooner or later lead to a recurrence of symptomatology. Marmor contrasted this model with an open-system model, which posits that enabling a patient to function more effectively in a particular area of life leads to an increase in a sense of mastery, self-esteem, and positive feedback from the patient's environment. Such feedback leads to further increases in self-esteem and mastery, resulting in still further impetus for growth and maturation. Change may continue to occur within the internal psychodynamic system of the individual without having to completely resolve all emotional conflict. Similarly, Wolberg (1965), in discussing the possibility of reconstructive change in brief treatment, noted that once a patient has gained an awareness of the relation of even a few facets of one's current personality distortions to past conditionings, and has then challenged some defenses, a chain reaction develops, slowly influencing personality in depth.

An emotional conflict does not have to be completely resolved during treatment for significant change to occur in a patient's life. A degree of successful mastery and resolution often stimulates further constructive efforts towards growth that continue to occur outside the auspices of the therapist's office. To continue work outside of therapy, however, the patient will need something to work with. In short-term psychodynamic psychotherapy, the therapist attempts to teach the patient a method of confronting and dealing with emotional conflict rather than attempting to root it all out. The therapist maintains confidence that while therapy of brief duration may not resolve all problems for a person, it furnishes the patient with an experience to be used for further problem resolution in the future.

Successful short-term therapy treatment enables the patient to experience a constructive mastery (however partial) of a particular conflict. Through this effort an attempt is made to help the patient learn how to identify and work on conflict for oneself. The patient is involved in a brief but intense experience of working on a problem in hopes of engendering a new way of looking at oneself and coping with conflict. Patient motivation, intelligence, and psychological mindedness pay great dividends in generalizing what is learned in treatment to future coping attempts. It is for this reason that such qualities are important as selection criteria.

THE IMPORTANCE OF CLINICAL EXPERIENCE

There is no substitute for clinical experience and acumen when employing short-term psychodynamic psychotherapy. This therapy is dependent on information and understanding gained from long-term psychodynamic psychotherapy. The therapist who is intent on using short-term therapy is encouraged to gain experience with the psychotherapy process from a long-term, open-ended perspective. With a few technical modifications (e.g., establishment and maintenance of treatment focus), brief therapy is an intensified form of long-term dynamic treatment conducted with carefully screened patients. Experiences with the various phenomena associated with long-term therapy allow the therapist to rapidly establish an optimal therapeutic environment and to effectively gauge interventions.

The interventions of the effective short-term therapy practitioner are characterized by an ability to quickly size up the patient's situation and willingness to intervene rapidly. The therapist relies on psychodynamic acumen developed through study and experience to quickly decide those topics most appropriate for exploration. The therapist avoids involvement with peripheral issues and concerns in order to identify basic dynamic patterns. Such work requires the therapist to use past experiences with similar patients and treatments. To illustrate:

> A female patient (MZ) presented with depressive concerns regarding the recent breakup with her fiancé. Discussion of her situation yielded a pattern of quick and intense involvement with men until a point of intimacy and commitment was reached. At this point, MZ found herself losing interest in the relationship. She felt guilty for hurting these men and very distressed that this pattern continually repeated itself in her life. MZ presented strong evidence of ego

strength in many areas of her life, including career. Her relationships with men, particularly when they involved sex, intimacy and commitment, were seen as her major problem area. The therapist's experience with patients presenting similar problem histories allowed him to rapidly focus in on the oedipal nature of this difficulty. A distant, competitive relationship with her mother was quickly identified. An ambivalent relationship with her father, in which the patient experienced both resentment and affection, was also clarified. Exploration of these relationships allowed the patient to rapidly identify the onset of conflictual patterns of reacting and to begin a profitable self-examination.

Effective therapy requires trust in one's theory and therapeutic approach. This is invaluable in confronting patient resistance. The therapist must have enough confidence in the therapeutic method to help the patient stay with the therapeutic task even when it is anxiety-provoking and seemingly unproductive. This comes with experience. Confidence and trust in one's approach occurs only after the therapist has repetitively experienced rise of patient resistance, has helped the patient accept and work through this resistance, and has come to see the patient behave in a more productive and mature manner.

The therapist works with patient resistance in a manner that respects the patient's need for security and at the same time attempts to convey insight and understanding as rapidly as possible. The therapist flexibly flows from one point to another on the triangle of insight. If interpreting the here-and-now relationship between patient and therapist is too threatening, the therapist may clarify a conflicted reaction pattern using contemporary or past relationships. Different parts of the triangle (patient–therapist, patient–contemporary, patient–past) are more easily examined depending on patient dynamics. The short-term therapy practitioner is flexible in laying the groundwork for the patient's exploration and working through of problem areas.

To work effectively, the therapist must sensitively gauge the depth of interpretations. In his work with brief, dynamic technique, Malan (1963) experimented with the depth of interpretations. A major question was: Should interpretations be made only in terms of current life problems, or should they include the developmental roots of the patient's neurosis as well? Malan noted that one of the possible lengthening factors of therapy was therapist preoccupation with developmentally deeper and deeper feelings. Perhaps, then, it could be argued that one way of shortening therapy would be to keep interpretations superficial. Depth interpretation was additionally feared because it increased treatment duration by fostering regression and deepening patient dependency. In his studies, Malan found these fears to be groundless. Sensitive depth interpretations were a crucial element of his method of brief treatment.

Although there is agreement as to the productivity of depth interpretations, their effective use requires skill and experience. Malan (1963) stressed that it is essential for depth interpretations to focus on the circumscribed area of conflict. The therapist gauges the depth of interpretation according to what the patient is capable of accepting and working with. An interpretation brings to the patient's awareness some aspects of intrapsychic or interpersonal functioning. The therapist helps the person learn about oneself as rapidly as possible without the patient abandoning the collaborative venture due to fear or inability to comprehend the therapist's intervention. An interpretation must be deep enough to create therapeutic tension and uncertainty regarding present coping strategies, yet not too deep to frighten the patient or increase defensiveness. In short-term therapy, the therapist continually works to keep the therapeutic task at an optimal level. Such work requires a strong understanding of the therapeutic process acquired through supervised experience of brief and long-term treatments, thoughtful study of the literature on psychotherapy, personal psychotherapy, and a wide array of personal experiences including involvement in the arts, sports, and academic pursuits.

CHAPTER SEVEN
Termination

Therapists have struggled with termination since Freud introduced hypnosis, talking, and forming relationships as elements of psychological change. In the original case of Anna O (Breuer and Freud 1895), concerns about attachment, dependency, and separation became conflicted issues for both patient and therapist. It was with this patient, treated by Breuer, that Freud identified the transference relationship. This occurred as a result of Freud's observations of the development of a complex dependent attachment between Anna O and Breuer, and of Anna O's phantom pregnancy when informed by Breuer that their relationship must end (Jones 1953). Since that original case, therapists have been concerned about the nature of the dependent attachment that develops during treatment and have sought ways to constructively use and resolve it.

The prototype of termination in psychotherapy is the separation–individuation process. Initially, the child develops a sense of self and self-esteem through the feeding, nurturing, and emotional relationship developed with its mother. The manner in which the child experiences the gradual change and movement from total dependence upon its mother to a sense of autonomy plays an important role in how future change, loss, and endings will be experienced. The therapist–patient relationship, which involves dependency, mutuality, and autonomy, provides a unique arena to reexperience the vicissitudes of the parent–child relationship. In the process of giving up the therapeutic attachment, the patient has an opportunity to confront, explore, and modify reactions to loss, separation, and autonomy. The elaboration and resolution of grief work regarding the loss of present and past objects increases the patient's capacity to invest in new objects.

Management of termination in short-term therapy is of critical importance and may often determine the success of the treatment. The time-limited nature of this treatment offers a ready vehicle that may be used to explore and resolve issues of separation and loss. The techniques used to work with termination issues are similar to those used throughout the treatment. Active confrontation of patient resistance to working through the termination process, examination of feelings elicited by the here-and-now patient–therapist relationship, and the recovery of repressed/suppressed affects related to past separations and loss are of key importance.

UNCOVERING VERSUS SUPPORTIVE PSYCHOTHERAPY

To understand the various means by which termination may be approached, it is helpful to review the distinction between uncovering and supportive psychotherapy. Strategies for managing termination in uncovering and supportive psychotherapy differ. They are determined by the manner in which the working and transference relationships are utilized. The therapeutic relationship may be conceptualized as having a realistic component, which helps form the therapeutic alliance and facilitates the work of therapy, and a transference component, which includes patient distortions and misperceptions of the therapist. These distortions, remnants and derivatives of long-standing attitudes and reactions brought by the patient to the treatment, are stimulated in the relationship with the therapist.

Supportive treatment is provided to patients who have limited ego resources and are unable to observe and deal with the immediate aspects of the treatment relationship. In this treatment the therapist curtails examination and interpretation of complicated transference responses. While the therapist encourages and supports the development of a warm, positive, trusting relationship, the focus of therapeutic attention is on the problems the patient has in situations outside of treatment. The therapist functions as a parent, a role model, a coach, an expert in behavior relations, and a host of other helpful figures. Feelings elicited during termination are dealt with as normal, expectable phenomena. The therapist provides a variety of ways to help the patient separate from treatment, such as reducing frequency of sessions or periodic check-ups. The therapist maintains the stance of a benevolent expert. The patient is helped to disengage from treatment by focusing on the cognitive aspects of the therapy, such as a review of treatment gains and development of future preventative strategies. Patient affect regarding ending, while not avoided, is framed in terms of the naturally occurring sadness to be expected when losing a source of support and gratification. No attempt is made to undo resistances against termination feelings. The emphasis is on a continuing relationship with no effort made to resolve the transference component of their relationship. Rather than focus on the termination of the relationship, the therapist may instead emphasize a continuing interest and availability to the patient (Dewald 1965). The following example illustrates termination in a supportive treatment.

AB was a 27-year-old man who sought therapy for work-related difficulties at the suggestion of a work supervisor who felt AB's job was in jeopardy. AB found himself procrastinating, missing deadlines, and, in general, withdrawing from other staff members. He was depressed and was quite concerned that he would lose his job. AB related an emotionally barren childhood. His parents divorced when he was three. He reported seeing his father only sporadically. He described his mother as an angry, bitter woman who had little nurturance to offer. The therapist felt AB had a schizoid personality structure with minimal ego resources and a tenuous yet somewhat satisfactory adaptation to life demands. AB was highly defensive and firmly entrenched in his mode of dealing with the world. He had never been in treatment before and was pessimistic about its helpfulness.

Treatment focused on modifying his procrastination and withdrawal at work. Minimal attention was given to genetic interpretations or here-and-now examination of how AB's problems were reenacted with the therapist. AB showed little interest in intrapsychic exploration and became noticeably anxious and defensive when he experienced tension in his relationship to the therapist. He maintained that he wanted to "fix" this present problem and get on with his life.

Treatment progressed well, with his efforts at work earning him a commendation from his supervisor. Upon discussing these improvements, the therapist brought up the possibility of soon ending weekly treatment and moving to bi-weekly meetings. The therapist framed bi-weekly meetings as an indication of AB's progress. AB responded with a mixture of pleasure and fear. He was pleased that the therapist also saw the progress he had been making but he also was afraid of cutting back too soon. The therapist asked AB to think about it during the week. AB returned for the next session expressing a readiness for the new format. They agreed to meet bi-weekly for the next few months as a prelude to ending regular meetings. The next few sessions focused on a continued monitoring of AB's improvements by identifying and reinforcing the constructive changes AB had made in his life. The therapist encouraged AB to express his feelings about his progress and the impending termination but didn't attempt an in-depth analysis of these feelings. After three months of bi-weekly sessions, AB stated he was ready to stop coming regularly. The therapist supported his decision and cautioned AB not to be alarmed if his symptoms temporarily returned, for this was a normal occurrence. This intervention was meant to prepare AB for possible symptom recurrence in order that such occurrence would not take him by surprise and jeopardize his confidence in the therapy and the therapist. The therapy ended with an agreement that AB would seek more treatment whenever necessary. In addition, the therapist asked AB to drop him a card in about six months to let him know how he was doing. Due to the patient's history of emotional deprivation and tenuousness of relationships, the therapeutic strategy focused on avoiding the experience of termination as a significant abrupt loss and on the maintenance of an ongoing relationship.

In uncovering psychotherapy, the therapist focuses on the patient's real and distorted perceptions of the therapist and their relationship. These childhood reaction patterns, in the form of attitudes toward the therapist, become a major area of attention. The therapist takes a confrontive, exploratory stance and attempts to identify, understand, and work through conflicted intra- and interpersonal reactions in order to strengthen the ego, broaden the range of coping mechanisms, and increase the patient's flexibility and spontaneity. In terminating an uncovering psychotherapy, the therapist encourages an examination and explanation of the feelings this experience stimulates. These reactions represent real phenomena related to ending the present relationship, as well as derivatives from earlier losses and separation experiences. The therapist encourages the patient to emotionally experience and examine the pain, sadness, and anger associated with loss involved in the present as well as in previous losses. Such work allows the patient an opportunity to rework old feelings and to develop new coping skills in order to deal with the inevitable separations and losses of life. A case example follows.

CD was a 24-year-old woman who sought therapy when her fiancé terminated their relationship two months prior to marriage. CD was distraught and wondered if she would ever have a lasting relationship. She vacillated between rage towards her former fiancé and concern that something was deeply wrong with her. The assessment interview suggested CD was a moderately well-integrated individual who functioned well in most situations (e.g., her career) but had considerable difficulty in her relationships with men. An open-ended treatment focusing on an examination and exploration of these difficulties was agreed upon.

From the onset of therapy CD was preoccupied with her feelings toward the therapist. She was surprised by his empathy and understanding. She repeatedly compared her father's attitude towards women (and herself) with that of her therapist. As therapy progressed, CD explored and modified her views towards men, including her deep resentment and mistrust, as well as her tendency to idealize as a defense against her anger and as a means of gaining male attention and acceptance.

After 13 months of treatment, CD began to demonstrate what seemed to be significant and stable changes in her reactions to the therapist and to other people in her life. Although CD had less to talk about during the session, she faithfully attended. At this point, the therapist brought up the issue of how long they would continue to work together. CD had little initial reaction to the therapist's question but missed her next session. When she returned, she refused to discuss her absence. Upon exploration, CD related that although she also had been thinking about termination, she felt hurt and rejected when the therapist brought it up. She stated that although she knew it was irrational, she felt like the therapist had seduced her into treatment when she was vulnerable and now was abandoning her. She was hurt and angry. The next few sessions focused on CD's attachment to the therapist that had developed over the past months, especially her feelings of abandonment and rejection. The therapist tied these reactions to similar reactions she had experienced with her fiancé and her father. This led to meaningful progress regarding her feelings of self-worth and her capacity to value and respect herself.

Following this phase, CD began to discount the therapist and treatment. She felt that he was trying to teach her a lesson, that she should not be dependent on anyone. She questioned whether such independence was realistic and if the therapist knew what he was doing. The therapist pointed out that she was struggling with her conflicts regarding dependence/independence. He also helped her consider that her devaluation of therapy might be a way of making an ending easier. She responded with tears and an expression of sadness in leaving someone who meant a great deal to her. In the following sessions the therapist helped CD maintain a focus on this pain, as well as on her fear of being on her own. As CD finished her grief work around ending therapy, she stated that it was time to schedule a last session. Treatment ended three sessions later.

TERMINATION APPROACHES OF
MALAN, SIFNEOS, DAVANLOO, AND MANN

Malan (1963, 1976), Sifneos (1972), Davanloo (1979, 1980), and Mann (1973) have offered methods of approaching termination in brief, dynamic treatment. Their ideas are briefly summarized.

Malan

For Malan, the role of therapist is to encourage exploration of unresolved issues stimulated by termination. Typically, feelings regarding earlier losses of parent figures are elicited. In addition, Malan believes that as termination approaches, the focal conflict often is reactivated and termination becomes another opportunity for further work on conflicted material. For example, the patient who has worked through performance anxiety may reexpress this theme during the termination process by becoming preoccupied with whether this therapy was superior to that of a close friend.

Malan views termination as the time to organize and consolidate emotional gains and cognitive constructs regarding a few specific issues. Encouraging a cognitive integration of the therapy tends to counteract the diffusion that some patients experience at the end. Malan initiates the notion of a time limit quite early in the assessment and recommends the time limit be established in terms of a date. On average, the experienced therapist works with the patient 18 sessions. Malan suggests that trainees work with a longer framework, but no more than 30 sessions.

Sifneos

Sifneos advocates that the therapist explain the brevity and time-limited nature of treatment when the focal issue is formulated and agreed upon. Though treatment typically lasts an average of four months, an exact date for termination is not established until behavior change in target behavior has been achieved. Sifneos consistently calls attention to the focal issue and accompanying behavior change. Termination becomes the phase of treatment that marks the behavior change and acknowledges that both participants have worked at and accomplished a goal.

During the termination phase, the therapist addresses the patient's natural ambivalence, which is expected when the inevitability of separating is acknowledged. The therapist focuses on this normal and predictable reaction as another learning experience. The therapist highlights the patient's disappointment and sadness, as well as the patient's positive feelings of increased self-esteem, competence, and autonomy as a result of having initiated personal change in the treatment. In addition, the therapist helps the patient establish an attitude that the self-awareness gained in psychotherapy can be applied to future experiences. Sifneos feels that separation is facilitated by taking a future-oriented stance that involves an active application of what has been learned in therapy to relationships outside of therapy. This strategy prompts the patient to deal with immediate external reality rather than to develop regressive dependencies.

Davanloo

Davanloo takes a very optimistic view of the success of brief treatment and does not see termination as presenting more difficulty than any other aspect of treatment. He implements a flexible approach to termination and suggests that length of therapy be related to the patient's ego strength. Well-functioning patients can deal with a focal issue in 5 to 15 sessions. Those patients who are capable of handling the reality demands that face them on a day-to-day basis, but also report emotional conflicts in several areas of their life, are treated in 15 to 25 sessions. Patients with more severe personality disorders are treated in 20 to 30 sessions.

Davanloo feels that the well-functioning patient, with a relatively sound ego and cohesive sense of self, does not necessarily experience an overwhelming sense of loss at the end of the treatment. Such patients may experience therapy as a realistic adjunct to their coping strategies and are capable of working in treatment without forming an intense or complicated dependency attachment to the therapist. Patients who have experienced important losses at critical times in their emotional development will often respond with mourning during termination. In such cases, it is essential to reexperience and rework the loss in a stable therapeutic relationship. Treatment often involves work on two focal issues. The first revolves around the presenting problem (e.g., a relationship difficulty). The second focal issue involves the patient's experience of loss. Not infrequently, the two are interwoven. For example, a patient with fears of involvement and commitment may find these difficulties intimately related to unresolved feelings concerning a childhood loss. The inability to work through and accept an early loss may make it difficult to develop other attachments that could also be lost. In such situations, it is essential that feelings accompanying the development of the therapy relationship be worked through with the therapist at termination. Ending of the therapy relationship becomes a metaphor for the previous loss.

Davanloo's suggestion that termination not be viewed as an inherently traumatic loss, but rather as an opportunity to explore and deal with unresolved feelings concerning past and current relationships, provides a very helpful cognitive framework. Both therapists and patients, for their own reasons, are frightened at termination. Underlining the realistic aspects of loss and using the termination as a learning experience is an antidote to therapists' grandiosity about their own importance to the patient.

Mann

Mann (1973) outlined a treatment format organized around selecting patients and developing a treatment focus in which time is the major issue. Mann's approach to termination places a major focus on the patient's inability to accept the limits of time, the relationship of time and separation conflicts, and the ultimate issue of dealing with death and mortality. Termination assumes major importance as a vehicle to examine attachment, loss, separation, and the finiteness of relationships. Mann recommends that only patients who can tolerate the frustration of the termination and are able to cope with strong affect be accepted for this approach. Treatment is strictly limited to 12 sessions. The time limit is established after the focus has been delineated, typically after several meetings.

A key issue in Mann's format is the definite and irreversible decision about the time of termination. Mann believes that throughout treatment, patients are aware of the inevitability of termination and organize their defense mechanisms to guard against the pain of this loss. The therapist's task is to help the patient examine repetitive defensive strategies dealing with these feelings. A predictable phenomenon is that the patient frequently forgets the termination date. The therapist keeps raising to awareness the patient's attitudes regarding time and incorrect perceptions of the passage of time. Near the end of treatment, the patient often experiences negative feelings toward the therapist. These feelings often take a form and intensity analogous to negative feelings toward other figures (e.g., parents, lovers) who have frustrated them. For example, patients who have experienced parents as rejecting or as setting unfair limits will often experience the deadline of termination as unfair and rejecting.

The firm establishment of a termination date permits the patient to examine present and past reactions to separation and loss. As the patient experiences these feelings and attitudes, the opportunity is provided to master these emotions and, in the process, develop an increased capacity for functioning more adaptively with the time-limited nature of various aspects of human experience. Mann notes that during the termination phase of treatment, themes of anger and abandonment, guilt toward parent figures, sadness that has accompanied losses, and wishes to be reunited with people who have died are frequently elicited, providing an opportunity for therapeutic work.

TERMINATION AND THE ASSESSMENT PHASE

Preparation for termination begins in the assessment phase of treatment as the therapist evaluates the patient's past experiences with separation and attachment and introduces the idea of a time limit. In doing the historical review, it is necessary to pay attention to previous attachments and separations and to determine whether losses have occurred at important developmental phases. Learning about the patient's history of separations and responses to loss helps predict how the patient will deal with termination. Attention should be given to the patient's previous experience with teachers, coaches, physicians, and other significant caregivers. Frequently, the patient's attitudes and feelings toward these caregivers come to be reflected in the therapy relationship and signal to the therapist the kind of relationship the patient has either valued or had negative feelings toward. These attitudes help to forecast the nature of the transference.

The therapist must additionally assess the patient's response to the time-limited nature of treatment. The patient may, for instance, feel that the problem cannot be dealt with in the time offered and that therapy in the offered time frame will be superficial. It is often helpful to explore previous therapeutic relationships to learn if the patient has had brief contacts with therapists or relationships of significant length and/or involvement. Those patients previously involved in long-term treatment may need special attention around setting a termination date since their expectations of therapy may differ from what is to be offered.

Failure to accurately assess the patient's willingness and capacity to benefit from a time-limited treatment may lead to an impasse. A case example follows.

EF was a 28-year-old graduate student who presented with feelings of loneliness and depression. EF related that he had recently entered a graduate program and, due to academic demands, was unable to develop new relationships. The therapist was impressed with EF's intelligence and motivation and felt that EF's difficulties were primarily the result of a conflict stimulated by his entrance into graduate school. They agreed to meet weekly for eight sessions. EF's feelings of isolation and disorientation in a new environment were the focus of treatment.

The initial meetings went well with EF reporting improvement. In the fifth session, the therapist reminded him that they were halfway through their work together. EF reacted with sullen withdrawal. Upon exploration EF stated that maybe they should just quit now instead of waiting. He stated that it was hard for him to trust anybody and that the therapist was making it more difficult. The session ended without resolution. As EF left, he sarcastically remarked that maybe he'd come back and maybe he wouldn't. The therapist was concerned about this turn of events. Upon reviewing this case with his consultant, several issues emerged: (1) the obtained history was incomplete and included little information about EF's relationship with his family of origin, and (2) although the working relationship was generally productive, any hint of tension or negative affect would prompt EF to regress into a hostile, defensive stance.

EF missed his next session and appeared for the following one 20 minutes late. Exploration of this resistance led to a discussion of their last meeting. EF related feeling overwhelmed and abandoned when the therapist stated that therapy would end in 4 sessions. Although he believed the therapist when he said that they had talked about a time limit in the initial session, he had been so anxious that he had paid little attention to it. In fact, he felt so in need of help that he would have agreed to anything. A more careful study of EF's history found that EF's mother had been chronically ill with numerous hospitalizations and that he had been raised by his father, whom he found to be dominant, controlling, and emotionally distant. EF was embarrassed to talk about his mother and didn't want to invite feelings of sympathy from others. Over the years, he had learned to present himself positively and to avoid bringing up his past.

Although the therapist was initially impressed by EF's intelligence and motivation, he failed to carefully consider the patient's past and present difficulties with relationships and how this would affect his ability to rapidly develop an effective therapeutic alliance.

With new perspectives of EF's history and how his self-esteem functioned, the therapist referred EF to an open-ended treatment.

TERMINATION FORMATS

In implementing short-term psychodynamic psychotherapy, there
are three formats for establishing a termination framework. Use of
each format depends on the patient's character structure, level of
functioning, and presenting concerns. The first approach works
with a rigid ending based on a specific number of meetings. This
format is most useful with moderately well-functioning young
adults in the midst of transitional crises in career choice and/or
marital and social relationships. These patients tend to be dealing
with what Erickson (1963) described as the early adult issues of establishing career and love relationships. These treatments can be
conducted with time limits of 10, 12, or 15 meetings.

In assessment, the therapist has determined that the patient
has ego strength, flexible defense mechanisms, and evidence of the
capacity to deal with the time-limited nature of termination as an
example of similar issues in one's life, especially the issues of dependency and autonomy. These patients tend to be struggling with
giving up the comforts and securities of their adolescence and entering into more adult tasks requiring commitment, responsibility,
and emotional give and take. In this approach the issues of separation, loss, and the treatment time limit are kept in the forefront of
the therapy process. The termination date is firmly held. Extending
treatment reinforces the neurotic belief that responsibility for one's
life and change in one's behavior may be accomplished at a point in
the future that is never quite reached. As the termination date approaches, ending is dealt with in terms of how the patient is dealing
with the focal theme and the time deadline. For example, some patients feel positively pushed by the deadline and work harder.
Others feel disappointed, angry, or cheated that there is not enough
time, blaming the therapist for not offering more time or being crit-

ical of themselves for not doing more or accepting the therapy in the first place. A case example follows.

> GH was a 25-year-old man who sought therapy for marital concerns. GH was disenchanted with marriage and dissatisfied with his wife. These feelings were heightened by their recent decision to begin a family. GH presently did not want children but had agreed in order to avoid conflict. GH spoke in melancholy fashion about his high school and college life. He had enjoyed his adolescent freedoms and found many aspects of his present life to be constricting. He also felt very guilty for feeling this way. GH wanted therapy to help him reach some type of resolution to his distress.
>
> The therapist gained the impression that GH possessed good ego strength and was a well-functioning, although somewhat immature, individual. An agreement was made to meet for 12 sessions and to focus on his feelings about being married and his general reactions to growing up and assuming responsibility.
>
> An effective therapeutic collaboration was quickly developed with GH gaining many insights into understanding his present dilemma and in converting these insights into change. To facilitate awareness of the time-limited nature of treatment, the therapist would announce at the onset of the session the number of sessions that were left and encouraged GH to consider its implications. In the initial sessions GH had no reaction to the therapy time limit. However, in the sixth session, GH reacted by asking the therapist why he always brought up that therapy was limited to 12 sessions. GH stated that he originally paid little attention to this but now it was becoming irritating. He angrily went on to state that the therapist was trying to control him, to tell him what he could do and how he should live his life. The therapist commented on the similarity between GH's present reaction and how he felt limited and controlled in his outside life, particularly in his marriage. GH was struck by the similarity of his feelings. He also identified a parallel between his reaction to his wife and to the pressure he had felt from his father to complete his college degree as soon as possible so he could join the family business. GH used the next sessions to explore his feelings about not being in control of his life, as well as the underlying conflict of wanting to be dependent yet independent. As GH developed an understanding of this dilemma and how it played out in his life, his anger and resentment with the therapist for setting time limits subsided.

In the ninth session GH reported that therapy was very helpful, that he was learning a tremendous amount, and that he would like to continue. He related that he was no longer angry with the therapist and that he would like to continue because they were working so well and he had gained so much. He additionally stated that he felt close to some important insights and that all he would need would be a few more sessions than the original limit. The therapist called attention to GH's bargaining behavior and helped him explore the underlying motivations. The fears and anxieties regarding giving up the therapeutic attachment were examined in relationship to GH's difficulties in giving up his attachment to his adolescent freedom (i.e., dependency yet independency). In his remaining sessions, GH explored feelings and reactions to growing up and letting go. He worked hard and productively. GH came to the last session in a resigned yet optimistic mood. He agreed that it was time to stop; it had been a good experience and though he didn't like to admit it, the time limit had helped him confront issues in a way never previously done. He also shared a grudging respect for the therapist's firmness around the termination date. In the past he had usually been able to coerce others to give him what he wanted.

The second and more widely used format is implemented in those cases where an ongoing focal issue is identified with a patient demonstrating a neurotic level of functioning. These patients typically experience moderate anxiety and stress and have personal conflicts that interfere with obtaining optimal satsifaction in personal relationships. Themes in therapy frequently involve an oedipal conflict, sometimes expressed in problems of choosing and working toward career goals, but more frequently around relationship issues. These relationships may involve dating, marital issues, relationships with parents, or relationships with significant figures such as bosses, authorities, or peer competitors.

In these treatment situations, it is helpful to use several meetings to assess the patient, acquire a history, identify focal themes, and agree to spend a specific amount of time in dealing with a specific problem or problem constellation. The focal issues worked on in this format may or may not have specific separation and autonomy implications. Thus, issues of termination often become relevant later in the therapy as work on the focal problem is being completed. Treatment may last the entire agreed-upon time or may end before the original termination date. If progress is made before the entire allotted time is up, termination can be initiated. In addition to behavioral change, dreams of ending and alterations in mood and attitude may signal that termination can be addressed and worked through. In any event, when the agreed upon time is reached, patient and therapist end their work together. A firm termination date is needed here to fully gain the benefits of a time-limited approach. Patients requesting additional treatment are urged to take a break from therapy (a minimum of four to eight months) to get a sense of how they cope on their own and to more clearly identify those issues needing further attention. The therapist may, at such points, educate the patient as to the use of therapy at various points in life to deal with the emergence of new conflictual issues or situations or the reemergence of old problems. For example, a patient may seek six months of treatment while in college to work on an achievement-and-competition conflict and return to treatment later in life to deal with conflicted feelings of resentment and guilt regarding a first-born child. A case example follows.

> RV was a 29-year-old dental student who sought treatment for lack of self-confidence and inability to assert himself. RV was experiencing difficulties on his clinical rotations. He found himself "freezing" when performing tasks that were being evaluated. He also found it difficult to explain his work or defend his ideas with his supervisors. Although RV was bright and quite skilled, he was in danger of failing his internship. The assessment phase of treatment lasted 2 sessions. RV was found to be an appropriate candidate for short-term therapy. The focus of treatment was his anxiety with autority figures. An agreement was made to work weekly for about four months. Since his birthday fell near the time of termination, it was decided to work until his birthday week.
>
> Treatment proceeded well with significant work occurring by means of the analysis and working through of the here-and-now patient–therapist relationship. RV was alerted to the half-way point

in therapy and had little reaction. He was more interested in working on his identified, focal problem. In the eleventh session RV reported feeling differently towards his supervisors. In addition, he felt he was behaving in a more confident, less intimidated manner.

RV came to the next session in an agitated state. While driving home after the last session the thought occurred to him that therapy could end soon; after all, he had all but accomplished his goals. RV felt anxious as he considered this and found himself ruminating throughout the week. He was frightened that he would lose the progress he had made and that he would revert back to being easily intimidated and to behaving like a "rabbit."

The following session focused on helping RV understand his reactions to the prospect of termination. These reactions seemed overdetermined. In part, they expressed the wish not to terminate but to start over. RV's feared regression also seemed to be the use of a well-learned neurotic defense (passivity) in order to cope with the anxiety elicited by the thought of ending. RV's feelings about leaving the therapist were closely examined. He felt he would be vulnerable and helpless. He was dependent upon the therapist for help, even though it wasn't quite the type of help he had thought he would get. The therapist related these feelings to RV's focal problem. His fear of authority figures was examined in terms of his underlying dependency needs. This work proved fruitful. With increased understanding, RV's self-confidence improved and his fear of ending lessened.

After working through his resistance to termination, RV began to express feelings about ending in a less conflicted way. He had grown fond of the therapist and would miss working together. The therapist encouraged expression of these feelings and helped RV examine them in light of past relationships with significant others. As RV worked through and sorted out his feelings about separation, he stated that it was important for him to express his appreciation and caring to the therapist because once before he missed the chance. His grandfather had unexpectedly died, and he had never told him he loved him. He wanted to tell people how he felt before it was too late. This led to grief work around his grandfather and also his therapist. Treatment ended on the agreed-upon date. RV expressed sadness, as well as a readiness to get on with his life.

The therapist's task during this process was to help RV identify, express, and examine his feelings around ending the therapeutic relationship, and if possible, relate RV's reactions to the focal problem. The treatment was seen as a success although RV had not completely resolved his transference to the therapist. Such a task would require long-term work and was not needed to assist RV with his focal concern.

   Important to the success of this case was the therapist's management of his feelings regarding therapy and the termination. The therapist also found it difficult to end treatment. He had enjoyed their work together. RV was an interesting patient who was able to make productive use of the psychotherapy relationship. There were other reasons for the therapist's difficulty in terminating. RV's degree of improvement had stimulated the therapist's narcissistic desire for perfection. At times he found himself wanting to continue therapy in order to urge RV to greater and greater gains, thus gratifying personal needs to be seen as a great therapist. The therapist would occasionally find himself concerned that RV had not improved enough and should therefore stay in treatment. These feelings seemed to stem from the therapist's perfectionistic demands, as well as his dependency conflicts and fears of aloneness (i.e., if RV still had work left to do, therapy would not be over). These and similar feelings are often experienced during the termination of brief treatment. The therapist found weekly contact with his consultant to be extremely helpful in identifying and working through his reactions to termination in order to present to RV the most optimal therapeutic environment possible.

   A third format for managing termination is used for those patients who present more severe character problems indicative of preoedipal conflict yet, in addition to their disturbance, also possess certain positive traits (e.g., motivation, psychological mindedness) that counteract what would generally be a poor short-term psychodynamic psychotherapy prognosis. These patients may profit from brief, time-limited treatment if it is kept highly focused on a specific problem or problem constellation. Careful assessment is of critical importance in establishing a treatment plan. Of key importance is the therapist's awareness of the patient's underlying dependent character structure and the use of a time limit and a persistent focus on the agreed-upon problem to avoid undue development of a regressive attachment to the therapist and therapy. The therapist must be prepared to actively confront and interpret the acting out of patient resistance to termination. This acting out is often more impulsive and self-defeating than that of the less conflictual patient and requires greater therapeutic attention to limit setting and focus maintenance.

> KL was a woman in her early forties who sought therapy while in the final phase of divorce proceedings in order to deal with feelings of failure and inadequacy. The therapist assessed that KL had certain strengths in the form of intelligence, personal reflectiveness, and a sense of determination. He was also aware of significant conflicts regarding attachment and dependency. In particular, he was aware of the hostile, dependent nature of her marital relationship and felt the potential for a similar unproductive relationship in the therapy. He believed that a brief treatment could be helpful to this woman, provided a focus could be maintained and undue regression avoided. An agreement was made to work for six months with the goals of exploring her sense of failure around her marriage and of adjusting to single life.
>
> KL made slow but steady progress in treatment. She coped well with divorce proceedings and began to establish new support systems. Of key importance in this treatment was the maintenance of the therapeutic focus. KL often attempted to engage the therapist in discussing other issues, especially her chronic bitterness with her mother. The therapist dealt with these maneuvers by attempting to interpret KL's material in terms of her focal concern; if that was not possible, he confronted the change of topic and explained that it was not helpful to their work. To keep KL problem-focused and to avoid undue regression, the therapist often referred to the amount of time they had to work together. KL occasionally mused about having to end therapy so soon. At such times the therapist empathized with the difficulty involved in giving up a helpful relationship. In addition, he reminded KL of their agreement and encouraged further work on KL's presenting concern in order to gain full benefit from the therapy.
>
> KL seemed to accept and work well with the therapist's interventions, which were aimed at facilitating a strong working collaboration on her focal problem, avoiding digression onto issues not resolvable within the limits of treatment, and discouraging undue regression in therapy and dependent involvement with the therapist. However, at the session prior to ending, KL appeared in a disheveled

state. In an agitated and angry manner she complained that all her progress was gone: her new friends weren't stimulating, she missed her ex-husband. The therapist interpreted KL's reactions as an attempt to avoid ending. Rather than focusing on the deep-seated dependency conflicts underlying these reactions, the therapist focused on KL's wish to break the therapeutic contract and on the need to follow through this agreement in order to optimally facilitate KL's self-esteem and self-respect. The therapist attempted to keep the therapeutic attention on resolving the present impasse without an in-depth examination of KL's dependency conflict, since such an examination would be difficult within treatment limits. She was helped to look at her sadness and anger at not getting what she wanted, but this was kept focused on the therapeutic relationship, with her feelings of frustration and deprivation toward her mother being less attended to.

At the final session, KL was less anxious and depressed. She stated that she had overreacted the previous week and that things were not as bad as she had painted them. She felt there was something to seeing a task through, and when she had made that decision, she began to feel better about herself. The remainder of the session focused on recapping the course of treatment, highlighting her gains, and saying good-bye.

When treatment has not progressed sufficiently in this format, the therapist has two options. The patient may be accepted into a longer-term treatment. This is to be considered when the patient is currently experiencing a high level of stress and conflict, and/or the therapist feels that a strong, and ultimately productive, alliance is established. High levels of stress and a weak alliance may indicate the need to transfer to another therapist. A second option is to offer the patient periodic therapeutic contact after the termination. This may take the form of check-up sessions or the opportunity to return when a crisis state is experienced. Periodic therapeutic contact is to be considered when treatment has stabilized the patient but few inroads have been made inducing psychic change. Periodic check-ups and doses of therapy to deal with crises are particularly valuable for those patients who possess strong dependent needs and have potential to develop an excessively dependent attachment. Such patients are able to continue their connection to the therapist in a controlled and modulated fashion. Paradoxically, this option is also helpful for patients who fear reliance on others and need to see themselves as independent and on their own.

TIME, DATES, CALENDARS

Although the calendar year is January to December, people maintain their own individual calendars. In all time-limited treatments the therapist must be aware of the natural life cycle of how people work with the calendar and the demands of work, career, or family. For example, parents, teachers, and school children follow the academic year of September to May. In the world of fashion, showings are seasonal. When considering time-limited treatment, it is helpful to learn how the patient works and uses time, and to propose a time framework within the patient's natural cycle of beginnings and endings. For example, the college student may be offered therapy for a semester or school year. The more the therapist is able to arrange treatment to coincide with the various aspects of the patient's schedule, the more likely therapy termination can be a natural part of the patient's experience.

PATIENT REACTIONS TO TERMINATION

New Problems/Symptoms/Regression

Patients near the end of treatment will often bring a new problem, have a regressive return of symptoms, or express a feeling that the treatment has made no change at all. This reaction often represents fears about ending and should be addressed from that vantage point. In dealing with such phenomena, a therapist must respond to the patient's concerns and assess whether negative changes have occurred. Abrupt dismissal of patient concerns is unempathic and hinders the development of a collaborative investigation into the various origins of the patient's concerns. The idea may be introduced that ending therapy can be a frightening experience and that patients often respond by temporarily regressing back to where they were when treatment began. It is crucial to help the patient examine his/her concerns as being related to the difficulties involved in giving up a helpful and meaningful relationship. It can also be helpful to help the patient explore previous endings with significant individuals in order to shed light on current feelings. Termination of treatment often involves a repetition of the conflicts and affects that occurred in response to earlier loss.

Desire for Complete Understanding

As the end of treatment nears, the patient may express a wish to continue therapy to learn more, explaining that the therapy has been a helpful experience, and a new way of looking at relationships and life has been introduced. The therapist may find this a difficult request to deny, especially if treatment has progressed well and the patient is found to be exceptionally interesting. The therapist's curiosity about the complexity of the patient has been stimulated. In addition, it is particularly gratifying to have a patient who is committed to further therapeutic work and understanding.

The wish for continued treatment in order to reach complete self-understanding is often a rationalization the patient uses to avoid fears of separation and autonomy. Rather than give up the close attachment that has developed and deal with the painful feelings of loss, the patient attempts to seduce the therapist to continue the therapy. Failure to respect and work through the original treatment agreement may encourage the development of a therapeutic misalliance, which would have negative effects on the internalization of the therapist as a positive, growth-promoting introject. In addition, it is often the case that when further treatment is initiated, the patient's intense interest in understanding quickly dissipates.

Bargaining

Another theme that comes up in the termination process is criticism of the chosen deadline or ending time. Patients may bring up anticipated stresses or events during which it would be helpful to have the therapist available. The patient may state that the deadline was established in haste without a genuine consideration of what could be accomplished. These concerns about the time limit have the flavor of logical renegotiation or bargaining. Logical rationality and the importance of an external event are used to avoid working through the sense of loss. Rather than work through feelings of closeness, loss, and dependency, the patient uses a "mistake" about time to try to extend the deadline.

Once again, the therapist must take seriously the nature of the reality event or reason that can serve to prolong the therapy. Efforts to dismiss the patient's argument on a logical basis will usually be ineffective and should be avoided. It is best to redirect the patient to feelings involving attachment, termination, and dependency. It is often helpful to focus on the interpersonal struggle between patient and therapist to help demonstrate that bargaining for more time is often an indirect way of expressing closeness and involvement. Typically, when the fear of letting go emerges, the therapist can profitably focus on some variant of the following: (1) relationships come to an end, (2) not every ending is logical, or (3) ending a relationship is not an abandonment.

Anger

Patients frequently express anger toward the therapist during termination. This reaction is most often seen in treatments with a set number of sessions in which themes related to time, responsibility, autonomy, and dependency have been major issues. Patient anger may take many forms including criticism of techniques, personality of the therapist, and the arbitrary decision of the therapist to establish a treatment deadline. This anger is complex and overdetermined, representing a defensive denial of therapeutic attachment, as well as a reaction to feeling abandoned.

Management of this anger can be difficult for the therapist since it is frequently directed at the therapist's helpfulness and competence. It is essential that the therapist accept the anger nondefensively and explore what is happening in treatment to stimulate this reaction. The patient's expression of anger is often a coping mechanism that permits one to feel in charge at a time when he/she feels insecure. The anger may also mask patient sadness. The task of the therapist is to help the patient experience and see the defensive nature of the anger.

Devaluing Treatment

At the end of treatment, patients occasionally devalue or belittle the therapy. The patient may indicate that therapy was superficial, that a core issue has been left undone, or that the improvement made was a function of time, some external event, or other relationship. Belittling treatment is a subtle and complex defensive maneuver that may help the patient avoid confronting the meaningfulness of the therapy and the impact of its loss. The maneuver permits the patient to avoid acknowledging the importance of the therapy relationship and working through feelings about the termination.

Desire to End Early

Patients may indicate that improvement has occurred and ask to stop sessions prior to the original agreement. The request to stop early may appear rational and as being in the best interest of patient and therapist, usually saving time and/or money. The patient often focuses on the importance of symptomatic improvement as the major determinant of treatment duration and offers the therapist the benefit of working with additional patients who have a greater need of the therapist's time. The therapist should not accept this rational ending too quickly.

The important tactical issue is not to focus exclusively on symptomatic improvement as the major criterion for ending treatment. The desire to end early often represents the wish to avoid the experience of grief and the mobilization of conflicts around separation. The patient may thus attempt to avoid the work of mourning the therapeutic relationship by forming the attitude that one's problem has been solved and then quickly terminating. Though the therapist cannot force the patient to remain in treatment, it is crucial for them to explore the possible meanings of the wish to stop early.

Therapist Idealization

Another mode of dealing with the complex nature of the feelings elicited by termination is for the patient to idealize the therapist or therapy. The patient may focus solely on the positive aspects of treatment: symptoms have remitted, self-esteem is positive, the therapist is great, the interpretations were unerring, change could not have occurred without this particular therapist. The expression of pleasure at termination is common and marks the conclusion of significant work and accomplishment in a meaningful relationship. In some cases, however, the positive is overdone and serves a defensive purpose to avoid negative feelings associated with the termination. In dealing with this patient reaction, the therapist should accept these feelings nondefensively and should examine this overdetermined reaction in the same manner as patient anger or devaluation of the treatment. The patient who adopts such a positive view of treatment may be defending against experiencing termination as an angry abandonment. The idealization is often intended to help the patient avoid feelings of anger regarding the loss, and secondarily to enlist a positive response from the therapist. Such patients must be helped to see that they can end the therapy with both positive and negative reactions. Having a negative thought or criticism will not spoil the treatment or destroy the relationship with the therapist.

COUNTERTRANSFERENCE

Countertransference is viewed as the therapist's emotional reactions to the patient developed during the treatment process. These reactions often stem from unresolved conflicts of the therapist, and/or the impact upon the therapist, of the patient–therapist interaction, especially the patient's conflicted interpersonal strategies.

Therapists conducting brief treatment must be alert to the influence of countertransference reactions in their management of termination. The characteristics of this therapy, including its brevity and the use of a termination deadline, offer an especially fertile soil for the therapist to express conflicts around dependency, separation, narcissism and identity.

Dependency

Therapists struggling with dependency conflicts often experience difficulty during termination. Such individuals may enjoy the parental aspects of the therapist and experience a reluctance to relinquish their attachment to the parent. Through a complex identification with the patient, vicarious nurturance may be gained while in the role of offering help to others (Malan 1980). Therapist dependency issues may make it difficult to help the patient with such resistances to the termination process as the presentation of a new symptom, the plea to continue, or the wish to end early. Working on a new symptom may gratify the therapist's wish to take care of a problem. Offering to continue therapy would allow the gratification of a mutually dependent relationship. Conversely, accepting a patient's wish to end early (without working through termination issues) may be an unconscious expression of anger toward a patient who does not behave in a dependent manner toward the therapist.

Separation and Loss

Therapist conflicts around separation and loss, often intimately related to dependency issues, may also create difficulties during the termination process. The therapist's unresolved feelings regarding loss and separation may lead to an undue sensitivity to the termination process. This may result in an undue preoccupation with termination throughout the therapy and may communicate to the patient that there is an inherent danger in terminating. In addition, such preoccupation with termination may reduce the amount of therapeutic attention given to the agreed-upon focal problem. Therapist sensitivity to loss and separation may also result in an attempt to keep personal conflict repressed/suppressed through a defensive denial of importance involved in working through patient feelings evoked by termination. The therapist may discount the importance of termination when discussing it with the patient. Efforts may be made to deal with it solely in a cognitive, experience-distant manner. The therapist may also avoid the issue entirely and rationalize this as an attempt to help the patient resolve the focal issue as fully as possible.

Narcissism and Perfectionism

Difficulties with termination may also be related to therapist narcissism and conflicts regarding perfectionism. Brief therapy with limited goals challenges the therapist's need to resolve all the patient's problems. Therapists whose self-esteem is overly dependent on dramatic and complete modification of patient dynamics and interpersonal strategies will experience frustration with brief treatment formats. This frustration may be expressed during termination by means of anger toward the patient for not improving enough, or the temptation to add a few more sessions to add a bit more resolution to the patient's problem. Narcissistic overinvestment in therapeutic results may also make it difficult to help the patient realistically examine and consolidate therapy gains. Anything less than dramatic improvement may result in narcissistic injury to the therapist.

Rigid, perfectionistic treatment goals may make it difficult to assess therapeutic progress. The therapist's conscious/unconscious strivings towards some ideal in therapy may make it difficult for the therapist to "let go" of a patient who has used therapy productively yet is also still working toward further gains and growth. The therapist's inability to let go of an imperfect or incomplete product may convey to the patient a devaluation of the progress made in treatment. In addition, through identification with the therapist's perfectionistic strivings, the patient may internalize a demanding, nonaccepting attitude that is nonconducive to the continued development of emotional well-being.

Identity

A final therapist conflict often stimulated by the termination process is uncertainty regarding professional and personal identity. Therapists struggling with such issues may find patient's resistances to termination especially taxing. Patient regression, bargaining over the deadline, and requests to change the treatment format may stimulate the therapist's preexisting insecurities regarding being a therapist and being able to help people. The therapist may react to these resistances by developing doubt in the viability of the treatment format for this particular patient, and/or the therapist's ability to facilitate change by use of this format. Such feelings may result in the therapist overtly or covertly supporting the patient's disinclination to work through a termination.

Lack of a stable and secure identity may cause termination difficulties of another sort. Therapists struggling with identity concerns often quite readily accept and conduct "new and exciting" therapies without adequately studying the method and integrating the underlying theory. In regard to brief therapy, this may result in a less-than-adequate selection of patients and subsequent inability to successfully implement the treatment strategies. Treatment impasses may be highly evident as termination approaches due to insufficient treatment progress, and/or the patient's inability to give up the therapeutic attachment due to the development of intense and complex dependency strivings.

Use of Countertransference

During the early development of dynamic theory, countertransference reactions were seen as detrimental to analyst neutrality; for that reason, they needed to be guarded against. As dynamic theory evolved, increased attention has been given to the interpersonal and interactional component of the patient–therapist relationship. In the development of interactional ideas, clinicians realized that to eliminate countertransference feelings was not only impossible, but disregarded the valuable therapeutic material in the therapist's reactions to his/her patient. The therapist began being viewed not only as a neutral figure but a barometer of the interpersonal and intrapsychic mechanisms of the patient. A greater acceptance of the use of countertransference reactions has evolved in the continued progress towards the understanding and modification of the patient's conflicted interpersonal strategies. To illustrate:

> ZB was a 25-year-old graduate student who sought brief treatment to work on his ambivalent relationship with his father. As the treatment deadline approached, ZB's thoughts and feelings about ending were increasingly focused upon. While discussing these feelings in one of the final sessions, the therapist became aware of a vague uneasiness. Though the content of ZB's material suggested a readiness to terminate and a desire to be independent of treatment (i.e., he had

accomplished his goals, he was looking forward to therapy being over), his manner of expression (i.e., voice inflection, facial features) evoked a wish in the therapist to offer continued meetings.

In supervision the therapist's reactions were examined in terms of his own dynamics and needs. The therapist gained increased understanding of his personal need to provide continued nurturance in order to feel worthwhile. In addition, supervision was used to help identify the interpersonal strategies used by ZB to evoke such feelings in the therapist. In the remaining sessions ZB was helped to confront his ambivalence around dependency and how this conflict was enacted in his relationships with others. This work added a new piece of understanding regarding his relationship with his father.

The therapist is not "bad, inadequate, or hopelessly neurotic" because he/she feels conflicted or disturbing feelings towards the patient or the treatment. What is crucial is that these feelings are explored to: (1) facilitate the therapist's ability to intervene in a flexible and helpful manner and (2) increase the patient's understanding of his/her intra- and interpersonal dynamics.

ROLE OF BRIEF THERAPY IN AN INDIVIDUAL'S LIFE

Short-term psychodynamic psychotherapy is a treatment format that can be useful throughout the patient's life. The core elements of this therapy offer a framework for therapist and patient to meet intermittently, at predetermined points, or at nodal points of change. Psychological growth and the need to deal with developmental tasks continues throughout life. Career shifts and changes in family constellation through birth, death, divorce, or altered personal expectations require adaptation. Just as it is necessary to care for different parts of the body, an individual must deal with different aspects of psychic change and growth. From this vantage point, a patient could be expected to return for psychotherapeutic consultation at various times in life as new and trying experiences are faced.

References

Abrams, S., and Shengold, L. (1978). Some reflexions on the topic of the 30th congress: affects and the psychoanalytic situation. *International Journal of Psycho-Analysis* 59:395–407.

Alexander, F. (1925). Review of *The Development of Psychoanalysis,* by Otto Rank and Sandor Ferenczi. *International Journal of Psycho-Analysis* 6:484–496.

———— (1944). The indications for psychoanalytic therapy. *Bulletin of the New York Academy of Medicine* 20:319–332.

———— (1954). Some quantitative aspects of psychoanalytic technique. *Journal of the American Psychoanalytic Association* 2:685–701.

———— (1956). *Psychoanalysis and Psychotherapy.* New York: Norton.

Alexander, F., Eisenstein, S., and Grotjahn, M. (1966). *Psychoanalytic Pioneers.* New York: Basic Books.

Alexander, F., and French, T. (1946). *Psychoanalytic Therapy: Principles and Applications.* New York: Ronald.

Alexander, F., and Selesnick, S. (1966). *The History of Psychiatry.* New York: Harper & Row.

Balint, M. (1969). *The Basic Fault: Therapeutic Aspects of Regression.* London: Tavistock.

Balint, M., Ornstein, P., and Balint, E. (1972). *Focal Psychotherapy.* Philadelphia: JB Lippincott.

Bauer, G., and Kobos, J. (1984). Short-term psychodynamic psychotherapy: reflections on the past and current practice. *Psychotherapy* 21:153–170.

Bellack, L., and Small, L. (1978). *Emergency Psychotherapy and Brief Psychotherapy,* 2nd Ed. New York: Grune & Stratton.

Bibring, E. (1954). Psychoanalysis and the dynamic psychotherapies. *Journal of the American Psychoanalytic Association* 2:745.

Brenner, C. (1980). Working alliance, therapeutic alliance, and transference. In *Psychoanalytic Explorations of Technique,* ed. H. Blum. New York: International Universities Press.

Breuer, J. and Freud, S. (1895). Studies on hysteria. *Standard Edition* 2:1–310. London: Hogarth, 1955.

Davanloo, H. (1978). *Basic Principles and Techniques in Short-Term Dynamic Psychotherapy.* New York: Spectrum Publications.

_____ (1979). Techniques of Short-Term Psychotherapy. *Psychiatric Clinics of North America,* 2:11.

_____ (1980). *Short-Term Dynamic Psychotherapy.* New York: Jason Aronson.

Dewald, P. (1965). *Psychotherapy: A Dynamic Approach.* New York: Basic Books.

Eisenstein, S. (1980). The contributions of Franz Alexander. In *Short-Term Dynamic Psychotherapy,* ed. H. Davanloo. New York: Jason Aronson.

Erickson, E. H. (1963). *Childhood and Society.* Vol. 1. New York: Norton.

Fenichel, O. (1941). *Problems of Psychoanalytic Technique.* Trans. D. Brunswick. New York: Psychoanalytic Quarterly.

Ferenczi, S. (1919). Technical difficulties in the analysis of a case of hysteria. In *Further Contributions to the Theory and Technique of Psychoanalysis,* ed. J. Rickman. London: Hogarth, 1950.

_____ (1921). The further development of an active therapy in psychoanalysis. In *Further Contributions to the Theory and Technique of Psychoanalysis,* ed. J. Rickman. London: Hogarth, 1950.

_____ (1926). Contra-indications to the "active" psychoanalytic technique. In *Further Contributions to the Theory and Technique of Psychoanalysis,* ed. J. Rickman. London: Hogarth, 1950.

_____ (1955). *Collected Papers.* Vol. 3. *Final Contributions.* New York: Basic Books.

Fine, R. (1979). *A History of Psychoanalysis.* New York: Columbia Press.

Flegenheimer, W. (1985). History of brief psychotherapy. In *Treating the*

Oedipal Patient in Brief Psychotherapy, ed. A. Horner. New York: Jason Aronson.

Ford, D. and Urban, H. (1963). *Systems of Psychotherapy.* New York: Wiley.

French, T. (1958). The reintegration process in a psychoanalytic treatment. In *The Integration of Behavior.* Vol. III. Chicago: University of Chicago Press.

Freud, A. (1936). *The Ego and the Mechanisms of Defense.* London: Hogarth.

Freud, S. (1905a). Fragments of an analysis of a case of hysteria. *Standard Edition.* 7:7–122. London: Hogarth, 1953.

———— (1905b). On psychotherapy. *Standard Edition.* 7:255–269. London: Hogarth, 1953.

———— (1909). Notes upon a case of obsessional neurosis. *Standard Edition.* 10:151–319. London: Hogarth, 1955.

———— (1910). Wild psychoanalysis. *Standard Edition.* 12: London: Hogarth, 1958.

———— (1912). The dynamics of transference. *Standard Edition.* 12:97–108. London: Hogarth, 1958.

———— (1913). On beginning the treatment. *Standard Edition.* 12:121–144. London: Hogarth, 1958.

———— (1914). Remembering, repeating, and working-through. *Standard Edition.* 12:145–157. London: Hogarth, 1958.

———— (1916). Introductory lectures on psychoanalysis. Lecture XXVII. *Standard Edition.* 16:431–447. London: Hogarth, 1963.

———— (1923). The ego and id. *Standard Edition.* 19:1–60. London: Hogarth, 1961.

———— (1925). An autobiographical study. *Standard Edition.* 20:1–71. London: Hogarth, 1959.

———— (1933). New introductory lectures on psychoanalysis. *Standard Edition.* 22:5–249. London: Hogarth, 1964.

———— (1937). Analysis terminable and interminable. *International Journal of Psycho-Analysis* 18:373–405.

Fromm-Reichmann, F. (1950). *Principles of Intensive Psychotherapy.* Chicago: University of Chicago Press.

Gill, M. (1979). The analysis of the transference. *Journal of the American Psychoanalytic Association* 27:263–288.

———— (1982). *Analysis of Transference.* Vol. 1. New York: International Universities Press.

Glover, E. (1956). The indications for psychoanalysis. In *On the Early Development of the Mind.* New York: Internal Press.

Goldin, V. (1985). Problems of technique. In *Treating the Oedipal Patient in Brief Psychotherapy,* ed. A. Horner. New York: Jason Aronson.

Greenson, R. (1965). The working alliance and the transference neurosis. *Psychoanalytic Quarterly* 34:155-181.

Grotjahn, M. (1966). Franz Alexander: western mind in transition. In *Psychoanalytic Pioneers,* eds. F. Alexander, S. Eisenstein, and M. Grotjahn. New York: Basic Books.

Hartman, H. (1958). *Ego Psychology and the Problem of Adaption.* New York: International Universities Press.

Hinsie, L., and Campbell, R. (1977). *Psychiatric Dictionary.* New York: Oxford University Press.

Horner, A. (1985). Principles for the therapist. In *Treating the Oedipal Patient in Brief Psychotherapy,* ed. A. Horner. New York: Jason Aronson.

Jones, E. (1946). Review of *Psychoanalytic Therapy: Principles and Applications,* by F. Alexander and T. French. *International Journal of Psychoanalysis* 27:162-163.

_____ (1953). *The Life and Work of Sigmund Freud.* Vol. 1. New York: Basic Books.

_____ (1955). *The Life and Work of Sigmund Freud.* Vol. 2. New York: Basic Books.

_____ (1957). *The Life and Work of Sigmund Freud.* Vol. 3. New York: Basic Books.

Kernberg, O. (1975). *Borderline Conditions and Pathological Narcissism.* New York: Jason Aronson.

Klein, M. (1948). *Contributions to Psychoanalysis, 1921-1945.* London: Hogarth.

Kohut, H. (1971). *The Analysis of the Self.* New York: International Universities Press.

_____ (1977). *The Restoration of the Self.* New York: International Universities Press.

Krohn, A. (1978). *Hysteria: The Elusive Neurosis.* New York: International Universities Press.

Kuiper, P. (1968). Indications and contraindications for psychoanalytic treatment: a symposium. *International Journal of Psycho-Analysis* 49:261-264.

Langs, R. (1981). *Classics in Psychoanalytic Technique.* New York: Jason Aronson.

Levin, S. (1960). Problems in the evaluation of patients for psychoanalysis. *Bulletin of the Philadelphia Association of Psychoanalysis* 10:86-95.

Lewin, K. (1970). *Brief Encounters: Brief Psychotherapy.* St. Louis: Green.

Lipton, S. (1977). Clinical observations on resistance to transference. *International Journal of Psycho-Analysis* 58:468–472.

Mahler, M. S. (1975). *The Psychological Birth of the Human Infant: Symbiosis and Individuation.* New York: Basic Books.

Malan, D. (1963). *A Study of Brief Psychotherapy.* New York: Plenum.

———— (1976). *Frontier of Brief Psychotherapy.* New York: Plenum.

———— (1980). *Individual Psychotherapy and the Science of Psychodynamics.* Boston: Butterworth.

Mann, J. (1973). *Time-Limited Psychotherapy.* Cambridge, Mass.: Harvard University Press.

Marmor, J. (1974). Psychoanalytic therapy as an educational process. In *Psychiatry in Transition.* New York: Brunner/Mazel.

———— (1979). Short-term dynamic psychotherapy. *American Journal of Psychiatry* 136:149–155.

———— (1980). Historical roots. In *Short-Term Dynamic Psychotherapy,* ed. H. Davanloo. New York: Jason Aronson.

Masterson, J. (1976). *Psychotherapy of the Borderline Adult.* New York: Brunner/Mazel.

———— (1981). *The Narcissistic and Borderline Disorders.* New York: Brunner/Mazel.

McGuire, M., and Sifneos, P. (1970). Problem solving in psychotherapy. *Psychiatric Quarterly* 44:667–674.

Menninger, K. (1958). *Theory of Psychoanalytic Technique.* New York: Harper Books.

Palino, T. (1981). *Psychoanalytic Psychotherapy: Theory, Technique, Therapeutic Relationship and Treatability.* New York: Brunner/Mazel.

Rank, O. (1907). *Der Küenstler.* Vienna: Heller.

———— (1924). *The Trauma of Birth.* New York: Brunner/Mazel.

———— (1936). *Will Therapy: An Analysis of the Therapeutic Process in Terms of Relationship.* New York: Knopf.

Rank, O., and Ferenczi. S. (1925). *The Development of Psychoanalysis.* Trans. C. Newton. New York: Nervous and Mental Diseases Publishing Company.

Saul, L. (1967). Goals of psychoanalytic therapy. In *The Goals of Psychotherapy,* ed. A. Mahrer. New York: Appleton-Century-Crofts.

Schacht, T., Binder, J., and Strupp, H. (1984). The dynamic focus. In *Psychotherapy in a New Key,* ed. H. Strupp and J. Binder. New York: Basic Books.

Schafer, R. (1973). The Termination of brief psychoanalytic psychotherapy. *International Journal of Psychoanalytic Psychotherapy* 2:135–148.

———— (1983). *The Analytic Attitude.* New York: Basic Books.

Sifneos, P. (1961). Dynamic psychotherapy in a clinic. In *Current Psychiatric Therapies.* New York: Grune & Stratton.

———— (1964). Seven years' experience with short-term dynamic psychotherapy. *Selected Lectures, 6th International Congress of Psychotherapy.* London. 1964. New York: Karger.

———— (1967). Two different kinds of psychotherapy of short duration. *American Journal of Psychiatry* 123:1069–1073.

———— (1968). The motivational process. *Psychiatric Quarterly* 42:271–279.

———— (1972). *Short-Term Psychotherapy and Emotional Crisis.* Cambridge, Mass.: Harvard University Press.

———— (1979). *Short-Term Dynamic Psychotherapy.* New York: Plenum.

Singer, E. (1965). *Key Concepts in Psychotherapy.* New York: Basic Books.

Small, L. (1979). *The Briefer Psychotherapies.* New York: Brunner/Mazel.

Sterba, R. (1934). The fate of the ego in analytic therapy. *International Journal of Psycho-Analysis* 15:117–126.

———— (1951). A case of brief psychotherapy by Sigmund Freud. *Psychoanalytic Review* 38.

Stone, L. (1961). *The Psychoanalytic Situation.* New York: International Universities Press.

Strachey, J. (1934). The nature of therapeutic action in psychoanalysis. *International Journal of Psycho-Analysis* 15:117–126.

Strupp, H. (1973). *Psychotherapy: Clinical, Research, and Theoretical Issues.* New York: Jason Aronson.

———— (1977). A reformulation of the dynamics of the therapist's contribution. In *Effective Psychotherapy: A Handbook of Research,* ed. A. Gurman and A. Karzin. New York: Pergamon Press.

Strupp, H., and Binder, J. (1984). *Psychotherapy in a New Key.* New York: Basic Books.

Sullivan, H. (1953). *The Interpersonal Theory of Psychiatry.* New York: Norton.

Tarachow, S. (1963). *An Introduction to Psychotherapy.* New York: International Universities Press.

Thompson, C. (1952). Sullivan and psychoanalysis. In *The Contributions of Harry Stack Sullivan,* ed. P. Mullahy. New York: Science.

_____ (1964). *Interpersonal Psychoanalysis.* New York: Basic Books.

Waelder, R. (1936). The Principle of Multiple Function. *Psychoanalytic Quarterly* 5:45–62.

Winnicott, D. (1965). *The Maturational Processes and the Facilitating Environment.* New York: International Universities Press.

Winston, A., and Trujillo, M. (1985). The uncovering process. In *Treating the Oedipal Patient in Brief Psychotherapy*, ed. A. Horner. New York: Jason Aronson.

Wolberg, L. (1965). *Short-Term Psychotherapy.* New York: Grune & Stratton.

_____ (1977). *The Technique of Psychotherapy.* 3rd Ed. New York: Grune & Stratton.

Zetzel, E. (1956). Current concepts of transference. *International Journal of Psycho-Analysis* 37:369–376.

Index